Spiritual Harvard

Conversations on how religion is taught, studied,
and practiced at America's oldest university

Werner de Saeger

Table of contents

Preface

The objective of this book is to give readers an insight into the way religion is currently taught, studied, and practiced at Harvard University. Although religion is studied in various ways in almost all of the different schools, particularly in the College and The Kennedy School of Government, the center of all activity with regards to theology and religious studies is undeniably Harvard Divinity School. Situated in a quiet, leafy area of Cambridge, at the fringe of the Harvard campus, it is here that scholars and students focus on the study of religion in its many varieties. I hope that the interviews with faculty members and students in this book will give readers a taste of the diversity and pluralism which is unique to the Divinity School, and a perspective on its multidisciplinary and open-minded approach to the study of religion, as well as draw attention to the particular challenges of teaching and studying religion in both the secular framework of Harvard University and the wider world.

It would be a great challenge, perhaps even an impossible task, to capture the smörgåsbord which Harvard Divinity School really is. If one were to select a different group of individuals, be they scholars, students, or alumni, many different topics would have been addressed, and without doubt several different analyses would have been offered. Yet I hope that these twelve interviews, if read together, will draw a polyparadigmatic portrait of both academic and religious life at the Divinity School, providing readers with a picture of the Harvard way of approaching religion in academia.

I'd like to thank the professors and students who were most kind in answering my interview questions and I would also like to express my gratitude towards those many other friends, faculty members, and staff who made my time at Harvard an unforgettable one.

Furthermore, I also wish to thank those who made it possible for me to study at Harvard Divinity School, namely the Committee on General Scholarships at Harvard University, the Office of Financial Aid at Harvard Divinity School, the Belgian-American Educational Foundation, the Hoover Foundation Brussels, and finally the Fernand Lazard Foundation in Belgium.

It was while studying at the Hebrew University of Jerusalem in Israel, and at Leiden University in the Netherlands, that my initial idea to study religion at a graduate level in the US became a solid plan. My gratitude therefore, goes to the academics, both in Jerusalem and Leiden, who directed me to Harvard and with whom I discussed strategic ways to acquire knowledge and expertise in the study of religion.

My intellectual exchanges with David Little, the T.J. Dermot Dunphy Professor Emeritus of the Practice in Religion, Ethnicity, and International Conflict at Harvard Divinity School, were crucial in my decision to go to Harvard, and my gratitude to him is beyond words.

Lastly, my thanks go to Harriet MacMillan and Mariah Whelan who kindly assisted me in the final stages of this book project.

Werner de Saeger
Oxford
October 2013

Professor William Graham

Former Dean of Harvard Divinity School and current Murray A. Albertson
Professor of Middle Eastern Studies (Faculty of Arts and Sciences) and Member of
the Faculty of Divinity

Could you describe religious education at Harvard in general?

It's structured in terms of three kinds of programs. There's the undergraduate concentration, which is an undergraduate major within the college, and then there are only two Master's programs of any size or weight that are both within the Divinity School. One is more oriented towards preparation for going on to doctoral work, towards academics generally, or a broad range of careers. In fact, people go into a hundred different careers out of the MTS [Master of Theological Studies], but that's one of the programs.

Then the other master's program is the MDiv [Master of Divinity], which is a smaller program. About 40% of MDiv students go into ministry of one kind or another. The larger majority either go on to do more advanced studies, or they go into other professions—particularly service professions. Then they're finding doctoral studies here, which are all handled out of the offices of the same committee. It is a committee of the Faculty of Arts and Sciences, but it's a joint committee between Divinity and Arts and Sciences with half and half memberships from each faculty. And that joint committee, which is a degree-granting committee in the faculty of Arts and Sciences, reports out two doctoral degrees. They report Ph.D. [Doctor of Philosophy] degrees to the Faculty of Arts and Sciences, and then they report out Th.D. [Doctor of Theology] degrees to the Divinity School faculty.

Over the last thirty years, the two degrees have grown to be virtually indistinguishable. It used to be that the Th.D. had an additional theological component, particularly in terms of Christian theology. Now they really require almost exactly the same thing. So those two degrees remain our two doctoral degrees. Essentially, we have graduates of those two degree programs who go and do almost exactly the same kind of jobs, the same kind of teaching jobs in colleges, universities and occasionally, although less often, in seminaries or divinity schools.

Here we have seen an overview of the degree programs both at the Divinity School and at the Faculty of Arts and Sciences in the Yard—there is collaboration there, obviously—what about the teaching of religion in the other schools?

There is an occasional course. We have had a scholar for several years studying religion in conflict, in particular, in the Kennedy School. The former Dean of the

Divinity School, who was here for three years, Bryan Hehir, also teaches religion and human rights issues in the Kennedy School. There are occasionally courses in the Law School on religion, there is a center for Islamic legal studies, and there are faculty members in the Law School who teach Islamic legal courses. There are also some Jewish legal courses in the Law School. There are a few specialists here, I'm not sure exactly how many but at least one, who specialize in Talmudic law. There have also been, on occasion, scholars in public health who've had some interest in religion and public health and were more particularly interested in ethics. So sometimes the ethicists in several of the schools may overlap with religious ethics or religious concerns in their courses.

However, there aren't that many generally. There have also been a few courses, for instance in Social Medicine in the Medical School. We have a couple of scholars who had joint appointments between Sociology and Anthropology. So, religion creeps into a number of places. It's true that in palliative care at the Medical School, they have had a course there in Religion and Issues in Palliative Care for several years. We actually have one of the teachers of that course as a post-doc here this year. We are working with them to perhaps develop cooperation between the Divinity School and maybe Arts and Sciences, in addition to the Medical School, in the area of palliative care and end of life issues.

So, I think that there are a number of places where religion crosses over into curriculum besides in Arts and Sciences and Divinity, but they're the two places where most of the people who would consider themselves specialist in religious studies are based. Almost all of them are in those two faculties.

These courses are organized without supervision from HDS?

That's right, absolutely, yes. They are totally decentralized in that regard. We have nothing to say or any desire to have any control over courses in other faculties.

Have you seen any evolution during your time here as Dean at HDS, in terms of interdisciplinary work? Do you seek it out as a growing field or do you see that as something of a hype? If it's lacking, what are the obstacles preventing more interdisciplinary work?

Well, there's not enough exchange between schools as far as I'm concerned, in the area of religion in particular. I think that part of that is simply that faculty here at Harvard or in almost any of the faculties, are usually pressed to the limit in terms of the demands on their time both from outside the university and from within. So it's doubly difficult. Also, a big university like this, with an awful lot of traffic through the university from abroad and from around the country, has extra pressures. It's very difficult for people to carve out the time to pursue interdisciplinary projects, but they do from time to time, in terms of co-teaching courses. We have had some co-teaching with Kennedy School people in the past.

As a scholar for roughly thirty years prior to coming over to be Dean of the Divinity School, I've never been a member of this faculty, but from the moment I started teaching as a young assistant professor in 1973, I taught courses that were open to Divinity students. Here, I co-taught courses with members of the Divinity faculty and with an American historian. I also co-taught with members of other departments, our basic doctoral seminar in the English department. So the co-teaching and certainly the cross-registration of students have taken place for a lot longer than the last few years that I've been over in the Divinity school.

So it's certainly a long history of a great deal of fluidity. Students, particularly very good students, which we have a lot of, tend to move very quickly to find the people they want and the courses they want wherever they are in the university. The best students move the fastest, in my experience. So you do help guide a lot of traffic around the university when courses are taught from other faculties. It may be only a scattering in any one course, but the cumulative effect there is a lot. In terms of interdisciplinary connections and projects, I don't feel that we have enough of the many humanities in general. I think the sciences have been better at this partially by necessity, partially due to the swift movement of modern science. Particularly in areas like biology, and engineering, and so on. There are a lot of fields flowing together that thirty five years ago were not even imagined to be together.

I think particularly Biological Engineering is a good example here, where we've had even undergraduates doing senior theses and work in engineering and biology. It's moved very quickly in the sciences and a lot of other areas; however, in the Humanities, in my mind, they should always in some way be interdisciplinary. I think that it's particularly important in the Humanities, even more than the Social Sciences, because rarely does one focus on the method that you use to study things in the Humanities. This is changing in the Social Sciences. I think that even within their indications in Economics and Sociology and so on, there are more and more attempts to draw upon a lot of other disciplines in addition to their own narrow disciplinarian approach. I think it used to be the case, maybe forty or fifty years ago, when a lot of Anthropology departments felt that you trained somebody to do Anthropology and then they could choose to go anywhere in the world and learn the language and apply their method there.

I would like to think that Humanists have always been subject-oriented, that's why I don't like the term 'disciplines' in the Humanities. I feel like we're not a group of disciplines by and large; certainly we use certain disciplines like close reading of text or historical method. We do use methods and disciplines if you like, but by and large our fields are focused more on topics and problems that require both close reading of text, historical methods, sometimes anthropological methods, sometimes sociological methods and so on. My own mentor, Wilfred Smith, somewhere in an obscure publication, said something once that has always stuck with me. I stumbled across it when I was a graduate student. He said, "Interdisciplinary studies are a ladder to get out of a hole into which the true scholar never falls." [Laughter] So there is a certain amount of hype around, as you said, interdisciplinary studies.

I really do think that good scholars have always been forced to be, or by choice have been interdisciplinary. I do think that we are beginning to see, even within the Humanities, a lot less structure around departmental organization and departmental fields than, for instance, when I was training in the 1960s. Fifty or sixty years have made a great a deal of difference in that regard. Now I think, in terms of the study of religion, it has developed throughout the last twenty years or so that many more people in other fields have realized that they need to study religion somewhat seriously, because it becomes very important to politics. I think literary people have always known religion was important in literature. But I think now there is a renewed sense that one ought to know more about the religious background of the materials that they're dealing with even in fictional texts, let alone historical texts or others. So, I do feel that there is more to interdisciplinary study now than, a half century ago. I think we still have a ways to go.

Have other things changed dramatically during your ten years as a Dean here at HDS, in terms of either student population or the methodology of religious education?

I don't think a lot of methodology has changed or even a lot of focus has changed. I do think that a couple of things have happened. I think that—and this is just something that has probably been happening since time immemorial, but certainly for the last ten years that I've watched here—I've seen the quality of our student cohorts significantly increase. The best at any time is as good as the best in any other time, but the spread that you get now is, I think, much narrower than it was even when I came in. A lot narrower than the students I taught here or even some in the college twenty years ago. There was a much wider divergence of quality, capacity and ability at that time than there is now. I think that our Admissions group keeps reporting every year. They say, you know, "It keeps getting harder and harder to make the choices, because we have an ever stronger cohort to pick from." We have found in the last three years—we've started requiring the GRE results for our Master's applicants, which had never been done here before. In fact no other Divinity School except Chicago requires that for Master's candidates. We decided to do it because most other Harvard graduate schools have a requirement of either the GRE, or GMAT, or some other graduate exam.

Mostly, I was interested in trying to see us get a handle on the quality of our students vis-à-vis other cohorts. I thought this would help us get that and, in fact, it has. It did cut our number of applications, but we feel like it probably cut off the bottom of the pool, and we dropped, I don't know, thirty five percent or so. We lost a lot of applicants, but the quality of the whole pool stayed extremely high, in fact, the quality of the whole pool got better. I think a lot of that was because I think people who maybe realized that they probably were just applying with little chance of getting in decided it was not going to be worth it if they also had to take an extra set of examinations. I have a feeling that that seems to be what we're seeing in terms of looking at the data, now that we're beginning to get enough data to judge.

We also now have compared our GRE scores with all the other graduate schools for Master's candidates and we compared extremely well with everybody else. So we can see that there's no lagging in quality here over any other Master's program. In fact, we're better than some other cohorts and some professional schools, in terms of the mean or the median, the mean is higher. I think that's shown us that we are getting really high quality students and we're still admitting probably a higher percentage than a lot of programs do. We get a very high percentage of qualified—very highly qualified—applicants now.

What caused that change? Were there global events that triggered that change?

I don't know. I think that in some ways, it's just the competitiveness from schools through … at least at the higher levels of people who are going to go on to do higher education and then particularly to go on to specialized education beyond the undergraduate baccalaureate, you know, the BA degree or the AB degree. Those who want to go there are a self-selecting group. They often come out of very strong schools, private or public, and they've already been through a lot. I think the competition to get into very good colleges is now much, much more severe. So the top of the spectrum of intellectual quality and ability of kids coming through the school system, particularly secondary school system and then into the colleges, has been getting more and more competitive.

Part of that is numbers. You have more people competing for roughly the same number of spots in high quality schools, particularly by the time you get to college, and you already have that happening even in the secondary school level. So the competition starts very early now and the quality of training is better in the better schools around the country. I don't think overall the quality of training in American schools is nearly as good as it is in Europe, as statistics show. But I think the competition is beginning to get much fiercer. So the very good have really already come through the mill by the time get there, they come through a college and do extremely well—because almost no one is going to get into any of the Harvard Graduate programs if they haven't done extremely well in their early work. You know, they may have other things to compensate for a B+, A-, average in a few cases, but mostly at the Doctoral, and at the Master's level even, we are looking at people who have A records. They have A- or A records with very few grades below that.

So you're picking from a quarter of people. Part of that is just population growth. We've grown by about sixty percent since I was applying to college, maybe by one hundred percent, I don't know. So the cohort that you're up against is definitely bigger now.

Do you think this is accompanied by a growing interest in religion in general?

Of course. In terms of religion, I do think that the last thirty years have pushed more people to think seriously about maybe studying religion and dealing with it, that's certainly true. And, you know, the number of jobs in the academy have also gone way up since the 1960s, if you look at the growth within religion department positions. I'll bet, I mean I haven't seen statistics on this, but I would almost guarantee that it's certainly well more than two-fold. It might be four-fold. Now there are so many schools that had maybe one or two smaller schools, maybe one or two teachers of religion—usually a teacher of the Hebrew Bible and maybe a teacher of the New Testament—that was about it, particularly in state schools and so on. Now, you have religion departments, even in small places, ranging from four or five to twenty in many colleges or universities where there would have been at most five people or ten people, fifty years ago. So I think that's a change.

If we go back to the difference between the MTS and the MDiv program, are students in the MTS differently prepared to study religion? Are they more prepared to engage critically?

No, you know, you would think that, and I think I almost thought that when I came over to be Dean, having not been in the faculty. I hadn't seen much of this, and I had certainly not seen applications and so on. In actual fact, we now find that we have as many as fifteen students every year who shift from the MTS to the MDiv, not the other way. Maybe one or two will go the other way, but it's rare. It's usually that people will go and do the extra year to get the MDiv, so even the MDiv is often used as simply a three-year track—particularly if you're in something like biblical studies where you need several languages. Or if you're in Islamic studies, it makes sense to do as many years as you can before applying to the Ph.D. unless you already have the languages under your belt.

So, some of it is just functional like that. It often has nothing to do with people's spiritual orientation, or training, or anything. It's often just a matter of getting a three-year degree to get the things you need in order to do what you want to do. So that's one thing, however it is true that probably more of the people who have applied initially to the MDiv are at least considering, if not ordination, then some kind of a, let's say a church, or temple, or mosque, or whatever kind of related preparation. We have a handful of Muslims and Hindus, we have at least a number of Buddhists who do the MDiv, most of those people are thinking of going back to be leaders in their own communities of some kind. So there certainly is that element of people with more of an orientation to do practical training to work in religious service organizations; maybe as hospital chaplains, or prison chaplains, or college chaplains.

People like that will gravitate more to the MDiv to begin with, but a lot of the MTS people began to get interested in that and we have a large number of MTS students who take the field education courses that are designed for the MDiv program, but that are open to everyone. So quite a number of MTS people like that practical element, to get that experience. It's very much harder for me now to generalize about the two cohorts as radically different. There was a time when the name MTS was probably originally conceived, it was probably formed within idea that it would be basically a preparation to do doctoral studies specifically, and you probably wouldn't get anybody who was trying to then go on to do something in religious work. Now that's just not an assumption you can make. It's also true that both MDiv and MTS students also go on and do degrees in other professions, they go on to be lawyers, or doctors, or business people. Sometimes they do them in tandem while they're here, but from both programs you find that happening, and you find people going out from both programs to NGOs, to government work, or civic work of some kind, people going to relief organizations or other kinds.

I find that service professions are frequently the targets of both MTS and MDivs when they finish, even if it has nothing to do with religion, because I think they tend to be people who are maybe looking for how to make their life's work spiritually meaningful in some fashion. Even if they want to be a lawyer or a businessman, they may decide, "I really would like now to sort of get my own head together better about how I want to approach my life philosophically, religiously, and so on." So the MTS in particular can be a degree for what we used to call "the seekers" if you like. They don't know quite what they want to do, but they want to do some more. I mean it can be an advanced AB degree for some of these people, particularly for some who haven't done religion before, but decide, "I really ought to learn something about religion," so it's almost an advanced humanities and social sciences degree if they want it to be.

It's very hard to pigeon-hole either group with one descriptor, because they are so varied in both groups. Even within MDiv, only about forty to forty five percent actually go into ordained ministry of some kind.

Recently I interviewed Harvey Cox, who was talking to me about the way we approach religion these days. One of the things he told me is that we might be too easily satisfied these days, because basically what we're trying to be is good neighbors. We're trying to be tolerant and get along.

And we were wondering together, "What's the next step? How can we grow above that?" My second part of this open question to you is, therefore: Everybody speaks about interreligious dialogue. How can we make sure that we're not having just two monologues?

I'm afraid I have a sort of jaundiced view about most interreligious dialogue efforts when they're formal efforts. They are always described like that, because I can get two monologues more or less speaking past each other usually. My notion is somewhat different. My vision of what the education here is, and I could be wrong, but it's been the vision that I work with. It's what I call the tertium quid, that is, that people come here to study, and we try to bring as diverse a group of neighbors as we can bring. So we bring Muslims, and Hindus, and Buddhists, and Zoroastrians, and Jews, and Atheists, and we bring all these people together. They all study in the same classes and courses. They don't do—I don't know that we even have a course in interreligious dialogue here.

Occasionally we have one particular class with visitors and so on, but we don't have anyone really who specializes in interreligious dialogue. So what I think happens, and what I hope happens, is that people get together and you have a Hindu and a Jew in the same class, and they are working together on something like let's say, the ethics of end of life care. And it's that tertium quid, it's working on a third thing that's not each other. I think that throughout so much interreligious dialogue you're working on each other. My feeling is that the way to really make progress is to work on a third thing together that you both care about, and then first of all you discover they're human just like you. They share the same humanity, that's the first discovery.

The second discovery is that this Hindu next to you, or this Jew next to you, or this Muslim next to you, or this Christian next to you—whoever it may be—that this person is just as smart as you are, just as faithful to their tradition, and in the light of their faith they are just as committed. They have the same kinds of depth of concern about the right things; about suffering, about the suffering world, about justice, about human rights, about, you know, ethical conduct towards one's neighbor. They have all of these same kinds of things. They may be expressed differently. They may have different names and so on, but you begin to discover this and that's really the common humanity again. It's also the common culture of humanity that is very different in every part of the world, but it's also very similar.

It's both very different and also shares many things. I think it's that discovery that I would like to think happens by not focusing on interdisciplinary theological interchange. I will say this: we have, for instance, one of the leading people in the world in Comparative Theology here in Frank Clooney. Frank is carrying the notion of comparative theology to a very different level, which I think is also very important. I think that for people who are really interested in interreligious dialogue or whatever, that Frank's method is a lot more interesting and fruitful than let's say, just straight interreligious dialogue. What he tries to do, if I'm understanding the things that he writes and says correctly, is to bring two traditions into juxtaposition so that one can learn from the other. And each, let's say the thinker in each tradition, the theologian in each tradition, the scholar in each tradition who's committed to that tradition, should recognize that he or she can find something in the other tradition that makes them say, "Wow, now that would be interesting. How could we use that in our tradition?" So that vision of theology begins to influence Catholic theology or vice versa.

If you really get people doing this seriously, I think that's a much more fruitful way to think about it—as a supplicant, or as a learner and a student. You come and you sit at the feet of another tradition, and try to say, "Well, what can my tradition actually benefit from in this tradition?" So you're actually looking at it in a very constructive way, and you're not saying, "Well, we know they're both really alike at heart, because of course they really are alike at heart," the way a lot of the perennial philosophy people would like to have a say. You know, that there's one God and one central reality that is somehow bringing all the traditions together at the core of things. Even if you believe that there is one God, I think you would not necessarily believe that God is trying to manipulate like a master puppet for all of the various traditions to come together. People have developed religion. A religion is a human creation. God may not be. Some people argue that He is, but God may not be. Religion certainly is. It's natural that there are as many religions as there are cultures, or languages, or whatever else, because even within traditions, people vary quite sharply according to their culture, and family, and all sorts of other things. So, I think discovering that in a pluralistic intellectual environment, like I hope the Divinity School is becoming more and more all of the time, that you can each discover in this kind of environment a model for the way the world is probably going to necessarily be in the next hundred or two hundred years, even more that we can imagine right now. I mean just in my lifetime, it has certainly changed more than I probably could have imagined fifty years ago or sixty years ago. But it has, and I think it will probably continue to do that, only at an accelerating pace.

However, there still is the problem of religious illiteracy and widespread ignorance, even within religious research. Can Harvard, and specifically Harvard Divinity School, play a role on a more international level as well or are we just playing in a local field?

Well, it's hard to know. I mean certainly a lot of our graduates, both Doctoral graduates and Master's graduates, come from around the world, but also go out to act in the world, in our faculty or around the world all the time. A lot of them study other parts of the world, that is all happening. But the issue of religious illiteracy is a rather large problem today, I mean right in American society itself, as you can see from the Pew survey. I think from 2008 on, you probably know, the statistics are pretty horrifying. People often don't even know very much about their own tradition. You know, there was forty-some percent of Catholics who did not know that transubstantiation is a Catholic article of faith and worse things. That was not the worst.

Lots of Christians didn't know that Martin Luther was—I mean lots of Protestants did not know—that Martin Luther was central to the Reformation. I mean, the level of just literate understanding is really hugely low in this country and probably in a lot of other countries. Probably less so in the countries that are multi-religious in a very major way, for example in Malaysia, where you have substantial portions of the population who are different from one another and not just minorities who are different. America is such a melting pot that we're just used to every third person being different, but different in a hundred different ways. So it's probably more understandable that people don't bother to learn about people down the street if there's only one or two of them. But I think when you begin to have a mosque in your neighborhood or a Hindu temple in the suburbs or whatever, people ought to sit up and look around and say, "You know, I've been a Jew all my life, but what is this about, you know, what about the Hindus?" They meet people, they work with people, they begin to ask some questions and then they begin to learn. I'm hoping some of that learning will go on, but I also think that we probably need—my own theory, my base interest, is in undergraduate education—a liberal arts education. That's why I really went into scholarship, because I really believed in the American ideal of a liberally educated public. We're not getting it now. We're getting thirty-some percent of people through higher education. This country ought to be seventy-some percent and it's not. We should be getting people through some kind of advanced education even if it's vocational education. We're not getting that, so we're failing in our education. I do despair sometimes, but I really do feel that in our general education curricula around the country we ought to, at the college level, have in some measure of issues of religion, faith, and historical tradition of religions. Some of that should be somehow integrated much more successfully into core curricula or general education curricula.

We're actually doing better with that now with the new general education curriculum in the college than we ever had in the two previous curricula that I taught, in the college under both the old gen. ed. curriculum of the late Forties that lasted until the late Seventies, and then the core curriculum. It was possible and you could sometimes get courses with some religion in it, but now we have two or three areas really, maybe even four areas, of the new general education curriculum in which religion courses can play a significant role, particularly culture and belief. That area is the most significant. I'm teaching a course in culture and belief right now, and you know, a lot of the faculty here and in the Yard who do religion are teaching courses in those areas. So I think we're doing better here now, but I wish we were doing this all around the country—a lot better than we do it.

I feel like some of this illiteracy at the level of the educated citizenry reveals that the 'elites', if you like, are often religiously illiterate, because they've never had to confront or take anything that really deals seriously with religion. A lot of the people that have done, let's say, history courses in the past, disparaged religion or ignored it or whatever, unless maybe they were teaching, you know, a particular period and place where they couldn't ignore it. It's hard to ignore religion if you're doing 16th Century Europe. Reformation and renaissance historians tend to know something about religion, but an awful lot of others don't and they frankly have ignored it in a lot of the classrooms.

I think today that it's getting hard. I find more and more Doctoral students, just as I find more scholars out there, but more and more Doctoral students here in the History department, the Anthropology department, the various Social Sciences departments, and also in Literature and so on, who are coming over and doing graduate seminars or just even general courses in religion, because even they realize that their research is compromised if they don't know something more sophisticated about religion than just the usual content that you get if you come through sort of a normal run of courses. I think there is recognition in the actual world that people need to be more religiously literate. I'm not sure as regards general society, although I think people recognize that religion is important. I don't know how much religious literacy is growing, I really don't know. If our school system were a little bit better, maybe it would grow better. You should to talk to Diane Moore about this or maybe you already have.

Do you think the relevancy of religious education is not being debated anymore at the college, institutional level?

No, I think the relevance of the study of religion, at least, is certainly not being debated. I know when I was hired here, my very first job was a new position in the Faculty of Arts and Sciences in this Committee on the Study of Religion and Near Eastern Languages, which was my special area of Islamic Studies. But in the Committee on the Study of Religion there was a reason for the position being created, because they had so many students asking for ad hoc programs of concentration in religion. Undergraduates said that and they already had the Doctoral program at that time that was being administered by the Committee. So the Committee decided to add somebody to work on this and I worked with the Chairman of the Committee at that time, Richard Niebuhr. He and I worked together for a whole year to create an undergraduate concentration in Comparative Religion. I came there as a comparativist, he came there as the Season's Scholar of Religion and Theology, obviously.

So we started that in 1974. It was voted through in the spring of '74 and we started with the first group in the fall of '74. At that time, and talking to all of the luminaries of the faculty here from John Rawls to, you know, to any number of other people in the faculty at that time, there was a lot of mistrust of having anything that had the name religion in it in the Arts and Sciences world, particularly with regards to undergraduates then. But what won the day for us was that this was comparative religion, this was a course that was worldwide in scope. It was open to people to study any religion. We weren't trying to produce people who were going to go into Christian ministry or the rabbinate. It was for people who wanted to understand religion better, and that message got through. Now, I don't think you have to make that argument except with a small handful of people. I think people recognize that we ought to be studying religion like we study politics, because it may not have been a good thing in human history, but it's a pretty important thing, you know. I think that's much more common now.

You've been the Dean for ten years, how do you align faculty and students, knowing that everyone is completing a highly individualized program of study and research? How can you manage such a diverse group of people and how can you create a community with all these people doing their own things, sitting on their own island?

Well, you know, it doesn't seem to work like that very much. I think that people see themselves as being in a common enterprise. We demand, even in the MDiv program, that people do serious work in a second tradition outside their own. So even if they come here to prepare themselves for Buddhist leadership, or for Protestant leadership of some kind, or for Jewish leadership, whatever they're coming here to train in, they still have to do work in something totally unrelated to their special area. So I think people assume that what they're studying here is religion, even if they're specializing in this religion, my religion, or his religion, or her religion, or whatever. They nonetheless feel, "we're all kind of doing religion," and I think that's the way most of the public events here go. The people come from all quadrants to lectures, and so forth, and then questions come from all quadrants.

I really find that today, being in an open lecture and question period in the Divinity School or in the Yard that involves religion is much more like it used to be in seminars and courses fifty years ago within comparative study or the history of religions where you explicitly were always bringing up counter cases from another religious tradition. You're always looking at religions in juxtaposition as a part of your professional training. Now I find people do that as a matter of course. It's very comfortable for people in the same audience. Here people talk about, "Well, the Buddhist idea about this is X," and somebody else stands up said, "Yeah, but in Islam we think Y," and then discussion can go on about that. No one thinks that's exotic, or odd, or remarkable. It just is something that people of any persuasion may raise in a question.

So I think that is indicative of what happens in the student body, I mean certain people do have affinity groups and people do have their religious communities that they all gather in for worship and so on, but I find that people don't stay in their affinity groups exclusively at all, in my experience here in the last decade. I find the students really move around a lot. The very fact that the students hold these … they're not interfaith services at all, but they hold our Wednesday services. Every week, a different religious group or even a different social interest group hosts. They might be gay and lesbian, or it might be the Sikhs, or it might be, you know, Orthodox Jews, it could be any group here and they will take the worship service on and everyone is always welcome to come in. People are welcome to simply sit and observe. They're welcome to participate. The very fact that the students are open to try to do something that allows other people of other faiths to participate, not to try to dialogue or to 'do dialogue' … they always say, 'to dialogue.' I don't like that as a verb. Anyway, not to 'do dialogue' about it or engage in dialogue about it, not to compare anything, but simply to explain themselves to people who don't know about it and to show what their worship looks like, or what their thinking looks like.

This is the kind of atmosphere that I've been very pleased to see here. It produces this sort of easy … I don't know if you can even call it tolerance, there's always with tolerance or toleration is a sense that well, I can get along with them despite the fact they're an idiot, you know. There's always this sense that they're misguided or whatever. I mean, toleration can be very positive or very negative. I'd like to think that the kind of toleration that emerges here is again one that is not focused on toleration but …

Respect?

Simply, yeah, just having a broader perspective and feeling comfortable with people who are very different, and not being threatened by them. Also not feeling that you've got to prosthelytize them, you know?

Mutual respect …

Yeah, so there's a mutual respect. You appreciate that, you know? You're not out to convert X or Y—we're here to talk about and learn from each other, and also learn something about each other in the process.

Obviously there are social events, Community Tea and so on?

Yeah, and again, you'll find people from a huge variety of communities. The leadership group for Life Together and whatever goes on in the worship services and so on. It's not all one denomination or one tradition, at least in my observation. I am sure there are places where the cooperation is ragged and places where people are resistant. Some of them are bound to have moments of frictions, moments of some—I'm not saying everything is—we're not all dancing around in a circle singing Hava Nagila, you know? It's not that kind of interfaith community either. I think it's an interfaith community where people at least take each other seriously.

Even if they know they disagree from the get-go, I think they're willing to give them a listen, a hearing, you know? To give people a hearing even though some people are offended at times by the religious views of somebody else. There's almost no question that they are. On the other hand, the fact that they've come here means that they've come here with the willingness to say, "Okay, I know who

I am. I'm not going to have to push that on everybody else. I'm going to learn about everybody else, but I'm not necessarily—I'm not going to feel threatened." Occasionally, I've had students come in and talk to me, because they did feel threatened, more often political and social conservatives than religious conservatives to be perfectly honest, because you know, there's a very liberal strain here. I mean, there's no question that we probably by and large teach liberal religion here, whether it's liberal Islam, or liberal Judaism, or liberal Christianity. I'm sure the proponents of the faculty who teach probably lean in that direction in their own lives, personally and intellectually. I'm sure the majority of the student body are also probably socially liberal and maybe politically liberal as well. But there's a strong group of people who are are conservative. At times I think they feel marginalized, so I almost feel that the social/political marginalization is maybe more frequently glimpsed than religious marginalization, although sometimes they go together.

However, in my view as an alumnus, I think that the presence of these conservatives is crucial.

Oh, I think it's absolutely crucial. In fact I think that probably we should try a little harder in our programming to have more people who jar the liberal consensus politically or socially. There have been—there were a couple of programs here in the last presidential campaign here where people, you know, we can't control this, but the panelist or whatever, came in and really became overtly political here, usually in a strongly liberal way. You have to remember that this was at the end of eight years of the Bush administration, and people were pretty frustrated, and so liberals in particular were ready to really sound off, because they really felt that they had been unheard for eight years and more than that actually; really actively attacked. I think things that they said in that period were often hurtful to conservatives, both political and religious conservatives at times. I had several talks with both groups at a couple of points. But to their credit, I think in each case the people who were offended realized that they wanted to bring it up and talk about it, they didn't want to just fester with anger about it.

So they came and said, "Couldn't we talk about it? Have a meeting and talk about this?" and so on. So we did this on a couple of occasions. I think that's probably the important thing, but I do worry that we don't have enough diversity of religious views even within traditions here. The Buddhists that are here, the Muslims that are here, or the Jews, or the Christians that are here, are always on the liberal end of the spectrum, or they wouldn't be here anyway. Although as I say, probably our largest single group is Christians, if you would count for instance Evangelical and Pentecostal, or just Evangelical, which I would assume includes Pentecostal Christians. If you look at that group, at least the last time I did a couple of years ago, that group obviously belonging to many different denominations or none at all, they outnumbered everyone except the Catholics, I think, here at that time. The Catholics are almost all women of course, you know. Not all, but a great number of them, certainly in MDiv they're mostly women. So both groups were big in the sixties. The next group is probably the Unitarians. There are about fifty or forty-eight or something. After that came the largest of the Protestant denominations and so on. So it was interesting to me. I mean, granted, there were several denominations represented, but the very fact that we can have that many people who self-identified as either Pentecostal or Evangelical was, I thought, significant, because I like to think we have that diversity as well. I would like to keep that kind of number here, because I think it is important, exactly.

While I was a student here, I saw some brilliant young scholars come in. However, I heard some voices say that it is quite a challenge to be a professor here at HDS, because not only do you need to be brilliant within your specific field of expertise, you're also required to know something about religion and society generally, and you need to be able to do some comparative studies. That is required of every professor here right now. So, here's my question—how big is the challenge to find new faculty members? How difficult is it also to retain the existing faculty here, because some have left as well?

There are some who've left, certainly. We've had pretty good luck though with our junior faculty now. I think the major factor in junior faculty retention is the ability to come in knowing you have a shot at tenure. When I arrived, my home faculty of Arts and Sciences, and Divinity, we both went to a tenure system at the same time, about a year and a half by the time I came here, maybe even in the first year I came here. Before that Harvard had never had a regular tenure track system. Of course they had tenure, but at least in the Sixties, Seventies and Eighties, I think the average was about eleven percent that, certainly in Arts and Sciences, got tenure.

When I arrived here at the Divinity School it had been twenty years since anyone had been tenured from inside. Margaret Miles had been the last person tenured from inside. So if you came in as a junior person you assumed, as I did when I started teaching at Harvard in '73, that from the beginning you were up against it. I didn't even think I wanted to stay at Harvard. I just took it, it was a job. But I saw people who really felt, "Well, I am going to do everything I can do to get tenured at Harvard." Generally, they were disappointed. So the system changed hugely at that point.

Since that time we have tenured six or seven junior people who have come up. We have lost one junior person, two junior people, but both were really for personal reasons, not for academic reasons. So now, I think the big change for junior people is the fact that they have an opportunity to actually be considered for tenure. I think that's the big factor, even in retention that's a big factor. We have lost several scholars. We're more likely to lose senior people though than the junior people, because senior people, you know, were often prepared to move for various reasons; money, divorce, there are thousands of reasons people in their career move for, of course. So that's always going to happen. The challenge of this comparative focus ... well, we don't demand that anyone does comparative work at all. We do try to pick people who have had some exposure and are interested in more than just their narrow specialty; whether that's exposure within one tradition or exposure across traditions.

So I do think the faculty is more conscious of getting people who are a little more multifaceted than the old model. Some of it has to do with the field areas, particularly in traditional Christian studies where if you were a New Testament person, you did New Testament, and of course you did a bit of Coptic, and a bit of Syriac. However, you really didn't have to know anything else apart from the Hebrew bible and so on. You really didn't have to know anything about Islam or Hinduism as I've said, and not really about post-biblical Judaism. So, that is just changed in the sense that if you do religious studies anywhere now in a good Doctoral program, you're going to be exposed to that anyway.

People here at Harvard have had to be exposed to that in Doctoral work here since the 1970s. Everybody for years has had to do a common exam that for many years was a history of religion exam. So they had to do questions on the history of religion around the world, in various centuries. They had to do methodological reading and they had to do something in another tradition. That started in the late Seventies. Since that time, and I think a lot of other schools have done the same thing, you can't just train in one narrow tradition and not learn something about others.

What about the economics of studying here? By this I mean—this is a group of very gifted students who are using their brains or intelligence to focus on religion. They're investing a lot of money even if they're on scholarships. Is it, in the 21st Century, something that can be justified?

Well, I think it's justified, but I don't think it's sustainable over the long haul. I don't think our university model, in the States at least, or maybe not anywhere, is sustainable for another century. I really think the economic model that we've got needs to find other ways. At Harvard, we do a lot of it with endowments. In the Divinity School, the mostly heavily endowed faculty in the university, far more even than the Arts and Sciences which is the second most, we're dependent on over seventy percent endowment for our annual budget. Arts and Sciences is over fifty and every other school is well below Arts and Sciences, so overall the university is thirty percent dependent on endowment. That's a big amount of money on endowment. It's very good if you got a very big endowment.

On the other hand, if you're trying to expand and grow things, it's a very risky way to do this. I think the economic model is a problem. We have managed to bring our financial aid levels here to a level that Doctoral students pretty much across the university get full coverage. They don't have real financial problems now. It was not always that way, but it's been that way the last ten or fifteen years, just because of competition.

Master's students, however, across the university we have now fairly advanced in financial aid. I'm almost certain in fact, that we give the very best financial aid of any school in the university. We give ninety percent of our students at least half tuition, seventy percent at least full tuition, and a small percentage, ten to twenty, I would guess, get full tuition plus stipend. That was a big change. We managed to do that because of the good years of endowment gain in the early 2000s after I came. I was very lucky, because when I came, we were probably covering maybe thirty to forty percent of our students. We had many more students, because they had to work part-time, and work jobs. They were having to borrow great amounts of money, and we still have people borrowing some. People still have to stretch sometimes to pay the half tuition, but by and large now, no one really has been turned away from here for a Master's program because they can't do it financially. So that's a great thing. Whether we can sustain that or not, I honestly don't know.

The financial times are not going to get easier over the next few years. We're going to have more expenses. We're going to have maybe, you know, no more money. So one of the places that we may have to find that from is by rolling back a little bit on the high level of financial assistance. I hope they don't have to do that, but they might. We might have to roll many more students back to half-tuition. We may not be able to cover ninety percent on half tuition anymore. We have ninety percent with need or ninety-one, ninety-two percent sometimes. Right now we give every one of those half tuition. We certainly give out more money and tuition aid than we take in tuition. So we are not tuition linked in the way most schools are. Most schools; business, law, and medicine, they depend on people borrowing huge amounts of money, but then having salaries where they can pay it back.

Our people don't go out to salaries where they can do that, nor do people in several of the other small faculties, but they're still taking on a large debt load in those faculties. I think we're doing better with that, but I don't know whether it can be sustained, so I'm cautiously skeptical.

What about the future? Is there a clear strategy for HDS, and for religious education at Harvard in general?

I think not. I think religion, the study of religion at Harvard in general, is still under review and rethinking. How it's going to fall out, we don't know. There's an outside committee that we worked out for the president to appoint this past year. They have not reported yet. I think we really don't know yet. I think the key challenge will be trying to get better synergy and planning among the seventy, eighty, ninety faculty at Harvard who do religion very seriously as a specialty of some kind. If we were able to do that and have a coordinating body that could do that, we would actually be better off, because we could more quickly and easily plan faculty appointments. We could more easily admit students and work more on curricula together, so that we don't have one group working on the undergraduate curriculum, and one on the Doctoral curriculum, and one on the Master's, you know? This is not the most efficient way to do things. So, I think it's mostly going to be a matter of trying to develop structures that are a little more efficient and a little more nimble than the structures we have now. We do pretty well with very old structures, but we could do better. So that's my hope, that's all.

Matthew J. Lyons

I am a dual citizen of both Canada and Great Britain, also making me a citizen of the European Union. My parents were both born just outside of Liverpool, England. My father was a blacksmith, who was the son of a blacksmith, who was the son of a blacksmith, and my mother was a social worker and family therapist. My father also entered the social work field.

In 1989, when my mother was seven months pregnant with me, my parents moved from Liverpool to Ontario, Canada, to Niagara Fall, and that's where I spent the first eight years of my life. Following this, we moved to Atlanta, Georgia, where I spent the next 12 years or so. After that I found myself here, studying at Harvard grad school, right after completing my undergraduate degree in Religious Studies at Georgia State.

As regards my religious background, the closest thing to religion that I experienced would be a Carl Sagan Workshop or something similar. Books like Carl Sagan's *Cosmos* and Stephen Hawking's *On the Shoulders of Giants* and *A Brief History of Time* vaguely informed my perspective. This was the closest thing to a general existential orientation that my mother and father instilled in me. In terms of ethics and morality, there was no direct or discernible religious correlation.

So you remain aligned with the family tradition, if I understand correctly?

I have great difficulty in self-identifying, using language to place myself within denominational bounds is an extreme challenge for me. I mean, it's something that I kind of bristle at, even attempting it is difficult. I find religion to be one of the most dynamic and compelling phenomena that the world offers for study and engagement. My relationship with it is so complex that it baffles even me—possibly especially me.

Did you specifically choose to major in religious studies during your undergraduate education? How did that decision come about?

Well, I ended up at Georgia State University because my father works there. He's actually now a Professor of Social Work. Currently, he's the Associate Provost, but he was a faculty member when I was leaving high school and going to college. My brother was already there and studying religion. So he was doing a double major in Religious Studies and Philosophy in his final year when I began my first year. I got recommendations from him about what would be interesting courses to take, just to sample things.

I took Critical Thinking in the Philosophy department and Introduction to World Religions in the Religious Studies department. I found that the department of Religion at Georgia State gave me the kind of tools that I felt like I was supposed to be given in a philosophy classroom. I began to study people's existential orientations and frameworks for understanding life, reality and ethics, on a large scale.

So it was the Religious Studies department, rather than the Analytical Philosophy department, that gave me the tools I was searching for. I found that the professors in the Religious Studies department were also very invested in the educational project. They were very engaged with the students' classroom experience and in tailoring their courses to the budding research interest of those students. This cultivated what I found to be a very nurturing environment. The experience of those courses was so positive that I really enjoyed sampling a variety of religious studies courses in my first two years before picking a major. I carried on with philosophy courses too, something I would not have done if it had not been so close to religion bureaucratically. I didn't really have to do anything very much extra to get the double major—a few courses rather than a whole other separate area of study. So, in summary, my brother took some courses and gave me some advice. We had both been interested in world religions beforehand, despite growing up without them to a certain extent. I don't know if you would say that we were without religion. You could make a compelling argument that we couldn't be.

But you did have a partially external view.

Yes, yes. We were growing up with that external view in the Bible-thumping South. However, we were simultaneously developing a real respect for institutions such as the African Methodist Episcopal Church, with whom I was working, playing gospel music. I found myself very fascinated by religion as a phenomenon and wanted to get closer to understanding its historical development. I now understand that development so much better, and I can understand the ways in which religions view themselves and their relationships with others. I feel like I've gone off on a tangent here ...

Were you happy with your experience in studying religion at Georgia State?

Absolutely. I was very, very happy with that experience. I found that the intellectual climate of some of the courses was profoundly more sophisticated and interesting than I had in any other courses in Georgia State, and truthfully than I've had in most of my courses at Harvard. In the particularly good courses at Georgia State, I found the experience to be much more edifying than in around about seventy five percent of my classes at Harvard.

While you were studying for your undergrad, you started thinking about grad school.

Why did you make the decision to go straight to grad school? Why did you elect to continue with religious studies? Was there an underlying compulsion?

I had a kind of a funny way of coming to it. Essentially, my brother and I had the same undergraduate adviser who has a Ph.D. from the Committee on the Study of Religion at Harvard, and was a Harvard Divinity School student. He's a Sinologist; he studies Ancient China. Although my brother studies Japan, they're both Asian religions. By the end of my first semester at Georgia State, my brother had been accepted into Harvard to study religion. So there was a bit of a train track set for me that I followed a bit like an ant—I followed the hormone trail that had been left.

So in your final year, which was 2009/2010, you applied to Harvard and only to Harvard?

Harvard and Yale, and I didn't get into Yale. I got admitted to Harvard and was awarded with the Presidential Scholarship.

Had you visited Harvard before or had your approach been purely speculative?

I had visited; I came to visit my brother. Actually, I came to Harvard before my brother ever moved here, I think. He'd been here and visited campus a couple of times and then my parents and I came up to set his whole apartment up and stuff like that for him before he had even arrived. So I was able to visit the campus and the whole Cambridge area before Adam even moved here. That was two years before I came.

Do you still remember your first impressions of Harvard?

Yes, I certainly do. My first impression of being in Cambridge, and Summerville in particular, was of setting up the apartment for Adam. It was a little later when I came back to visit Adam and was able to meet some of his friends who were fellow Harvard students that I got a real taste of what the atmosphere of Harvard was. I had the chance to go around the campus and talk to him about what his class experiences were like, and what the workload entailed, and all of those other things. I felt that there was certainly a mysticism to it when I arrived here. There was a sense of grandeur that probably kindled my aspirations quite significantly, urging me to try to come here at some point and experience it for myself.

So Harvard was a logical step for you?

Harvard, for me, was a logical step, yes, and not only because of the general pres-tige and the desire to go to a renowned Ivy League graduate school, but also because of the ways in which my undergraduate experience had shaped my research interests. I was particularly guided by both my adviser and another influ-ential person, Kathryn McClymond. Kathryn is now the chair of the Religious Studies department at Georgia State, and together they really influenced both my brother and I to form the perspectives we now hold on religion. They shaped our views on the study of religion, the relationship between religion and the Academy, and the dynamics between scholar and practitioner.

I think, therefore, that our understanding of the nature of religious studies scholarship and religious investment had become congruent with the atmosphere at the Harvard Divinity School. This is due to the fact that Kathryn McClymond and Jonathan Herman, the current Head of the Religious Studies Department and my former adviser respectively, are both Harvard trained.

Could you describe that atmosphere? What was so specific, what makes the atmosphere here so different?

I think if I had to describe the major landmarks of the setting, to say a rift or a divide would be inappropriate because it gives the impression that there's a stark contrast between two poles that cannot be bridged. That's not what I mean. I think that there is a membrane, a semi-permeable membrane, between academic, reli-gious study, or academic scholarship or religion, and what might be more properly termed "Religious Studies."

At HDS, I think that one of the most beneficial things about the environment for me here has been the utterly unapologetic intermingling of people who want to be ministers, chaplains and practitioners of any variety, who also have an interest in scholarship, with those who have an interest in the history of critical research and so on. Practitioners become integrated with "the other side"—anthropologists and eth-nographers and what you might call straight academic scholars. It's been in tracing the context and content of the distinction between those two camps—the academic and the confessional—that I have conducted the most fruitful research.

Are you also talking then about dialogue between MDiv and MTS students?

Definitely. But I also think there are certainly religious MTS students who are here doing confessional scholarship. I would have more difficulty thinking of an exam-ple of an MDiv student maybe who is utterly irreligious or who is doing kind of uninvested scholarship. Well, you can't do uninvested scholarship [laughter] but anyway, you know what I mean.

But for you, it was very clear you would prefer the MTS?

Yes, absolutely. I was trained at a state school and there was a heavy emphasis on the distinction between colleagues and data in the training that I had at Georgia State University. The idea was that they were not there to teach you how to 'relig', as it were, to use the verb. They are more interested in seeing that you understood a different world view than your own. They were concerned with ensuring that you experienced some empathetic and intellectually rigorous interaction with a cultural or religious tradition that was not your own.

So if we look back to August 2010, you arrived here and obviously you knew people—your brother was here—those were your first real steps at Harvard?

Well, my brother wasn't here in my first year, he was in Japan.

OK. You met your adviser, Professor Michael Jackson, some fellow students, you participated in the Orientation Days and so on. How did that go, those first days and weeks?

That's a really good question. I'll have to go back now and think what the four or so classes that I took in my first semester were. I took German for Reading, which was great. That was a really fun first half of the semester for me. I was in Existential/Phenomenological Anthropology with Michael Jackson. That's a great thing to be doing in your first semester at Harvard whenever one asks you what classes you're taking. "Well, Existential/Phenomenological Anthropology!" Everyone goes, "Ugh. Harvard."

What else now? Anthropology of the Religious, I was in and one more …

How did you find those classes? Were they very different from what you had been doing in your undergrad—the methodology, the content, the interaction with the teacher and fellow students? Did something change, or were you just continuing along the same path?

The German class was very much like a class that I would have done elsewhere. I would say that on average the students are a little more hard-working. The students are a little better prepared than you'd be at a State school that you can go to for free with a B average in Georgia. But it was basically just like school. It wasn't hugely jarring—there were certain aspects of the atmosphere that shocked me to a certain extent, certain aspects I found a little difficult.

For example?

Well, I felt particularly in one of the courses that I was in during my first semester, that there was a certain—there was an accusational tone taken by the professor. It seemed like the pedagogical goal of the course was to get the students to understand in a way that the professor didn't seem to believe the students ever could understand. That they were complicit in a system of hegemony that went back for centuries and that was somehow resting on their shoulders.

That was the most central negative aspect of my first semester here—really finding that at least some of the professors didn't seem interested in promoting a positive and nurturing learning environment. They seemed more interested in getting the students to submit to a certain pedagogical task or goal that this professor established.

That being said, I also had really positive experiences. I can't remember for the life of me what the fourth class was that I took here, but my experience in Michael Jackson's Existential/Phenomenological Anthropology class was absolutely fantastic. I found that I was being given the tools that I had needed to deal with the issues that I was presented with in the budding research interests I had.

At that point, nothing explicit had really taken shape, other than that I was interested in religion, ethics, and politics in the United States. I also felt that from the theoretical materials and the methodological frameworks that were given to us throughout that course—through excellent reading and excellent lectures—I was able to lay the foundations of my ongoing research.

What was your area of focus here at Harvard?

Religion, ethics and politics. I like to add, "and generally in the modern US."

Is there a specific subset within that bracket that you're focusing on? For example church and state relations or ...?

Well, yes. I came here more as a comparative religions scholar, with a general interest in the philosophy of religion. My undergraduate honors thesis was probably the piece of work that gave me confidence and propelled me into graduate school here. It was a historical study of the personal relationship between Nishitani Keiji, who was a Kyoto School Zen Philosopher in the 20th Century, and Martin Heidegger.

Basically, I traced some themes that I deemed to be resonant with one another in their philosophies, and in their lives; not the least of those being nationalist fascist totalitarianism. I did offer acclaim for a therapeutic dimension of the philosophy that they are putting forth, or the idea that they hold in some way a key to the proper existential orientation for human beings. So that comparative project kind of propelled me here.

But before I came here I was thinking about applying to social work programs. Ultimately, I didn't. My reluctance was that the field of social work in general did not have the social capital necessary to do the job that it is tasked with—which is to function as a safety net for impoverished people and for people who are dealing with serious problems in various communities.

I had been looking for a long time for a way in which to develop the social capital necessary to do the kind of projects that I think social work has the capacity to achieve with appropriate levels of funding and support. So as I was here studying phenomenological methods for anthropology and existential anthropology, I came to the conclusion that if I was to study meaning-making practices, storytelling and the narrative imagination, and the symbolic imagination of reality by homeless people or by impoverished people, we would get an interesting lens into their agency. I thought that through the telling of that story and the spreading of the story throughout society, we might be able to construct a compelling enough narrative that might help to influence the accruement of the social capital currently unavailable. I felt it could be hugely beneficial to social justice advocacy campaigns and social work more generally.

So, I found in the ethnographic research methods that Michael Jackson teaches a tool for taking the theories and methods of the academic study of religion and tying them to a concrete social justice advocacy campaign. This is one of the great difficulties inherent in the divide between colleagues and data. If you want to do this kind of academic research, the real question is, "How can we remain ethically engaged whilst seeking this kind of scholarly objectivity?" For me, this type of ethnographic research provides the perfect opportunity for that kind of work, in terms of listening to people's stories and resisting the placement of any kind of qualitative or normative judgment on those individuals' perspectives. But just really trying to do the work to see clearly what it is that they're trying to tell you about where they come from and how they see themselves. And then to publish that and to talk about how you understand it as best you can.

That seemed to provide the grounds for me to have an ethically and politically engaged role as a really, simultaneously productive scholar of religion, to study the religious imaginations of the urban poor.

What's important is seeing clearly what it is that they are trying to communicate about where they are from and how they see themselves. Then to publish that communication, and to talk about how you understand it as best you can. That seemed to provide the grounds for me to combine having an ethically and politically engaged role that functioned simultaneously with the study of religion, and the religious imagination of the urban poor.

Not only does that produce new knowledge and new scholarship in the study of religion, but also it hopefully has the effect of improving social capital for those urban poor. I hope to see, with some great effort over the course of a long period of time, some serious community development and poverty prevention work.

You clearly aspire to having an impact outside of the 'Ivory Tower'. You've shifted away from comparative religion and the philosophy of religion, to religion, ethics, and politics. Yet you could have shifted to religion and social sciences as well. Did you consider that?

I'm not sure if religion and social sciences was an explicit field that you could do when I came here. I don't think that it was one of the sub-fields. I think actually, I've heard of people doing it now. When I hear of people doing it now, I think to myself, "I should have, that would have been great." I didn't see it on the list of options so I checked the one that seemed the best.

I understand. Now if we move on to the student population here, was it different from Georgia State?

Yes. The student population is very diverse, which is great. I think one of the things that is extra fantastic about the Divinity School amongst other schools at Harvard is that it is particularly good about admitting non-traditional students. Students from impoverished backgrounds and students representing the indigenous traditions of various communities around the world are all welcome here. Perhaps my understanding is skewed by the fact that my knowledge of this school is more detailed, as opposed to the Kennedy School or the Business School or the Law School. But I really think that you find quite a lot of unusual people here—types you would not expect to find in the Ivy League.

I mean, for my part, you know, I came here from being a professional guitar player. I was playing rock & roll, R&b, hip-hop and actually also traditional African-American gospel music for a living in Atlanta. I kind of lived that rock & roll lifestyle during my undergraduate years. I was spending a lot of time with people who don't have education or academic aspirations, or even professional opportunities or credibility of any variety. People who might have criminal records and things like that. Spending a lot of time with what people just seem to describe here as the subaltern, or you know, people who are conceived of as the other, or the oppressed, or the downtrodden.

Those were the people I was spending the most time with before I came here, and I think that there are a lot of people who are that way, you know. From any number of different backgrounds. Whether you are a Mormon, or a Muslim, or you're practicing African indigenous traditions, or Buddhism or anything like that. I think one of the common threads at the Divinity School is a certain—and you know, maybe this term is a bit vague—but a certain alternative streak. There's a certain … it's almost a Bohemian atmosphere at the Divinity School, artistic types, unusual and eccentric people [laughter] …

Yes, I think that it's difficult to describe in any kind of one thematic sense because it is so diverse, there are so many different types of people. But I think at the Divinity School in particular, you find a lot more variety. I mean, I'm almost tempted to use all kinds of words now that don't seem appropriately academic. Like, you find hippies at the Divinity School, and you find the punk rockers and the metal-heads like me. [laughter] And you know, the poets and the artists and the musicians seem to gather here. They are all people who have aesthetic talents, aesthetic interests and aesthetic streaks. People with highly developed senses of beauty and art and things of this nature seem to be interested in religion and in ethics. Of course, there are also real streaks of liberalism, of feminism, of post-colonialism; you might say those are the dominant structures or paradigms for understanding the way that the community works here.

But HDS is also pretty good, I think, about trying to include more conservative voices—fundamentalists or evangelical forces. So the diversity really is the central descriptor that I would want to emphasize in terms of students' economic, religious and family backgrounds. You know whatever set of demographic characteristics you could try to describe somebody by, there's probably somebody from almost anywhere here.

Have you found that everyone operates on the same intellectual level? Because if the students are coming from very different backgrounds, as you're telling me, they must have had very different experiences in the study of religion. Is that right?

Well, that's a good question. Yes. Very different skill-sets. People have very, very diverse skill-sets here. I don't think there are many people here who are without some kind of a highly-developed skill-set. But you certainly find that people's research interests and the kind of development of those research projects over the course of their lifetimes result in them having very different skill-sets.

Does that impact upon the content and the intellectual level of classes somehow?

I think maybe it does.

Perhaps we could frame it like this. With regards to the classes, are there classes offered at different levels? I wonder how people cope with that, coming from different backgrounds.

Yes, yes. So one way to articulate the range of different courses that you can have, or different styles of teaching that you can deal with, or different pedagogical goals that different professors have, would be to set up two different poles, though there could be more. One pole would be David Lambert's *History of American Pragmatism*, which is essentially an intellectual history class which focuses very,

very deeply on sophisticated and dense American philosophy from the 19th and early Twentieth Centuries, which would be primarily for specialists who are going to pursue Ph.D.s in Philosophy or Philosophy of Religion. The skill-set that you would need for that is a hermeneutical one, you know, a philosophical one, an analytical one, and an historical one. And that might be one pole, or one example of a Divinity School class.

Let me think about a good example from the other side. Well, I must admit I wouldn't necessarily be able to come up with the best example from that other side because I sit on the side of the nerdy, historical, philosophically inclined kind of scholar. But you have course titles like, 'Eye Contact' and 'Inter-Being' or 'Pastoral Care for the Sick and the Dying', or you know, 'Preaching' and courses in 'Compassion and Ethics in Pastoral Care' and so on. These are much more practice oriented, much more MDiv oriented, since the MDiv is usually a terminal professional degree for people who are going to seek ordination and going to work as ministers or within their communities. That would set up in a certain way, two poles that might articulate relatively well, two types of things that are going on in the Divinity School that are relatively different.

You have philosophically, theoretically and academically oriented research and writing as well as in-class scholarship going on. It is really focused on developing an academic understanding of the nature of religion as a phenomenon. Then you have courses which are more designed to emphasize personal investment and are more confessional. They emphasize the kind of personal relationships of the people within the room, and the seminar discussions, and things like that. Success in the course, or the understanding of the readings for the course, the course material, is much more based on one's own ability to personally invest or to come into a relationship with the material that's covered. This would be opposed to having some kind of conceptual understanding of it, necessarily.

Matt, we've been talking about the different poles here, about different types of students. It seems to me, from my own experience here, that this is a highly individualized environment; everybody is doing their own study project, or research project. How is there a sense of community when everybody is sitting on their own island?

Well, that's very interesting. It's interesting that you would ask me too, because I live in the Center for the Study of World Religions, which is ostensibly the Community Center for Harvard Divinity School. I think there are a few different ways that you could look at the way that community exists at HDS and there are certainly upsides and downsides. There are certainly incredible benefits and some difficulties.

I think that people seem to interact quite well across the boundaries—their institutional, academic, professional, and religious boundaries. I think that there is a certain sense here at HDS that people, although they work on different things and often in opposite directions, are driven by a common cause or a shared sense of meaning and purpose that is developed through the actual concrete community that exists here. The fact of the matter is that no matter how specific you are in what you want to do or how much you try to stay on your side of the aisle, or within the community of scholars that you want to interact with professionally, you're going to be in classes with people that don't have the same research interests as you.

Whether that means that they're not interested in the same region to study, or whether that means they're not interested in the same religion, or whether that means … or if they're even trying to work explicitly to stop the type of scholarship and the type of work that you are doing, you'll be in classes with those people. You'll eat lunches with those people in the Rock Café, you'll see them walking around Divinity Hall and Andover Hall and the Center for Study of World Religions. You'll see them at public events.

And there's a real effort, I think, among people in the community to make meaning out of it, for people to feel like they can interact with each other across the boundaries and diversity. It's actually an incredible microcosm of American democracy more generally construed because the challenge is unity in diversity. How can we have some kind of meaningful, constructive, productive, and empathetic dialogue with one another whilst remaining true to ourselves and doing what we think is right, when the person that we're interacting with and dealing with can often have completely conflicting world views and values?

I think at HDS, partially because of how comfortable the place is and how well provided for we are, we can function as a real model for those types of interactions because people do seem to get along relatively well. As frustrated as people can get on a theoretical or professional level with people that disagree with them, at the same time there's not a whole heck of a lot of tension here. For the amount of diversity that you're dealing with, it's not a very tense place. Although, it can be—politically—depending on what you want to say. [laughter]

Am I correct in thinking that your social interactions, especially with your peers here, have enhanced your experience? Were they an integral part of your intellectual formation?

Oh, yes. The students have taught me as much as the professors have or more, absolutely. Not to besmirch the professors. I've had some really great professors here and some incredible classroom experiences. But that's what I was saying earlier. I have been training as a scholar of religion, and not as a religious scholar, amongst religious scholars and scholars of religion from all different walks of life. It has been a wonderful trial by fire, in terms of developing a methodology for pursuing research in the study of religion that is both true to my commitments as a scholar and palatable for the people I would consider data.

Did you participate in social activities here? For example, Community Tea or the frisbee team or …?

I wasn't on the frisbee team! I've been to Community Tea a lot. I went to Community Tea more in my first year and I haven't gone much this semester, more because of the way my schedule is set up on Tuesdays than anything else. But Community Tea is a fantastic environment for interacting with people across those boundaries and just loosening up for a little while. Living in the Center has been wonderful because people are here all the time. And there are events going on several times a week that mean I can just go down and sit in on a lecture for the Hindu Studies Colloquium, or something similar. Although I have no academic interest in that field, I can go in there and see who is there and talk to people in that field and learn about what's at stake for them in those scholarship and research avenues. You know, it doesn't have to be Hindu Studies, it's anything imaginable.

They have the Ice Cream Social every year, which is always a wonderful opportunity for people to kind of interact and cool off a little bit. I played at the Charity Ball last year. I'm playing at the Charity Ball again this year.

Did you participate in any religious services during the past two years?

I have a liminal position in religious services often, and it's very similar to the relationship that I had with the religious services that I was playing at in the African Methodist Episcopal churches in the rural South. Which was, essentially, that music is my main hobby and form of personal self-expression, and probably functions in a lot of ways for me in the manner that prayer might function for a more explicitly religious person.

I played for the Unitarian Universalists several times this year and I played for a few religious services in the first year that I was here as well. I played for the Opening of the Prayer and Meditation Room right before someone blessed it at the Center for the Study of World Religions in my first year here. I have always found that music has been the best medium for me in which to interact with religious ceremonies. Because I find such great difficulty and tie myself in such knots trying to work out conceptually where I stand—epistemologically, metaphysically and philosophically, on what's going on in religious ceremonies and religious worship—I am able to express myself well and express my support in spirit for what's going on among the people who are performing the religious ceremony or religious ritual through a guitar, without having to deal with the difficulties of expressing that through an analytical framework.

So I have participated in a liminal manner in religious ceremonies here, yeah.

Can you tell us something about that? Were those religious groups part of the school?

They're in Andover Chapel.

OK. Was that multi-faith?

Yes. Actually, I played in the Conference Room. Yes, we did play for the Seasons of Light Festival, which is the classic HDS moment. It's where everyone from every religious tradition that is represented at HDS or someone from every religious tradition that is represented at HDS gets up and does some kind of reading or prayer or speech or something like that from their tradition. We play music from all over the world, people representing all kinds of traditions. It's basically just a musical and artistic smörgåsbord of religious themes.

Any other religious services you went to?

I played for the UU's; I think I played in Emerson Chapel once. I've played for Nuestra Vos, which is a Latin American Community organization here on campus for I think, oh no, I can't remember now. Can't remember what I was playing for … [Laughter] But yes …

A variety of things.

A variety, yes. That's the nature of the game at HDS. If you're dealing with one religious tradition, you're dealing with them all.

Let's go back to your project, the homeless shelters. When you came here you were already heavily involved in the social dynamics of society—you were dealing with poverty from both theoretical and academic perspectives, but also from your personal interactions. How did your insights evolve? Did something change here?

Throughout the course of my experience here? Yes. While I was here, I developed the toolset that I needed, or was given that toolset, to tie productive scholarship in the academic study of religion to a really concrete social justice advocacy campaign for the homeless. I spent a lot of time before I came here walking around the streets of Atlanta, handing out sandwiches and soup to homeless people and just talking to them, spending hours and hours at a time. Just hanging out with people in the middle of the night under a bridge. And, you know, trying to figure out where this person was from, how their life had taken shape, and how they had ended up living on the streets. I got to hear so many different stories doing that kind of stuff in the four years of my undergrad at Georgia State. I didn't really come here thinking that I was going to necessarily be able to tie that kind of personal project, my investment in social justice advocacy, to the study of religion.

As I went through that first semester in Existential/Phenomenological Anthropology, and the Introduction to Justice and Rights course that I took with Francis Fiorenza—which was the fourth course that I couldn't remember in my first semester—as I went through, I began to realize that HDS is the kind of place where everyone is doing their own project and that is the kind of thing that the professors, at least the good ones, were interested in doing. It's not that they were forcing you to submit to some pedagogical administration; rather, they gave you the tools that were necessary to let you see how you could concretely undertake the project that you're really most invested in personally.

So as I started to study the ethnographic methods, and as I started to study the theories of justice, rights and transnational politics, I started to see some ways in which I could connect the conversations that were being had on a very theoretical level in the classroom with the issues that I was really interested in on an ethical and a political level, personally. These were, namely: poverty prevention and social justice advocacy for the urban poor.

So as I took more courses here and spent more time really thinking about what it was that I was going to be doing in my future and what I wanted to do with the opportunity that was provided by Harvard, I started trying to think about ways in which I could tie directly the study of religion to social justice advocacy without subordinating one to the other. Because I'm invested in the fact that I have to do really good religious studies scholarship in order to earn my place here. I have to be studying religion and you have to be doing some kind of new and interesting scholarship in order to make yourself worthwhile for the Harvard community. But at the same time, I wanted to make the community here worthwhile to the larger community.

So as time went by I started to think like, "Ok. How can I—" I was seeing different fields in front of me spread out and slowly started to see ways in which I could tie them together and synthesize all the information that I was being presented with into a workable project. As I went along, I started thinking about the ways in which Michael Jackson talks about storytelling and the way in which that storytelling symbolically structures people's experiences of reality and their opportunities for being in the world.

So I had that focus on storytelling and the politics of storytelling and its function. I can think of particularly one quote that he [Michael Jackson] has in the preface of his book, *Politics of Storytelling* which he takes from Habermas, which is essentially that the voices of the marginalized are often privatized, in the sense that they are not given any public voice. I thought, "Uh. This is really something. I can tie this ethnographic research and this study of religion, study of X, Y, and Z, particularly religious phenomena, to a really concrete social justice advocacy campaign." In the urban South, in a place like Atlanta with a severe homelessness problem and some serious poverty, it's important to emphasize that I'm not here to arbitrate metaphysically or theologically what is true or not true, especially as regards religious practices. I can make that distinction because I am a scholar of religion and not a religious scholar, as such. I'm interested in what seemed efficacious for people or what people find efficacious. So the question for me is, "In a largely Christian Southeast, what does the suffering of God, namely Jesus, do for people who suffer so much, namely the homeless? And to what ends are notions of grace, salvation, love, conquering death being put? Or to what use are they being put in people's lives and their imaginations? And how is that imaginative restructuring of the experience of reality actually fundamentally and concretely changing people's lives?"

You want to take the knowledge gained here at Harvard, continue with your scholarship, but also apply it to those less privileged.

Yes. Yes! Absolutely. There is a real Herculean task involved there in terms of getting theory and method and the academic study of religion to speak to concrete issues. That's a real challenge.

Did Harvard in any way change your own religious views? You came here with a very particular world view. Did it change somehow or are you still that same Matt Lyons that you were two years ago?

That's a really tough question. [Laughter] Surely, it must have ... surely, it must have changed me somehow, right? It had some kind of an effect.

Not purely intellectually, but personally?

Yes, on a personal level. I'm sure that it has.

A minor contradiction to the worldview that you just described at the beginning of the interview. A minor doubt?

Well, slightly. The world view that I described—I never had a coherent or specific world view so there is nothing to doubt. It's just ... I was not an ardent nihilist or anything of that nature. Before I came here, I wasn't really an ardent anything and I'm even more ardently not anything now than I was when I came here. [laughter] Nothing in particular, you know. I've found inspiration and beauty and truth in bits and pieces out there at the very least in every religious tradition that I've ever encountered. There's something really magical and something really wonderful about them, and I felt that way before I came here.

I'm trying to think about how to articulate specifically how, on a personal level, I've shifted since being here and that's really tough.

You weren't a seeker. You know, I've been talking to some people who were seekers. You understand what I mean by the word seeker? They came here, they weren't really sure, "Am I Christian?"

Right.

"Maybe I should become a Muslim or whatever, I don't know. I'm going to look for an answer. I'm going to search."

You might say I'm a seeker but I'm not seeking anything in particular and I was never—I never thought that like, maybe I'll find this in Islam and I can then convert to Islam. There's no seeking with an eye to conversion or seeking with an eye to finding a unified truth or a particular single methodology for orienting myself existentially that will solve my problems. I personally never expected to find that nor did I.

What I might say is that this is a commitment that I had made in an essay that I was writing in my undergraduate years, actually, in the Philosophy Department not in the Religious Studies Department. But I was arguing for Simone de Beauvoir against Albert Camus, basically, her writing in *The Ethics of Ambiguity* against his *Myth of Sisyphus.* I juxtaposed the two in an essay that I wrote in my undergraduate research, and I wrote more about it while I was at HDS. Essentially Camus argues that, "meaning is not something that we can find in human life, therefore human life is absurd." So the only proper way to deal with human life is through this kind of existentialist courage and individuality that he articulates so well. Basically, because of mortality, finitude, and suffering, life is meaningless and we're Sisyphus pushing the rock up the hill. But as long as we understand that, and accept that, then we can gain some kind of purchase on our reality or something like that.

Simone de Beauvoir says in *Ethics and Ambiguity* something like—if I was to frame it as a direct response to Camus, which it was not necessarily framed that way—that he misunderstands the nature of meaning from the ground up. Meaning never was something that wasn't moving. Meaning was always dynamic, meaning was always multifaceted, and it was never something that you could pin down. In fact, it's not something you can hold because you're kind of subsumed by it in a certain way. It's kind of holding you.

I would say that over the course of my time here I have become more deeply entrenched in the idea that grasping meaning that is purportedly one through particular religious expressions and religious traditions, for me, is something that could never be tied to a particular tradition, because of my understanding of the nature of meaning itself, which is dynamic and multifaceted and something that I can't quite put my finger on.

So I am … the shift has been that I have come even more fully aware of the fantastic complexity of the task of developing an existential orientation. I have become more aware generally of seeing how human life is and thinking about what it means. It has given me the opportunity and the resources to come face-to-face with the enormity of the task of human existential orientation or human life more generally construed or of trying to make meaning out of human life.

Matt, it seems to me that Harvard has given you, as I understand, a toolset of resources to grow intellectually and personally. Now, with all of this almost behind you, with you graduating in a couple of weeks, what next? What's the goal for the future? What are you going to do with all this knowledge?

The next few years? I'm going to go back to Atlanta over the summer and hopefully get a job teaching. I would like to do some ethnographic research more concretely than I've been doing here in my time at graduate school. I haven't really had the time to do the actual ethnographic research that I want to do. So the beginnings of that. I'll start talking to people. I'll start taking notes. I'll start writing field notes and developing my own placements in different locations around Atlanta and meet with the different people that I want to talk to. I want to learn a few languages, at least one, or two, just to put on the resume you know. And for my own edification.

I'll probably end up playing more guitar professionally, you know the Plan A is obviously still to make $10 million playing my guitar. So this whole Harvard business has been Plan B the whole time. So, you know, if on the off-chance that doesn't work out, I will try to do some work, possibly internationally, do some research, write some articles, get some publishing done, get some languages under my belt and reapply to Harvard. Try to get a Ph.D.

What advice would you give to a young fellow such as yourself, if you saw yourself two years ago? What would you tell him knowing what you know now?

I would certainly tell him what classes not to take. [Laughter] I would tell him, "You really don't want to take that class. That's going to be a nightmare."

But you have shopping period here to try out classes …

Yes. It takes a while. [Laughter] It takes a couple weeks sometimes and shopping period's only one class session, you know, so I would have recommended that I avoid some specific courses, and some specific faculty members who didn't seem

to take kindly to my presence at all. All of the clichéd stuff about taking full measure of the opportunity that's provided to you and the time that you spend here,
because really, you're living in rarified air going to school at Harvard. And you're
really dealing with unusually intelligent, unusually interesting people a lot of the
time.

And so I would have admonished myself to, in the name of getting less stressed
about graduate school, get a little more organized about my work and things of
that nature. And beyond that, really just to try to take full measure every day that
you're here that you get to spend on this campus and doing this for a living. How
lucky you are! How lucky I am! And how lucky I got!

And I think that if I could have a) avoided some courses and b) really taken full
measure of the fantastic fortune that I had in being able to come and spend time
here, and interact with the students and the faculty here, I would have … I think
just with those two, I would be very happy to … if I could edit the experience in
those two matters, that would be basically it for me.

Take advantage of more of the resources because there just is so much stuff that
you can do. You can get so much money out of this place if you just send them a
letter about how you want their money. They will send you the money, you know.
And that's really unusual.

**But that's tough as well, isn't it? The number of choices is so great that you start
shooting in all directions, instead of following one straight path.**

Yes. Certainly, a dearth of opportunity can function to motivate or inspire someone to do something very specific. So yeah, it's overwhelming. It is overwhelming.
I would admonish myself not to be as overwhelmed as perhaps I was, and just to
think really concretely about what I want to do and how I can use the resources
here best to serve.

There's one person that I want to mention, and this may not have anything to
do with what you're interested in. But the most helpful, and I would say educational, and supportive and the central character in my experience here—or one of
them—has been a gentleman named deacon Roy. Do you know deacon Roy? He's
a Custodian here.

He takes it upon himself to develop a relationship with some of the students.
He's very friendly, a very gregarious guy, and really takes it upon himself to encourage the students and to spend time with them and really speak with them about
how they're feeling about their stresses and about their interests and about their
insights and what their future is going to look like. He's an African-American
Pentecostal Christian. He's very much an in-conversation-with-God-on-a-daily-
basis type of a guy. And he has basically, Roy, the Janitor, has been the most educational, interesting, supportive person that I've encountered here at HDS. And he
will always for me be one of the central pillars of my experience at HDS. He's the

guy that sat down with me when I didn't get into the Ph.D. Program. I went straight to Roy and talked to him about it. He made me feel better in five minutes. He's the guy that supported me all the way through my stressful first semester here when I was in a class with a professor that seemed to want me dead, you know.

And he's the person that encouraged me all the way through my program, applications, and all of the work that I was doing to try to organize my future and orient myself in such a way that I was going to have a professional future. He's kind of— he acts, I think for a lot of students here, acts like a surrogate parent—a mentor; just a person who really acts as a resource and a wonderful, wonderful supportive character on campus.

I think that that just goes to show you what kind of a place HDS is and what kind of a community there really is here because there is this sense that a lot of people on campus know who deacon Roy is, and he's very, very highly respected. There is this sense that people are really grateful to him for—well there he is! [Laughter as deacon Roy walks towards us in the garden of the Center for the Study of World Religions]. Hey, deacon Roy! You'll never believe this. I'm talking about you!

Maytal Saltiel

I was born in the Bronx, actually in the Riverdale area, but only lived there for four years. We moved a few times, first to Florida and then I grew up mostly in upstate New York. I think my family background is a big part of who I am. My maternal grandfather is a Holocaust survivor who escaped and hid in the woods in Poland during the Holocaust. My grandfather on my paternal side is Sephardic and that part of the family is from Greece. Those two sides are very big parts of who I am and how I glean my identity, my Jewish identity.

My Sephardic side of the family say that they can trace their ancestors back to the house of King David, but definitely to the Spanish Inquisition and through Italy and then to Greece. History—knowing where I stand and on whose backs I stand—is very important to me and critical to how I see myself in the world.

I grew up in upstate New York in Albany, in a Conservative Jewish family—conservative as in the movement not as in the political stance—and went to Hebrew school. I went to youth group and summer camp and Israeli dance. Judaism was a very large part of my identity throughout middle school and high school, I would say that's where my friend group was coming from and that's where I claimed my identity and my community.

Then I went to college, to Johns Hopkins, and that was a really big shift for me because I was used to a very univocal Jewish community in Albany; this Conservative Jewish community. Going to Hopkins, there were a lot more different kinds of Jews; there were a lot of very religious Jews and very orthodox Jews. I wasn't used to that. I didn't necessarily feel completely comfortable with that.

I think Hopkins was very formative for me in trying to see where I fell in the Jewish community and really explore the pluralism of the Jewish community. I studied international relations because I was interested in diplomacy and bringing together different kinds of people having conversation across boundaries to form peace.

Had you previously been to Israel studying international relations? Did that have an impact on your choice?

Yes, my father did his graduate work in Israel at Tel Aviv University. So he actually moved back to this country because he met my mom and they got married. We almost moved to Israel twice. So every time we moved, it was almost Israel and then something about the family really kept us here.

Was that an Aliyah-oriented move to Israel or more career-oriented?

I think it was a little bit of both. My dad always wanted to go back to Israel but at this point he doesn't because of the political situation. He's just really not happy with how things went. So it was ideological but also was strategic in careers. They weren't just going to move back and see what happened. They had three young kids so that wasn't plausible. So, by the time I got to Hopkins, I had been to Israel I think three or four times.

Was your first trip to Israel with a Birthright group, or was it always with your family?

Before I got to Hopkins it was always family. I think the first time I went I was two and a half, so I had been a few times and I have family there.

There's a connection.

There's definitely a connection there. At this point I've been six times or so.

Israel definitely impacted my desire to study international relations, as a place where I'd love to see peace, the Middle East. Because who doesn't, especially as an eighteen year old? But during my studies I became jaded with politics and politicians and just sort of this fakeness, which just isn't me at all.

About the same time that that happened, I stumbled into the Inter-Faith Center in my college campus. So it was all sort of serendipitous. The Inter-Faith Center at Hopkins is a converted old Methodist church building where they have flexible shutters to cover up the Jesus images. Up top they have a Buddhist zendo, downstairs a Hindu prayer room, a Muslim prayer room and a library; it's a very flexible, multipurpose space and it's just incredible.

There were two chaplains there who deeply impacted my life. I ended up working for them as an office assistant and then I became an intern and it really shifted my whole perspective.

When was that during your undergraduate studies, exactly?

It was the summer between my second and third year. During my third year I actually went to London in the fall to study abroad.

How was your first experience studying there?

I wanted to go to the Middle East; I wanted to go to Egypt. My father was not having that. He was not sending his American daughter, Jewish American daughter to Egypt. So I found this Arabic program at SOAS. I had studied Arabic at Hopkins but it wasn't a great program when I was there, even now I know very little Arabic. But I wanted to get this international experience. I knew I should go to the Middle East and I didn't want to go to Israel because I had been to Israel so many times and I knew that I would go back again. So I wanted to experience something new and something different. London was very attractive to me.

It was intriguing and sounded like this great cosmopolitan city. I loved it there and it was wonderful and the diversity really drew me into the vividness; the expression of culture, of identity, and of religion from such diverse places was incredible. It reminded me of New York City in many ways but also so different. I loved it.

You stayed for one semester?

I stayed for one semester and then I went back to Hopkins. I loved that I studied at SOAS and that it wasn't an American program in London or anywhere because I didn't have any American friends. All my friends were from all over Europe and the world, and that's what I was always seeking out.

So then in your third year, in the spring, you were back at John Hopkins?

Yes. There was a conference that was happening at the Inter-Faith Center. It's called Coming Together. This was the second one. It was a gathering of students from across the country who were all involved with their chaplains in Inter-Faith work, Inter-Faith councils, things like that. I am a planner and an organizer, so the summer before I went to London, I was helping organize this. I became sort of the co-conference coordinator and in February the conference happened and it was wonderful. I got to meet people from everywhere and I felt really in my element. Bringing people together to talk, to have conversations where people will come to me and tell me how wonderful a time they had and how life changing it was … I was riding this high. That's when I really thought that my world changed. I was not going to go into diplomacy.

So there definitely was a shift in your thinking.

That was the major shift that happened. But Hopkins does not study religion, Hopkins is a scientific research institution.

How can you study international relations there then, without the religious element?

It's a great question. My senior year, I pushed for a religion department. I met with different deans, I gathered signatures and we didn't get a department but we got a class through the Anthropology department. It was something. I think they just wanted to shut me up.

So there you took your first class in religion?

It was really anthropology because they weren't looking through a religious lens very much at all, but I did and it was fun. I took photography and my final project was a thesis of spirituality which explored different artistic modes of religious expressions. So religion sort of slipped into my course work, but while I don't feel like I had any mentorship in an academic way, I definitely had it in a spiritual way. I was very close with my rabbi who was at Hillel. We saw eye-to-eye on many of the religious and spiritual aspects, but he left after my junior year to go be a rabbi in Dallas.

I think that was some of my shift too. I was losing some of this Jewish, religious leadership and connection and really finding guidance within the Inter-Faith Center. I would have long conversations with both the chaplains and the students. I remember I would stay up till 2:00am with a Sikh, a Muslim, a Baha'i and Mormon students and we would have long conversations about life and humanity and what we wanted to do with our lives. It was really profound. It kept being life-changing, I see that more on the trajectory of shaping who I am today. I said, "I can't *not* do this for the rest of my life, this is who I am." It really lit a fire.

So I had that Jewish foundation and then when I stepped into these circles with multi-religious belief and belonging, I thought I could strengthen my Judaism. By having these conversations, I had to know more about myself and I would ask people questions that prompted them to know more about themselves. In our differences, I think we put it together and it was beautiful. It was really beautiful.

So you'd already begun to think about dialogue and inter-faith work. When did you start thinking about applying to Grad school to study religion?

At the same time that all of this was happening I was also was tutoring downtown in inner-city Baltimore. For four years I tutored during my time in Hopkins and then afterward I helped to run the program in my last year. I also taught summer school in Baltimore the summer between my junior and senior year and that had a profound impact on me too.

What topics did you teach?

It was Elementary school, so everything. A good friend of mine from the Inter-Faith Center, a Baha'i student that I worked on the conference with, went and did Teach for America and he worked in the Mississippi Delta. So all through my senior year I would have these conversations with him. We talked about faith and we talked about religion, we talked about his students and the conditions that he was teaching in and he would tell me these stories that you just have to laugh at because otherwise you would cry.

But that really encouraged me, too. So I knew that working with youth was very important to me but it wasn't something I wanted to do for my whole life because I did want to go do this chaplain thing. But I applied for Teach for America and got it. I worked after graduation in 3rd and 4th grade Special Education classrooms in the South Bronx. So I sort of went back to the Bronx, this place that I felt an affinity with. I actually taught in the same building that one of my second cousins went to when he was in kindergarten.

But it was crazy and I had no preparation. I knew nothing about Special Ed. My administration was awful. They would play rap music on the PA system every morning and get my kids all riled up. All my students were emotionally disturbed, there were curse words and desks and punches flying across the classroom every day.

Did you get any kind of preparation?

So we had summer institute and I would say about three hours out of the whole summer were on Special Ed. It was pretty rough with very little support, so I only did it for a year and then I got a job offer back at Hopkins, so I moved back to Baltimore because the chaplain that was there when I was there went up to be the university chaplain at Yale. So they were still looking for a chaplain and they needed some help. So I became the Programming Coordinator at the Inter-Faith Center.

I saw this as sort of my test year as to whether or not I wanted to go to Grad school or do this. It was wonderful, I worked with student groups and I became more of an adviser. I planned programs and we did a lot of community service and a lot of conversational programs. I started a group for graduating seniors about what comes next. We just did so much and I loved working with students. They weren't that far removed in age from me but it was different, wonderful and refreshing. So I applied to grad school.

While you were working on various projects at the Inter-Faith Center, were you involved in individual counseling with students as well?

Sometimes it would happen, just because students would form relationships with me. There was one student in particular, who was a freshman, a Muslim kid, who would come in a lot and we would do what I would consider counseling, not in a formal sense, but he really needed help to work through some issues. I think I worked with other students like that too, not in a very formal setting but definitely counseling work was part of it.

So that was inter-faith work but from a very different angle?

Exactly. The students were all from different faith traditions. I worked with Hindu kids and Muslim kids and Christian kids and Jewish kids.

How did you develop that skill? How were you able to adapt so quickly, to be able to talk to students from such a variety of faiths? Was there something that helped you with that?

I think in some ways it's just sort of me. My parents told me a story that when I was about four, parents of kids that were friends of mine would call my parents to ask me to come over and calm down their kids, because they were very wild. So I think it is me. I think some of those skills were further developed through life experiences in high school. I was part of a program called A World of Difference that's run out of the ADL [Anti-Defamation League]; it's all about exploring this difference within high school settings and doing training to help kids understand that. You know, we learned that bullying is awful, about respect, and all of these very fundamental things.

I don't know if it's run anymore but it was a great program. So I think in these types of experiences, I believe in walking into them with a sense of humility. I don't … I will never know all the answers but I know how to listen and I don't know that I was taught that. I think I learn often by example but I think it's also just who I am and those were the skills that were exercised that year doing counseling and doing this work of bridging boundaries and building bridges.

So you did that for one year?

Yes. During that year, I applied to Grad school. I was thinking already and I didn't know much about what was out there because there's no Religious Studies program at Johns Hopkins. My chaplains had Master's of Religion, one from Georgetown while she was working and then one from an ecumenical institute in Baltimore. So they were very nontraditional, I would say. I didn't really know where to go. I think they had mentioned to me some programs and I started looking at Harvard. I looked at Harvard, Yale and The Pacific School of Religion—very random list. My family moved to California when I was in college. I have two brothers who live in Berkeley now and my parents live in Orange County. So I'm sort of bi-coastal at the moment. I thought it would be really great to be near my brothers in Berkeley and PSR is there. It looked like they were doing interesting stuff too, just on my visit there, but in a very different way to what we are doing here. I applied to Yale because my old chaplain, Sharon, is the chaplain at Yale so I thought it would be great to work with her.

Then I applied to Harvard because it just seemed so pluralistic and it seemed like that could work. I came and I visited all these places. In Yale, I felt it was very

Christian. They took good care of me as the Jewish student who was coming in but I knew that I wouldn't fit in there entirely. I was looking for things beyond just Judaism and Christianity and it didn't seem there were any students that fit the bill.

It wasn't such a hard decision, but it was a little difficult because I knew my internship experience there would have been great. But then I came here. I actually came to look at the school the day of the Billings Contest, the preaching marathon, and I sat in. I heard one that was from a Protestant and I heard one Jewish orthodox woman who preached on Passover. She preached about not inviting singles in and about the roles of single people within the Jewish community. It was amazing to see her up there in Divinity Hall preaching and it blew my mind. I talked to Dudley Rose and he was so nice. I definitely blew up Harvard in my mind, you know, "They have everything there! It's wonderful, it's pluralistic, I can take classes in every religion!"—all these things.

Can you tell us something about your first steps here on campus?

It was very different to my previous education, because people were talking about religion. The first person I met on campus was Kerry Maloney and that was different to anything that I had ever experienced before. I remember I was wearing this necklace with colored swirls in it and she comes up to me. I think she knew who I was already. I think she memorizes people before they get here. She starts exclaiming about how beautiful my necklace is and how she can see it's so much a part of my personality and it's so spiritual and these colors are coming together and swirling all these ways. I was like—OK, this is very different but I will go with it because it's awesome. I was used to being surrounded by engineers and here is Kerry Maloney. It was a big contrast.

I remember just how open and honest and eager everybody was. I remember talking to students and learning so much about them and learning about what makes them tick. In our first conversation, it was so honest and so open and everybody was nervous, everybody was excited. There was this collective energy about, "Yeah we're here, we're going to do it, it's great!" I think that was the Orientation.

Shopping period was a little more stressful in trying to figure out where I belonged in this whole school and where I wanted to take classes. It was easier as an MDiv because there are two required classes. I knew I wanted to get my language out of the way because I am not great at languages. I just had this one class left that I had to figure out. I had never experienced shopping period before, we didn't do that at Hopkins, we picked our classes ahead of time. I felt like I was a kid in a candy store and had to go to everything and that one remaining class had to be the perfect class.

The class I ended up taking was Buddhist-Christian Encounters with Don Swearer. Don Swearer was the head of the CSWR. I also had heard from my friend that there was going to be a class at HDS that sent people to the Parliament of the World's Religions in Australia in December and I thought—I've got to get into this class. So I talked to Don during Orientation. I think I said something like, "I'm excited about your class, I know nothing about Buddhism or Christianity."

Did you end up in Australia?

I did, three of us went from the class. We had to fill out applications for the first week or second week of class. So there I was, this new Divinity student still working with the framework from a very non-academic way of thinking about religion because I had never studied it before. It's a different way of talking about religion and religious beliefs and religious experiences when people are doing it and sort of this 'pop religion', as opposed to when people are studying it very seriously. That transition for me took some time. I remember getting papers back from Don saying you know, "This is way too normative," and I had no idea what normative even meant.

I was speaking from my 'pop religion' eyes because that's the only way I knew it, even within Judaism. I never was in a chavruta to study. I've done Hebrew school but it's a very surface level. There were some very small topics that I knew a lot about and went deep in but very, very few. So it was a different experience.

Was your second semester better? Did you integrate into the community?

Kind of. My second semester was one of my least favorite semesters here actually, because I set out my course schedule ahead of time and I thought it was going to be just on the basis of the names of the classes, the best schedule ever. I took Harvey Cox's class on religion in America. It was different to what I had expected. I felt at that point that I knew a lot about religion in America and I had experienced religion in America in different ways and that wasn't necessarily how he was portraying it. So there is this dissonance.

I also took Modern Jewish Thoughts which I thought was going to be awesome but the professor was also a dean in a school and so he was very busy and less interested in the class. Theories and Methods, I wasn't really happy with and Hebrew which I still struggle with.

So that was a pretty tough first year?

It had extreme ups and extreme downs. I went to Australia in December right before finals. Then I came back and took finals and went to Israel because I led a Birthright trip because I got connected really quickly with Hillel here. I led the trip, I came back, traveled around the country for three weeks and then started school again. It was also my first semester, travel around the world and then I came back to school again. So that was a lot.

In these classes, even those with content you didn't enjoy, how did you feel about the methodology and the intellectual level? Was the methodology different from Johns Hopkins? Did you interact with fellow students and professors?

I think it was very different. I think it differs here from class to class, but on the whole I would say that my professors are much more approachable than my professors were at Hopkins, much more open to having conversations. I think that I formed relationships here. I had one professor that I still remain close with at Hopkins, but that was it over four years. As regards to methodology, I think everything was different. I think studying religion as opposed to studying political science is different. Also, I think class sizes for me were different. I graduated five years ago so it's hard to think back to my classes.

Was there a difference in the intellectual level between MTS and MDiv students?

I don't think that intellectually I saw differences between MDiv and MTS students. I think approaches to the intellect and approaches to the class were a little different. MDivs were open to talking about their experiences in ways that MTS didn't as much. Intellectually, both were talking about the rigorous readings that we were doing and also how they impacted us. Though I had less at the time as an 18 year old, speaking of life experiences wasn't welcomed at Hopkins in the way that it is here, especially starting with Intro. to Ministry Studies. This became the norm, to talk about our lives and how the intellect interacts with the on-the-ground real stuff, which inspired me. You know, I think for my whole time here—and I know this has something more to do with the community but also the intellectual—that having tea dates and conversations one-on-one with small groups of friends about the reading and also about how it relates to our lives, has been fundamental in my learning.

It was very different. In Hopkins I was surrounded by all my friends who were engineers and scientists and weren't in my classes with me. Here I can talk about the intellectual outside the classroom and bring it in and there is this fluidity that was not apparent in my undergrad.

Were your fellow students at Harvard very different to your peers at Hopkins? How did the interactions differ?

People talk about diversity at HDS a lot, and it is quite diverse here. For me, I think Hopkins was much more diverse. My friend groups ended up being much more diverse, especially towards my senior year. I think this falls into different categories. I think one is what we study. Everybody here studies religion of some sort, so it's not really that diverse. I would be at parties with friends at Hopkins and they would be explaining to me, like, conic equations, ways of looking at the world that were very different from my own intellectually. They were thinking about physics and thinking about biology and chemistry and that was impacting their life experiences in ways that people here don't have because there is a focus on religion.

At the same time, there is a diversity of family and cultural experience, which at Hopkins was based on religious expression. I was friends with a lot of South Asians from different religious traditions, people from all over the world, whose ways of being in the world were deeply impacted by their family experience and their religious beliefs.

Here there are a lot of different kinds of people coming from different places but the religious expression is very similar and the ways of comprehending the world are pretty similar. So there is a diversity here, but also not. Part of it I think, for me, is being Jewish in a place where there are maybe twenty Jews and maybe five of them who show up. So for me being part of the Jewish community in a place where we study religion and we're interested in what other religions think means that being one of five Jews is being constantly asked questions like, "So what do Jews think about such and such?"

The amount of times I have been asked that question either overtly or very subtly … but I've known that that's what's on the mind of the person asking … it's numerous. I've been called out in class to be asked about Jewish experience. I have been asked one-on-one and I have been in sections where it's come out and everybody sort of looks at me and it's like, "OK. Let me see if I can dissect this somewhat for you." I think for me, some of that is that I am very outgoing and I don't hide my Judaism. It's a big part of who I am and so I know I put myself out there to be asked those questions.

On the other hand it shows a bit of a miscomprehension of the Jewish role, because how can you speak with one voice, representing the entire Jewish diversity?

Because nobody would ask the Christian students what Christians think about that, right? I think about this in the American context too. We live in this Christian world and to be a Jew is to be told you have one voice when it's the furthest thing from the truth. So there is that level of diversity and I think that for me, a lot of conversations both in student life and academics have been talking about marginalization and oppression and postcolonial decolonization and trying to fit myself into that lens. That world has been interesting and somewhat difficult, because I don't think of myself as being part of a colonial power, but also not colonized. Where do I as a Jew fit in? Being displaced, being diasporic, being all these things? It's also the same for Blacks and Latinos and all these people who have had to face these things. So finding my voice in the classroom and finding my voice in the student life around these issues has been interesting and has been continuing. It's interesting I think, because I am white and I can't hide that. But I'm also not white in the traditional way.

How did you become involved in student life?

I got to campus and during Orientation I was sitting with the Jewish students and Rabbi Finestone says, "We need a leader of the Jewish students." We all started looking at each other and Cecely comes over and says, "Well, I will do it." When I learned that she had two kids and lives in Providence so she commutes in ... I thought, "This poor girl, I can help her." So my first day of Orientation, I become the co-president of the JSA, step one. Then a group of us during Orientation were talking about how dance and movement has been really important to our lives. Day two, we formed Ministry in Motion and I've been heavily involved in that. So in the first two days of Orientation, I feel like I became intimately part of this community life—both Jewishly and in the larger class body. I think part of that is who I am. I was probably over involved in things in college and I knew that that's how I operate in the world.

For the Jewish Student Association, I was a co-president for the first two years of my time here and I would say I went to lots of different events and groups in that capacity. In my first year I hosted an Inter-Faith seder and had weekly, or bi-weekly, or monthly meetings depending on what the interest was. That was really important to me, to have that Jewish community here, as small as it was. That continued mostly into my second year. I also was very involved in Hillel and got close to the Hillel staff. I wouldn't say I was involved in many student events or groups at Hillel there but I would go. I love going to services on Friday nights and that Shabbat experience is very important to me.

In terms of Ministry in Motion, we started by dancing for an hour and a half every week in Andover Chapel. A different person will lead it every time, different formats of dance. I led Israeli dance once or twice. Sometimes we just put on music and moved. We're looking at how movement is our ministry and movement is self-healing and spiritual and creative.

My second year, we all got even busier and so things would sort of slip away. I still participated in Ministry in Motion but maybe once a month at that point. I was also involved in Intersections my first year, which was a group pulled together by two first years who were interested in looking at the intersection of identities, whether in academic study or experience. It became more focused in academic study and looking at marginalized identities within the academy.

Community Tea and Noon service, for me, are such fundamental parts of being here that I don't think of them as things that I've committed to. It's just part of my schedule. I go every week and it's such a fundamental part of my experience at

Harvard. So that's why it hasn't come up. But Community Tea once a week as this social place …

What's Community Tea like?

Community Tea is when students, usually, but occasionally staff and faculty members, will come to socialize, have a snack and tea. Announcements are a fundamental part of Community Tea in terms of getting a sense of what's happening on-campus. It's about being part of the community and knowing what events are planned, what communities are being formed. Even if I don't participate in them, having that sense of what is happening is critical for me. A lot of people leave before announcements. But that time period of 15 minutes of people just getting up and saying what's going on is great. Even when I'm not interacting with them one-on-one, I have a sense of who they are, where they're coming from and what they're engaged in, what they're interested in. That's been fundamental for knowing my community and knowing the diversity of that community and maybe the plurality of it.

Noon Service has been a different experience, but similar. In my last two years, I've served on the Noon Service committee. Noon Service is a 45-minute period every Wednesday at noon, in which a different student group will lead a—for lack of a better term—a worship experience. This vocabulary that we put on these services, these gathering times together, it does not work for every religious tradition and does not work for many. Worship has always sort of carried a different emotion, a different cognitive conception of what's going on, than I would classify for my own religious experience. But we have the vocabulary.

So, we'll have different Christian groups and Jews—we host once a year—we have the Muslims and the Buddhists and we have Improv. service, the Humanists, the Women's Circle, Hindus … so all different kinds of religious expression. Also, not necessarily just religious tradition, as in a world religion, the Noon service is a way of experiencing God and a way of experiencing spirituality that has been delightful and wonderful, informative and educational. It has really pushed my expansion of my understanding of the world.

For a Jewish Noon Service, how do you cater to the vast variety within the Jewish communities?

I think we're very deliberate in wanting to represent the students that are here and the community that is here. Our Jewish community is probably a lot more liberal than it is ultra Orthodox and so it represents that. We host Noon Service every year around Sukkot and we do it in the Sukkah. There's not a sort of natural format, like many of the Christian services have, that can fit into a Liturgy. It would be silly. So we talk. It's more of a learning experience, I think. We sing some songs. We talk about what's meaningful to us. We do the blessings over the Sukkah and the food. But it's a student created experience that reflects our interests—where we find meaning flexibly within Jewish tradition. You know, I would love to bring every-body to Shabbat service, so they actually have an idea of what my experience of Judaism is, but Wednesdays at noon it's not going to happen.

I think the conundrum that I face a lot at HDS is that I can now open up a Jewish Shabbat dinner at school, I make it big and then there will be more non-Jews than Jews. So something that we've done these past years involved me open-ing up my home and we have Shabbat services and sing songs and have dinner together. We've done it I think three or four times. There are non-Jews that come, friends of mine and others. They love it. One person told me it was their favorite religious experience that they've ever had, and this is a person who is going on to be an ordained Christian minister. It's home based and it's real and it's authentic. Something that we talk about in Noon Service a lot is that it's not to be a perfor-mance. It becomes a performance sometimes simply by how the space is created. There's a lot of work put into not making a performance and trying to be authen-tic, people's actual experience and what they would do in religious service. We have words that we open the service with and words that we close the service with. Those are the only things that happen from week to week. So it starts off sanction-ing the space to be this Noon Service and then the group is allowed to do whatever they feel most connected with. There's been push back on that even. We had a Situationalist service last year, hosted by the Situationalist group. Their claim was that even having that container in which to put a service in goes against their tradi-tion, goes against what Situationalists believe in. So it's been this interesting navigation. It's like, "Yes, we want to honor you in everything that you do and believe, but we are here at HDS and this is a particular kind of covenant that we've created within the community." But it's always dynamic and it's always sort of under these considerations. Year-by-year different conversations emerge about what is important.

Do you ever bring in external clergy to speak?

Some student groups will invite somebody to speak. Last week it was HDS Baptists and Charles Adams was invited to give the sermon, which was phenomenal and wonderful. But it's all sort of student-led and directed, and the Liturgy is put together by students.

Are there any other aspects of your social life that you'd like to discuss?

This past year I've been active in Life Together. I'm the Coordinator for Spirituality in Life Together, so that has made another big impact upon my student life. Life Together is ... we don't like to call it this but there's no other vocabulary for it

... it's the student government of HDS. We see ourselves as a radical democracy and egalitarian. It's not a hierarchy and we're elected to service positions. There are seven of us on the coordinating committee and all start to fall on equal line. Kristen Raley, who's the President has been wonderful in not asserting a hierarchy. So I work closely with Kerry Maloney, from the Office of Religious and Spiritual Life. My role feels sometimes like a chaplain and some students will come and talk to me. It's hard to discern why they come and talk to me, maybe it's just me and maybe it's because they see my face on things and they see me as this ... as the Coordinator for Spirituality. Part of it has been that for the past two years I've coordinated these groups called 'Hear and Now'. They are groups for spiritual accompaniment. They are small groups of students that come from different places around the Div School across many different boundaries, to meet once a week and to go through the year together, and to get to know one another in an intimate way that they wouldn't normally have had that ability to do. We dwell a lot on the academic here. To have that intense personal space, maybe beyond a friend group, has been really valuable. I participated in one during my first semester and now it's been going on for four semesters. I think that almost fifty people have participated and been part of the groups.

So we've done that and I've done an "In Conversation" series with Kerry. My big thing when I came into this position is that in the Div School we like to talk about talking. It becomes this abstract notion that we can sit down and talk to one another and really engage on the personal level and I just want to cut all that out and actually talk. So, once a month we invite a faculty or staff member and then a student to speak for five minutes during lunch time on a topic. We've had different ones every month. Then, we come around small tables with lunch and actually get the audience to talk with one another and to talk with the presenter about what it's meant in their lives and from their spiritual traditions. That's been really fruitful, really meaningful. I've gotten great feedback; it's allowed faculty and staff get to interact with students in a way they don't normally and vice-versa. We get to talk about topics that we didn't before. We typically talk about talking about talking without actually engaging them personally, and this is a venue where that engagement can happen.

This year my roommate and I live a few blocks away and we decided at the beginning of the year that we wanted to be very deliberate about our house and our space being community space. So we have an open tea time for two hours on Thursday evenings. Sometimes it's happy hour and often there are snacks. But everybody is invited and we get different people to come every week. It's a social space. I think it's been great for me, and hopefully for others, for forming a community and really engaging with one another and outside of these walls.

On the Harvard campus, did you participate in any kind of Jewish activities? You've mentioned earlier on in the interview that you went to Hillel …

I'm somewhat active in Hillel. My first year, I was pretty active. I was friends with the staff members there. My first winter, I staffed a Birthright trip with the assistant director, Michael Simon. It was a wonderful experience. I went on Birthright when I was 18 with people from all over the country. It was good but this one was I think much better run, much better facilitated, and had a greater reflection emphasis to it. For me, having these intense experiences requires personal and group reflection. Then after that, I would continue taking out some of my students for a coffee and tea and still do that follow-up work with them. I entered the Hillel world through the staff and not necessarily as a student, which is a different experience. I would say Jewish life on campus is strong. I don't know that much about it. I would say my interactions with the undergrads were because of Birthright and Conservative Shabbat services but not that much beyond.

I think Chabad is also pretty strong but I went only once so I don't know. That's not my community at all.

Did you specifically attach to one group or?

I have been going for the past three years to the conservative Minyan on Friday nights whenever I'm in town. So Friday nights has really been my place in the Jewish community.

In addition at Hillel my friend Hilly Haber and I were asked to lead the Graduate Student Seder, which was a wonderful leadership activity. I was happy with how it went. It was a big community, a very diverse community, all sorts of religious commitment and religious knowledge of levels. So we tried to play the field and do it all.

We talked about the Jewish Student Association of HDS, can you expand on that?

We have a Jewish Student Association. When I was the President, I think there were about 30 Jews on the campus, of all varying levels. There were approximately thirty who had somehow affiliated themselves as a Jew and checked some box somewhere. Some of those I'd never met before. I would say there's a very intimate but very active group of Jews. We're a part of Jewish community here in Cambridge. Year by year, what we do changes. Sometimes we would do weekly study or bi-weekly. We organize the Noon Service and we're trying to do more Shabbat dinners, we've had a latke party. Assorted events dependent on who is interested in what. We sustain conversation around that. There's also the Jewish Denominational Counselor out of the office of Ministry Studies, who comes and works with the

Jewish students. She comes once a week and does study sessions and other things. She also provides a consistency from year-to-year because the turnover is pretty rapid due to the short degree programs here.

Most of the Jews on campus are MTS. They are active MTS students within their larger community. There are a few who are MDivs but it's few and far between I would say. Maybe there are six of us now currently within that Div program.

Did you ever think about becoming a Rabbi?

I have thought about it but not completely seriously. I've never wanted to be a rabbi. It was never an interest of mine. I've never wanted to have a congregation. Going to rabbinical school for five or six years does not interest me. I have inclinations towards further Jewish studies but not necessarily committing to rabbinical school.

You've talked a bit about your experience of practicing your traditions within various Jewish communities over your life. How has that practice evolved over time? Has it changed during your time at Harvard?

I think it's been pretty constant. When I was at Hopkins, I went to Shabbat services every week, too. It's sort of been that that is my modus operandi of how I express and enjoy my Judaism. Holidays have always been important in my life, you know, since growing up. So I don't feel like my spiritual or religious practice has changed very much.

Did the academic study of religion change that?

I was actually talking to a Rabbi yesterday. We were talking about the vocabulary that is found in rabbinical school and divinity school. Divinity school has greatly impacted the vocabulary I use. What I mentioned earlier, it was a shock to systems to hear terms like 'spiritual' and 'calling'; these words are not used within the Jewish community at all. But I became fluent in that. I can speak that code. So knowing where I am and what community I'm with, means I can switch languages. I'm not bilingual or trilingual, but in some ways I am so I can communicate with the various communities in order to be understood. I think that the academic vocabulary, the Div School vocabulary, has probably impacted the way that I see my religion and my spiritual convictions because I wouldn't even use those words before. But I don't know that my actual belief systems or my practice has changed. Maybe just the way that I talk about it has changed.

Have you approached the activities you've engaged in here as simply a way to provide others with some experience of Jewish life and a change to connect with each other, or have they served as a more serious engagement? Have you experienced any significant intellectual or theological exchanges through them?

I think it has been both. I think it's been about allowing Jews to have an expression—a religious expression in this space, which is not common. But I also think that through text study, and having these conversations, does engage the academic and engage the convictional. I don't know that for me that that was so different to things that I've done in the past. So, yes, I guess I've grown and engaged more. Actually, one thing that has been different is that I never was part of a chavruta before coming here because I didn't think that I was learned enough to be part of one. One of the Hillel staff-members invited and encouraged me to join him in a chavruta my first year. That was really fascinating to me, because I used to see all the Orthodox kids study together but I always felt a barrier. I don't do it anymore because time-wise it's hard, but it's something that I value and I have more resources to commit to now.

What about your exchange with students of other faiths? Were there debates going on between Jews and Christians?

I don't think debate is the right word. It hasn't been an argument of whose God is the right God or anything like that. I think there have been exchanges around belief and belief systems and practice and ways that we've grown up and grown. So I would say there's been a lot of engagement, debate sounds like a negative word to me.

During your time at HDS, have you been able to forget that you were in a mainly Protestant setting, or were you constantly reminded through the context or atmosphere?

I think it was always sort of there, even just walking around this place, with that building, just seems very Protestant to me—the chapel space, all of these things. It's an under-whisper that's always there. I don't think that that blocked me from doing things or expressing myself, though. I don't think that I suffered from it. I think that it was the background for many of my professors but I think they were also trying to fight against it in different ways, different people through their scholarship.

Harvard has, therefore, not altered your pure religious practice in anyway?

I guess every year, it changes. It deepens throughout my life. I am hopefully maturing and growing in practice and conviction. I didn't take a huge jump with Harvard.

If you were to look back to your arrival here in August 2009 knowing what you know now, what advice would you give to yourself and your peers?

I think that when I entered HDS I was expecting people of many different religious traditions to be expressing and engaging in their religious tradition. I think we have many traditions and many expressions of spirituality or religion represented here, but not necessarily a plethora of world traditions. Spirituality and religious belief are expressed in less traditional and culturally specific ways than I was used to. I would definitely give a warning about that. But I think people at HDS explore the ability to be religious in ways that I never imagined. I was talking about improv as a religious expression; I never would have thought about that before coming here. Also, there is this women's circle. Thinking about women as a spiritual community has not really been present in my life in a spiritual way before.

Did you grow into feminism here? There are a lot of feminists here. Did it change your thinking?

I think I've always been a feminist. I grew up as part of a lineage of feminists—from my mother and my grandmother. I think that I've been provided more with the vocabulary here and experiences, and other people's experiences, in order to strengthen those feminist inclinations. I think talking about marginalization and oppression here, in these academic spaces, has strengthened my ability to speak out and bring the marginalized into the conversation. Before, talking about decolonization was never part of my vocabulary. Jews don't really talk about that. So it's been an ongoing conversation on how I, as an American Jewish woman, fit into the decolonization project and where do I fit into race relations. It's about speaking on behalf of marginalized people, and where my own history fits into this larger, global, oppressed context.

We've discussed Birthright and your connections to the Middle East. On a personal level, how do you mix religion and politics?

I think it's a very difficult question. I find a lot of conflict within myself—I'm often upset with Israel, now. I think a lot of their actions have not been moral and it disappoints me. It hurts me to the core, because I feel like I am connected to it and they are representing me. They are my voice in so many ways but they're not acting with my ideals. I'm also in trouble because I don't know where to go with this. I don't want to be said to be anti-Zionist. I love the state of Israel and I want it to exist. But I don't want it to exist the way it's existing right now. So for me, when I led Birthright, it was about presenting the complexity of the issue. I wanted to show them the gray areas and there's so much about conflict that is gray. A lot of my students came with those convictions, which made it a little easier. I can't accept that everything Israel does is one hundred percent right, but I still want it to exist and thrive. So where do I find my voice in all of that? I think it will continue to be a struggle.

You clearly have very specific expertise, being on the one hand a graduate in international relations and on the other, a theologian. Is there anything else you might tell young Maytal?

Most of the things that I've learned in school have been through conversations with my colleagues and informal and formal conversations with my professors. That dialogical engagement is the true learning. I mean, inside the classroom is wonderful and great—do your reading and talk in class and that's wonderful. Talking from the heart, I think, is the most important thing and that's the only way we're going to learn from one another.

So what does a Jewish girl do with her life after a degree in international relations and an MDiv from Harvard?

Hopefully, some time off! My goal is university chaplaincy so I've applied to a number of different places now. I think that with my skill-set and with my degrees I am well equipped to serve in a university community. Working around religion and meaning and spirituality and all those things—asking the big questions of the world. Also, I'd like to help students navigate those questions and navigate how they interact with one another and with their home communities, because it's often a hard gap to bridge.

An inter-faith setting would be my goal. Hopefully, there's a job out there that wants to pay me to do it. I get the most inspiration from working in places and with people that have this diversity, that are coming from different backgrounds and want to know what to do with those backgrounds and how to interact with each other. I like to be part of creating and forming that safe space around these issues that are the most tender and the most vulnerable for our hearts. It's my passion. It's my fire. I think that my degree and my experience here has prepared me for that. I've gotten the pastoral care, I've gotten the preaching and I've gotten sort of some of the fundamentals of how we look at and how we talk about religion and what's going on behind the words that we use. I got that in a very different way with an international studies degree. You know, asking what are those power dynamics that are present in the room and how we can say them out loud? Who's at the table and who's not at the table? Whose table is it and who's doing the inviting to the table? So, there are more theoretical, incredibly important questions to answer.

Professor Harvey Cox

Hollis Research Professor of Divinity

For someone who doesn't know Harvard, or doesn't know the Divinity School at all, how would you describe religion, religious life and religious education here at Harvard?

I think the first thing that would come to me is that it has been a growing and multiplying phenomenon over the last thirty four years since I came here. It was rather minimal in the beginning and it's just burgeoned in the last years. I think a lot of it is the general interest in religion across the whole population, especially in the last ten years since 9/11 but before that as well. We're still growing a lot of curiosity and the Divinity School is probably kind of the center of this. It's grown considerably since I was here. So, twice as many students and more, than twice as many than were here since I first came, which is forty five years ago now.

The other words that come to mind are decentralized and diversified. There are now courses on Religion and Law in the Law School, there's Religion and Medicine, there are courses at the Kennedy School on Religion in Politics, everywhere you look now it's kind of off-Broadway religious instruction.

A few years ago I was on the committee for supervising—it's called, The Study of Religion Committee, which is mainly made up of Faculty of Arts and Sciences and the Divinity School. Somebody brought this up, "What should we do about this? We don't get a chance to evaluate these courses," and I think the general sentiment was, "Don't even try." If the law school wants to give it, let's not try to monopolize the teaching of religion—let them go ahead. So, there's some of that going on. There is a very popular course now. Richard Parker gives a course at the Kennedy School in Religion and Politics, which is very heavily subscribed. There are other examples of this too.

That's the decentralization part. Then you also have an enormous and growing diversity. Islamic studies has grown enormously and, as you know, the search is on to fill a full tenure position in Modern Islam and Society. There are four or five other people here who teach a program at the law school on Islamic Law. There are two or three people in the faculty of Arts and Sciences of Life and Sciences. Interestingly, our new professor of Religion and Science is Achmed Ragab, who is a Muslim. He's an Egyptian Muslim. That was a surprise to a lot of people.

I took two courses with him. He's a brilliant young professor.

Oh, he's very brilliant. He's a great addition, I think. So, I would say growth, decentralization and diversity are the first things that come to mind when I respond to that question.

Would you, from your point of view, say that religious life at Harvard— the practice of religion—has grown as well?

Yes.

Are students becoming more religious, practicing more? Are new communities forming, or is church attendance growing?

Yes, to all the above. Again, it's quite diverse. There are dozens and dozens of student religious groups—everything from Unitarians to Bahá'í's, through to Baptists and Anglicans, Presbyterians, Jews, and Buddhists. It's all of that and it's interesting for me to see the attendance at Harvard Memorial Church. Admittedly, when Peter Gomes, may he rest in peace, was the minister there, he was a very strong preacher; but even since then, if you go to the church there on any given Sunday, you'll find it relatively full of faculty and students.

Now, my son went to Princeton, and I went down there a couple of times to visit when he graduated a couple of years ago. Princeton Church attendance is really quite low. I don't know why, maybe they're ... I can't explain it, but if you look at St. Paul's, the Roman Catholic Church here, or, if you're here on the Jewish high holy days, they need three locations now for students to go there. The Muslims have a big prayer meeting on Friday evenings here—a couple of hundred Muslims are usually in attendance. I've been to it a couple times. They're very open. They invite lots of people in, and make it comfortable for you. I could go on, but I think it's not just the study of religion, it really is the practice of religion.

You know, one of the things that's contributed to it, and you know about this, is the influx of Asian and Asian Americans. Most of them are Christians and they tend to be very serious Christians; they have Bible study groups and they have this and that, you know. Also, since Harvard stopped being, some years ago, a New England elite and students started coming from Mid-America, things have changed. More people came in, including both African American and White, with a family religious background that they brought along, which I think contributed to the general atmosphere of religious practice here. So, there are demographic reasons that are not entirely institutional for that.

If we could go back to the days when you started teaching here, which was several decades ago, and if we look at what has changed—how do the two compare?

The biggest difference of course is gender. We had hardly any women students, just a few when I first came here; now half of them are women.

So, this was an all male divinity school?

Pretty much. Not quite all male, let's say 90 percent, maybe? We just celebrated a few years ago the first women graduates, I think it was the 50th anniversary of the graduation. It used to be a boys' club.

When I first came here, there wasn't a single woman on the faculty—not one. No women at all, and now you look around ... I don't know what the proportion is, but I'd say a third, or maybe close to half, are women. That's a big difference. Also, the diversity. We have Jewish students, Muslim students, a couple of Buddhists. Interestingly, whilst they aren't a majority, the largest single group is Roman Catholic. Now, that of course would not have happened before the Second Vatican Council, which was itself forty some years ago. They started coming here then. In the Catholic group, most of them are women—women students.

Do you think there's a specific reason for this? Would most Catholic male students go to a seminary?

Yes. Women can't anticipate being ordained in the Catholic Church but they have all kinds of other positions. They can be, you know, parish administrators, they can be diocesan officers. They can be chaplains at all kinds of institutions—prisons, hospitals. They can do all kinds of things but they just can't be ordained to the Catholic priesthood. I think they are still reluctant to take them in most Catholic seminaries. I don't think they're going to admit women because it's designed to prepare people—men—for priesthood.

But that limitation actually gives them more freedom, in a sense, because they can go outside of the regular structures and come to a school like this one, to study in a different way.

Yes. Right.

If we probe a bit deeper into the kind of students that come to Harvard, we find that Harvard is mostly seen as a liberal place. There aren't many really deeply conservative students here—Evangelicals and Pentecostals.

Deeply conservative, maybe not. But we do have conservative students, we have a very active Christian Fellowship here. It's associated with the inter-varsity Christian Fellowship which is Evangelical or of divinity students.

And we do have some Pentecostals, especially among the Black and Latino communities, but still some White Pentecostals, who apparently feel more comfortable. I think one of the reasons they feel more comfortable about being here became clear to me when we were having a little orientation discussion with new students a few years ago. There was a Pentecostal student there, a White guy who had gone to Gordon Conwell, which is the evangelical school up on the North shore. He didn't like it. I asked, "Why not?" and he said, "Well Evangelicals all look at me as though I'm a somewhat defective Evangelical. Here, it's so diverse that I'm not viewed as peculiar in any way." He was sitting around with a group of students who were introducing themselves and they all said, "Well, I'm Anglican," or, "I'm a Unitarian," etc. and when it came around to him, he said, "Well I'm a Pentecostal." One of the other students said, "You're a Pentecostal? You speak in tongues?" and the student said, "Well, yeah. I do." And this other student said to him, "Cool, man."

We can have Buddhists, so why not a Pentecostal? So I think in that sense our diversity works to our advantage, even with some conservative students, who want to be in a more diverse atmosphere. The ones who want to be in a more sequestered and parochial setting with their own would not come here as students. Now, they might come through the BTI [Boston Theological Institute]. I always have them in my courses.

Could you explain how people from different schools come here?

Yes. Well, that was instituted shortly after I came here. It's really a coalition of the main theological schools in the Boston area and what it does is allow for cross enrollment for any student from Boston, Andover-Newton, Weston, all of those schools, and a lot of them take courses here.

I haven't looked at the numbers recently but the last I knew of it, somewhat more students come here as opposed to students from here go out to other schools. If you're an Anglican or Episcopal student here, you'd probably want to take a couple of courses at the Episcopal Divinity School. I think Andover-Newton has some very good courses in clinical pastoral training, for example. Other than that, it's mainly people coming in here. This has raised questions with our faculty sometimes, "Why are we doing this? We have our own students." But they always decide in the end, "Yeah, this is a good thing. Let's keep it going."

This also causes an influx of different types of students. As you said, some of them are maybe a little more conservative?

Yeah, some of them are.

And this causes interesting debates?

Yes.

Do students today come with a different set of career expectations or different goals compared to the students of the Sixties and Seventies? Are they here with different expectations of the Harvard experience or with different goals for their futures?

Well, we do have these different programs. We have the MTS and the MDiv so I think they sort themselves out more or less. If they're planning for some career in religious leadership, a parish minister or something, they all go into the MDiv. If they want to continue working on religion in journalism or in public life, or if they want to teach then they go into the MTS. I don't think that's changed that much here. Not since those two programs were introduced.

I had the privilege of taking one of your classes which basically was an ex cathedra class, which was taught in a group. Then, a part of the class was also a section in which we debated. Has this particular methodology of religious education changed from back in the old days or has it remained consistent?

Well, for me it certainly has not changed. It's probably increased in my own teaching. I've become more and more convinced that interactive teaching and getting these students to work together is the best approach, and even if they just work together in teams to prepare a report, it's a good pedagogical practice.

So that's the methodology part of it, but what about the content?

Well, I was teaching very much within the Protestant-Christian ambiance and I've done other kinds of things now. I think that's a big difference. I mean, I think everybody now does, to some extent, a little bit of comparative religion. That's a hard transition to make. It's a whole other body of skills and resources that you have to sort of re-train yourself to do, but I think a lot of people are doing that.

I also get the impression that everybody's doing a bit of religion in society.

Oh, yes.

Even in Biblical Studies.

That's right. Now there's a change.

Which is a challenge?

It is. When I first came here there wasn't very much of that. In fact, they brought me here, I think, partly to introduce that. Very little of that was going on. Now a lot of it is going on. That's happening.

When you started teaching here, Professor Cox, we were at the height of the Cold War. We don't hear so much about the Cold War anymore, but we do hear about the War on Terror and we see quite a lot of tension, especially where I come from in Europe but we see it here in the U.S. too and in particular there was some animosity towards Islam. Do you see a difference from teaching religion in a setting where Communism as an ideology is the enemy, compared with a setting where Islam is seen as some kind of threat towards political stability, towards democracy, etc?

It's really ironic, isn't it, that during the Cold War the big enemy was Atheistic Communism. They were godless communists, and now the threat some people see is that these people are just too godly. They're too religious. Let's tone it down, please. They're anything but Atheists or godless. Yeah, of course that is a very, very big difference.

When I was doing my doctoral work and started in teaching, the rhetoric was "making the Gospel known to modern man." And modern man was thought to be a kind of rational, scientific person—religion and the modern mind, that sort of thing. Whatever happened to the modern mind or the modern man? I don't know. What we had instead was this resurgence of religiosity, just everywhere you look all around the world really, not just here. Therefore, the agenda of theological discourse has changed fundamentally. It isn't the rational scientific person who is the supposed target. We're faced with a super abundance of different kinds of religiosity; some of it rather extreme, some of it not, some of it very, very diffused and unfocused. Now there is of course still that kind of modern skeptic out there's no doubt about that. That's still there and even more evident in the last few years with what they call the New Atheist and so on. Still, it's a fundamentally different theological agenda than when I started at least. One of the reasons—I've thought about this a lot—is that here we are now, two billion Christians living in a world with a billion Muslims and most people in America, including theological students, know nothing or virtually nothing about Islam. I mean, when they had to take a course, a required course in another religion, they loved Buddhism. It's a peaceful, pacifistic, quiet religion. Or they would take Hinduism maybe. Islam—very few wanted to do that.

Now there's enormous interest in Islam and there are more Muslim students here. I have Muslim students in virtually every class I get. So that has certainly emerged as a very important focus. I started thinking about this a few years ago and I wanted to make a contribution, you might say, to the peaceful coexistence of these two religious cultures in the world, so there wouldn't be a clash of civilizations or something else. But I'm too old to learn Arabic. So I offered a course a couple of years ago which I will offer again, I think next year, on the history of Christian images and understandings of Islam from the prophet until the present. How do Christians respond to it? How do they define it? How do they see it? How did it fit or not fit into their world view? How did that change over the years?

It's very fascinating and there's some good material on this. So I gave a course that was a seminar format; a large seminar, maybe fifteen to twenty students. And at least four or five in the course were Muslims. So we had a very rich discussion there. I didn't have to learn to read Arabic because I could use the Western-European languages and so on, as that's where a lot of this, or almost all of this material is to be found. That's only just only one concrete illustration of how the focus has changed. I gave courses here where I talked about Christian-Marxist dialogue. And who's interested in Christian-Marxist dialogue anyway?

Statistical data shows that here in the US, two particular 'religious' groups are growing very fast—Atheists, including radical Atheists, and also conservative Fundamentalist groups. Whilst the latter group tend to have a demographic advantage, compared to the Atheists, because they tend to have children—lots of children, how would you say that, compared to a few decades ago, the dynamic has changed? Would you say that religion is being criticized more, right now, than it used to be?

Let me slightly amend your description. The number of people who declare themselves to be Atheists whenever surveys are done in America remains relatively quite small. They do not increase. They're a small percentage. Those who say they have no religious affiliation, they're called "Nones" sometimes, that's the group that's growing, especially among young people. No affiliation. They don't want to be Atheists but they don't want to be followers. Many of them will say, "Well, I'm spiritual but not religious." Many of them will, some don't. So, the interesting group for me is not so much the Atheist.

Compared to Europe, here there are so many shades and varieties of belief from way over on the left wing humanist utilitarians to the staunch Rick Santorum type of Roman Catholics and there's something for everybody. It's like all the different flavors of ice cream you can get here—why be an Atheist? You can find something. But the Nones are, I think, a very interesting group, these people who say, "I'm not affiliated. I'm not affiliated." what reasons do they give? I have a student now who just wrote his Master's thesis, this was a very, very good student. He went over a thousand interviews and questionnaires with people who consider themselves to have been conservative Christians and who are now either Atheists or non-believers or Nones or something, and asked them, "Why? Why was it they left?" Two reasons: one was the capture of the alliance between conservative Protestants and Christians and right wing politics—"I'm out of here. If to be a Christian means to have that agenda, that's not me," they said. The other one was a problem with science. Isn't that interesting?

That is interesting.

Not for the Catholics. Catholics have other complaints about the Church and its rigidity and exclusivity and so on. But for these conservative Protestants, the question was more what in the Bible could be trusted given the evidence of modern science? Now that surprised me very much. I didn't think that was a big issue but it was for these people. That's pretty good empirical evidence.

It isn't really the Fundamentalists who are growing as rapidly. It's Evangelicals, which are different from Fundamentalists. They don't want to insist on the verbal accuracy of the Bible in everything; science, geology, its authority in religion and morals and so on. Evangelicals tend to want to be engaged in the society. Furthermore, Evangelicals in America—this is very important—are no longer a single political or cultural or even religious block. There are various wings now that are emerging. I just read this morning about the electoral support for Santorum, how his support and lack of support in certain places has demonstrated that there isn't any Evangelical voting bloc. They have their own views within a framework or within a horizon of possibilities. So, I think it's a healthy tendency, now that American products of Evangelicalism are maturing to some extent and diversifying.

Now, when you were discussing 'Nones' and that small group of Atheists here in America, do you think they attack religious education in general , and specifically the way it's presented here at Harvard? Do they criticize the relevance in general of a divinity school in a secular or semi-secular institution of higher learning such as Harvard? Do they see the relevancy? Is that something that's changed over the last few years?

Yes. A certain group of the Atheists are very outspoken in the following way: they say, "Not only are the conservative fundamentalist or religious people bad, but the more liberal, ecumenical ones are just as bad because they provide a front for the others. They legitimate religion and religion as such is bad, destructive, ignorant, and anti-progress."

There's a long tradition in America of a certain kind of vociferous Atheism, back to Thomas Paine and other people, right through American history. But there is a little bit of a surge right now. However, it's still somewhat limited but there is an Atheist-Humanist student club at Harvard.

Yes. That is fairly recent because that was founded while I was a student here. They're quite proactive, I must say.

They're very active, yes. They're Evangelists. But one of them took my course a couple of years ago.

I was with him, I think. He was sitting in that class, which was fairly large, and I remember him being relatively critical, to say the least.

It's interesting that he would want to take this course. I got to know him pretty well. One time he was right here, sitting in that chair and I said, "Look, I'm not going to try to convert you. It's not my job, at least in this role. But at the end of this course I want you to be the best informed Atheist, because frankly at the moment you are not. You're not a particularly well-informed Atheist. I want you to be."

He wrote a mid-term paper for me that was devoted to attacking how ridiculous the story of Noah and the Ark was. How could you get all those animals, et cetera. I said, "Please, if we're talking about the religion of eighth graders or fourth graders, perhaps. But come on, if you're going to be at Harvard and be the head of an Atheist group, let's have a sophisticated view." So, he agreed with that. I don't know whether he ever really got there or not but …

Is that a general criticism we can all make? That the level of debate between Atheists that are supposed to be radical, and others, is not always on a very solid level intellectually?

I'm afraid so and I wish it were better.

Do you think the relevancy of the Divinity School is still criticized by other faculty members of other schools, or the college, or the Faculty of Arts and Sciences? Is there still a question as to the relevancy of religious education at an institute of higher learning?

No, no, no. In fact, I think it's been enhanced because when it was mainly Protestant—almost exclusively a Protestant divinity school preparing people for ministry—there were some people who were complaining, when I first came here, "What's this doing in the University?" Now it is viewed as a school in which all the various religious traditions are critically studied and taught. You need to know about that in the modern world if you're going to be an intelligent participant in global society and so on. No, I don't think there's very much complaint on that score.

That might be due to the fact that the academic part of the study of religion has grown considerably. Also, the number of people graduating to specifically become a minister, to become ordained, is rather limited, I guess.

Yes. Yes.

I remember you giving a class on Fundamentalism in which you actually visited a few of the communities surrounding Harvard. I think you spoke about Opus Dei? They have a house here?

Yes. They do.

There are quite a number, quite a substantial number, of religious conservative movements surrounding the Harvard campus. For example, Chabad-Lubavitch.

Yes. They have a very active community.

Were you here when the Lubavitcher Rabbi came to the class that time? I devoted a couple of sessions to the Lubavitch movement as an example of Jewish fundamentalism. He heard that I was going to do this and he called me and he said, "What are you going to say?" I said, "Well, come and see. You're welcome to come." He came and I invited him to come up and say a few words afterward and he disagreed with what I said. That just contributed to the liveliness of it. I went over and visited the house over there and I did take a group of students to the Opus Dei house.

Isn't there a contrast here between the quite liberal, open dialogue we have here at the Divinity School and in general here in Harvard on religion and these rather conservative movements attracting students with free meals, free education, just outside of campus, after class hours? Is that a typical strategy of those movements to come and recruit students?

Well, they try. They try and I think having them here contributes to the mix. I mean, why not? Let them try. As long as they play by the rules, that's fine with me and they seem to. The reason why I was able to take a fairly good sized group of students over to the Opus Dei house is that I just got in touch with the Harvard Chaplaincy and I said, "I'd like to do this." They knew the priest who was in charge over there and he said, "Sure, come." So we did, you know? And then there are two or three comparable conservative Protestant congregations. There's a Presbyterian Church in town. There's Park Street Church which is like a moderate evangelical church. It has an enormous number of Harvard students. You just get on the subway here and go right on down to Park Street and there you are. They have dozens and dozens of Harvard students, maybe more. Especially international Harvard students.

So there are these places in and around the campus that wear a much more conservative flavor. [It's] a religious tradition that's being nurtured and I'm all for them. I defend their right to be here. What can you do? It's a free country. If they want to have the privilege of access to Harvard buildings and so on, then they a have to subscribe to the rule against proselytizing on campus. They have to say, "No, we are not going to do that."

Have you seen a growth in interdisciplinary work in the past few years? Have you seen a growth in exchange between schools? For example, the Kennedy School, the Law School, even the Business School?

Yes. All of the above.

Well, a lot of it comes at the level of ethical decision making in business, or hard decisions in science, or legal issues where the practitioners say, "Look, there are certain things that we can't think about clearly, simply on the basis of established legal scientific practices. We have to bring in a larger tradition of ethical discourse." So it's not so much the theological as the ethical, moral level, but it's certainly happening. There is no doubt about that, yes.

Do you see a difference between college students and Divinity school Students in the way they react to your classes, in the way they approach theology or religious studies in general?

You know, not as much as I thought there would be, no. The college students are younger generally and a little more naive perhaps but very eager. No, there isn't a big difference and I kind of expected to find that there would be but there wasn't.

Having discussed religious education at Harvard, we all know that you've traveled far and wide and visited many institutions, not only in the US but also abroad. How would you say Harvard is different in the teaching of religion? Is there one specific element that is really different, that substantially makes Harvard the best place to study religion?

When we ask students who come here, "Why did you chose Harvard as opposed to other places?" the reason given more than any other was, "I wanted to study with

a diverse and varied group of students and faculty. If I had gone to a Baptist theological school or Catholic seminary or Lutheran seminary or whatever, that would
not have been the case, but here it was the diversity and pluralism that attracted
me." I think that also we are an integral part of a big university with a lot, as you
can see, of back and forth exchange. We're not peripheral to the university and I
think that is distinctive. When my son was going to Princeton, my wife and I used
to stay at the residence hall while we visited him. I noticed even in several visits
there that Princeton Theological Seminary is quite separate from Princeton
University. It's even legally a separate institution. Some interaction but not nearly
what we have here.

Now, Yale is a little bit more integrated but I still don't think it's as much as here.
So that's, I think, an important distinction. A very important distinction and none
of the ones that I've mentioned have nearly the diversity in faculty and student
population that we have, nothing like it. It was a gamble here. I mean, the idea that
we decided we'd go in that direction was a risky step but I think it has worked out
well.

**So, we have evaluated these last few decades, and the change in religious
education we've seen here at the Harvard Divinity School in general.
At this point, what do you think is the future of religious education here?**

I think we have to do more in addressing the larger American and global society
from the perspective of religious traditions. We're at the stage now of enjoying
being diverse and getting along with each other and trying to be neighbors and so
on, and so the prophetic, critical element has not been advanced the way it should
have been. I think maybe in the future, we're really going to need to address
American society from that point of view, as apposed to a Paul Tillich or a Reinhold
Niebuhr, you know, good 'ole Protestant boys, who could assume that there was a
kind of Protestant Christian substance to our society. That's over now. We have to
address it from this newly diverse, ecumenically inclusive, religious community—
and it's global now. I mean, it's very, very global indeed. So that is a big bite to take
but I think that's the next step

**Are we just talking about linguistic changes here? Should we use different sets
of words that are more inclusive from a theological point of view, or should we
considerably change our theology, our religion, and religious education in
general?**

I think it's the latter. I don't think that simply changing the way we say it is going
to do it. I don't know what the changes should be or how the changes are going to
be made but I am spending a lot of time on this now and becoming more and
more convinced that it isn't just about getting along with Muslims well. We really

need to rethink the meaning of Christianity in the context of world religions including Islam, which can be viewed as a historical and culturally defined continuation of the same Jewish insight that Christianity has continued. I think we can see through these three; Christianity, Islam and Judaism, that they are much more closely related to each other than we have thought previously, and in various ways that I'm just beginning to grasp. I think that it has to be substantive.

When you talk about Islam, are you talking about the new insights that Islam brings from Jewish and Christian principles, and are you seeing Islam then, as kind of a natural evolution coming out of Judaism and Christianity?

Yes.

Should we rather embrace that wisdom and those fundamental principles that Islam brings us, instead of debating fiercely, or even fighting Islam as some people tend to do on a global level right now?

The answer is yes. We have to ask ourselves, "What can we learn from each other?" I think there's much that we can learn. You know, when you think of the fact that for 800 years—say, from 600 to 1200 or 1300—Islam was at the center of the world, reaching out to China, reaching to India, all across North Africa, up into Spain, and so on. Christianity was this … was in this little peninsula, stuck off on the edge of Asia, with the Orthodox Church there as well, but still rather underdeveloped culturally. Some big changes happened in the 12th, 13th, and 14th centuries, of course.

Consider too the way in which the Muslims picked up on the Jewish and the Greek heritage. They were the ones who brought Aristotle to the West, remember? All of that has been so disastrously overlooked, and not integrated into theological training, research, and teaching in the way it should be. What we now see here is this 'green threat' out there. "How can we understand it so that we understand the danger it poses to us?" I'm overstating this a bit, but that's a lot of what it is. I think it has to go way beyond that. By the way, in about two weeks I'm going to Morocco; I was there a few years ago and I'm going back as part of my continued effort to be in touch with Muslim scholars and leaders. I've been to Istanbul and Egypt and Jordan, and I'm going back to Morocco, and one of the people I'm meeting with is a man named Ahmed Toufiq, who is the Minister of Religious Affairs of the Kingdom of Morocco. He's bringing together some people for me to meet with. I'm taking this very seriously.

I have a few years left, I think, in my life—I hope, I pray—and I see this as a very, very important project.

It's very interesting that you've just published a book while I was here, on the future of faith...

Right.

After the conversion of Constantine, Christianity grew exponentially. Do you see or do you predict—as far as you can, obviously—a similar expansion of Islam? Do you see Christianity becoming marginalized in the future?

No, no, no, I don't. There will be some growth in Islam, and there will be some growth in Christianity, but I don't predict that kind of spurt. The globalization of Christianity is really just [within] the last couple of centuries. In fact now the majority of Christians in the world no longer live in the West. They live in the Third World—or what we used to call the Third World. Islam is not prospering well there. A lot of it is too reliant on Arabic and Christians really, almost obsessively, want to get the liturgy of the Bible into every language around the world, so it globalizes more easily. I don't think that's going to change, and I think Islam will not. The growth in Islam is mainly a natural growth from families expanding.

Not from conversion?

No, not conversion.

If we should approach Islam not as a "big threat," as you said, would you see the difficult elements of Islam, as we tend to see them in Western liberal democracies—such as human rights, women's equality, et cetera; some practices on the fringes of Sharia law—do we see them as just peripheral elements that will grow out of the regular practice of Islam? Or should we deal with them in a proactive way? How should we deal with them, in the context of religious freedom?

Well, let me just answer that by saying Sharia law, as I understand it, has developed as a way of reconciling the Qur'an with a vast number of local customs and practices and procedures. It's a process, Sharia law, and in some places it's taken pretty literally; in some places it's taken kind of as an inspiration of how you do these things. If you look at the variety of different regional expressions of Islam, such as in Indonesia and Morocco where you have women's rights and democracy. Turkey is ninety five percent Muslim ... there *is* evidence that Islam can not only adjust to democratic principles, but can even nurture them in some places.

So we have to give that benefit of the doubt, and still see that there are certainly some theocratic and authoritarian tendencies there. I'm more and more impressed as I read the history of the vast multiplicity and varieties of expressions in Islam.

There has never been a Pope, never been a college of Cardinals—nothing like that. So, I just wish I had started this earlier because it's such a vast amount of literature to become familiar with here. I wish I had more time, but I really don't.

Vincent Cervantes

I grew up in central California, in the city of Merced. It's a mid-sized city. When I grew up, it had a population of around 68,000. It has since expanded; it's somewhere around 80,000 now. I come from a Mexican family. My father immigrated from Mexico and my mom is a first generation U.S-born Mexican-American woman. I grew up in Merced for most of my life. There was a brief period, however, where I was living in North Carolina for four years. I was living in Woodland, North Carolina, which is in rural, eastern North Carolina. Then I moved back to California when I was in high school, and I graduated from there.

I think that their relationship with religion developed as I grew up. I grew up both Catholic and Pentecostal—because my mom's family was Roman Catholic and my father's family was Assemblies of God. Neither of them really wanted to budge over the other and they didn't really want to raise the kids one way or the other, so they decided they were going to raise us both ways—which was very confusing! It was confusing for me even at age eight. That consisted of me having to take Catechism classes as a Catholic and going through Communion and my confirmation and everything. I was also involved with the Pentecostal church. Sundays consisted of us getting up really early to go to Spanish mass first thing in the morning. Right after that, we'd go get breakfast. Then we'd go straight to the Assemblies of God church, come home, eat lunch, and relax for a little bit and then go back to the Assemblies of God church for the night-time service. That could go on for hours. Growing up, I was basically in church at least five days a week. I was baptized as Catholic and then I got baptized again when I was nine, at the Assemblies of God church.

You name it, church was there. Whether we were at choir practice, bible study, some fundraiser, a guest preacher—Church was in my life at least 24/7. That changed though, when I moved to North Carolina at the age of 12. We were just unable to find a church that met our needs. It was mainly over a racial divide. Where we were in North Carolina, you were either white or you were black; so to be Latino completely problematized the spaces. Racial segregation still existed where we were living, in the sense that people self-segregated. The white folks kind of segregated the black folk out. We weren't really welcome in the white churches, because we were too dark for that congregation. While they never said we weren't welcome, they didn't really extend a hand of hospitality to us. We would go to predominantly black churches and they were sort of like, "You're just a little too light for this area, too." At that point, my parents just sort of stopped going to church. They just stopped practicing, really. They're kind of agnostic now. I have yet to have this conversation with them about, "How did you go from being really conservative Catholics and Pentecostals to, "God may exist and sometimes I pray when I need to?" That was interesting, but actually when I got to high school, when I was back in California, the first friends that I met were Evangelical Christians. Throughout high school I remained an Evangelical Christian all the way up until 2006.

Did you abandon your Catholic groups? Did you distance yourself from your Catholic friends?

Yes and no. I would still go to the Catholic church, because it just felt right. I really enjoyed the tradition of it. However, I would go to an Evangelical youth group. I would still go to the services later on in the day that were more Evangelical orientated, up until the point that I went to an Evangelical college when I graduated high school.

How did that happen, and what did you study?

Initially I went off to Azusa Pacific University, which is one of the largest Evangelical Christian universities in the country. I actually started as a pre-med Biology major. In the course of a year I went through about half of their majors though, because I really did not know what I wanted to do. I ended up settling on Spanish, that was what I had started studying before I had left the school on October 18, 2006. I wasn't really studying Religion at the time; however, there were requirements that I had to still take Bible courses and that I had to go to chapel three times a week. Whether you like it or not, you're going to learn about religion in that context and that was fine. I was content with that—that was what I signed up for and at the time, I wanted a Christ-centered education.

On October 11, 2006 I came out publicly to the entire university by writing up a four-page statement, along with my partner—we've been together since that day—of what it was like to be closeted gay men at a Christian college. We posted these on a public bulletin board outside of the chapel, which were taken down immediately by the university. We re-posted them, and they were taken down again. We decided to then organize a protest at Chapel that night. We were holding signs and had duct tape over our mouths, declaring that we were silenced for being gay at this institution. Expecting only a handful of students to join us that night, we were joined by over 80 students that wanted to stand in solidarity with us. That was quite shocking, because I just did not expect that. I should preface this by saying that the University has a policy that says that homosexual acts or behaviors are prohibited.

No faculty members showed up to help us at all. There are over 250 Christian colleges and universities in the U.S. that have policies that prohibit homosexual acts or behaviors. This happened to be one of them.

I came out October 11th and exactly one week later on October 18th, I was no longer a student. I had to meet with the administrators about my actions. The meeting with the administrators was very interesting, we kind of tip-toed around the gay issue. It was more like, "Well, you know you organized a protest without asking if you could have a protest."[Laughs] "You posted on the bulletin board without getting permission to post on the bulletin board." Finally I just decided to come out and declare that this was really about the issue of my sexual orientation, and that's what we needed to address. Both my partner and I were being asked to leave the University at the same time.

Prior to that, I had spent over a year trying to change my sexual orientation from homosexual to heterosexual, including going through an exorcism at an Assemblies of God church, my home church that I grew up in. That was the summer prior to me coming out. It was very traumatic and at that point I was almost done with Christianity. I was just … when I realized that it wasn't going to work, I wasn't content with that. I still believed that God wanted me to change, but something must be wrong with me, that I couldn't change. I contemplated suicide and the plan was thankfully abandoned. It was at that point that my boyfriend at the time, and now partner, read me a Bible verse. It was Isaiah 54:10: "Though the mountains be shaken, the hills be removed, yet my love for you will not be shaken or my covenant of peace be removed". That was enough for me to take a step back and rethink how I was approaching my life in relationship to Christianity. I decided for a moment that I didn't want to have a relationship with Christianity and that was fine, at least for me at the time. I knew I had to go back to this Evangelical Christian university. So the conversation with the administration ended with us being told that, "It is about time you reconsider whether this community was ever meant for you." We took that as our cue to exit. We decided to withdraw ourselves. At this point I was in my second year. He was a junior, I was a sophomore.

The school never addressed what happened. They never told the rest of the student body that we had withdrawn or what went down. There was never any mention of what had happened, but everybody knew what had happened. I got tons of emails and responses from people even after the protest, everything ranging from, "I support you; I'm so proud of you," to, "You should die of AIDS, you should never have come here," and "If I see you on the street, I'm going to physically attack you."

At this point I didn't want to stick around to see what the university was going to officially do to us. I just felt that my safety was in jeopardy and that I'd rather just leave now. At this point, they'd made it very clear that it was not a home for me anymore. Quite honestly, it was after that that I became interested in religion. [Laughter]

After that I joined a non-profit organization called 'Soulforce' that works for the freedom of lesbian, gay, bisexual, and transgender individuals from religious and political oppression. They were organizing a bus tour. It was going to be the second year of this bus tour, called 'The Equality Ride', and it would visit Christian colleges just like mine—colleges that had policies just like the one that I had experienced, so it was perfect. That's when I decided to join and they followed along the lines of Gandhi and Martin Luther King in practicing relentless non-violent resistance. We were visiting Christian colleges and universities that did not want us there and sometimes would arrest us as we showed up. That was the case, that I was arrested on this ride for showing up at the schools. I was arrested at Baylor University for writing, "God loves all" in sidewalk chalk in front of their chapel. I spent over 28 hours in jail.

It was actually in jail where I came to the realization that I wanted to study religion. Because I was sitting there, wearing black and white stripes—I did not know that prisoners in the U.S still wear black and white stripes—that blew my mind! I was in a cell that had a twelve-man capacity and there were thirty five of us in there. I was very confused, scratching my head. Eighteen hours ago I had been put in jail, and for some reason I'm in a jumper. I'm being treating like a prisoner for writing "God loves all" in sidewalk chalk. I just could not make the connection as to why that made sense and why the school would think that makes sense too, because of my theology. It was at that point that I decided, "I want to know why Christianity cares so much about this gay issue." There had to be answers somewhere but I wasn't getting them. I thought, "This is what I want to study." After I was done with 'The Equality Ride,' which ended in the spring of 2007, I went back to school. I went to junior college to fulfill general education requirements. I went to Merced College, back in my hometown, so I could get the units that I needed to transfer back to a university.

Tell me about the process of transferring back to university.

That was interesting because I kind of felt like I had missed out on my college experience. I went to the University of California, Riverside as a Religious Studies major. It was interesting because during my freshman year at my Christian college—well, for the first semester that I was there I did the whole college thing, but after that I was still struggling with my sexual orientation. I had priorities other than being a college student and so it was really interesting when I went back to college, because I did not feel like I was the same age as people that were in my class. I felt like I went from being eighteen to thirty overnight. I went there to study religious studies and that was my priority. I kind of shocked the department. They were so intrigued to find somebody who came in with such strong research questions and had research projects in mind. I guess that had not been their experience with other majors.

Can you tell me about those research projects and your focus during this period?

My focus was on Evangelical Christianity and I initiated independent studies during my time there. My first independent study was a focus on gender and religion.

I did a project focusing on homosexual relations in pre-modern Europe, to find out the historical roots of homophobia in Christianity. I did another research project on non-violent resistance and my paper for that was, "Okay, I just spent two months on a bus following these strategies; is this effective? Is this an effective way of getting this message, this theological message across?" That was my project and my Honors thesis.

Did your understanding deepen?

Oh yes, definitely. I was really focusing on the social relationships that existed, and the ways in which religion wasn't talking about it because it was so normalized, which I thought was fascinating. That it wasn't an issue to talk about homosexuality because the category of "homosexuality" didn't exist in their vocabulary. It was perfectly normal if a grown man wanted to have sexual relations with a younger man for the sake of sexual pleasure, that was just the norm. That intrigued me. I was like, "Okay, so at what point did it become not the norm?" [Laughter] So I spent time exploring that. I rediscovered that in the '70s, that kind of became more of an issue.

Your second thesis asked whether or not the protest methods you'd previously used were effective. Were they?

My answer turned out to be: it's effective for particular audiences, and in some cases it's not. I still felt like there was this tension between the ways in which the Stonewall riots were so effective, and in what ways did it take violence to offer rebirth. I felt frustrated with that project because I ended with more questions than answers. I had realized that non-violence works for some groups, but at what point have too many gay people died because they're not fighting back? That was my main question. I just didn't have an answer for it, and I ... to this day, I still don't have an answer for it. What's the most effective way of getting this message across?

I took a course [in] my first semester there, called Evangelical Religion, Culture and Media. It was taught by Jonathon Walton, who now teaches here. My paper for that course was on Evangelical masculinity. It was a very short paper because it was just a semester paper but I wanted to do so much more. I could have kept writing, and I wanted to keep writing. I decided that I was going to turn that paper into my Honors thesis, under the mentorship of Jonathon Walton. That was what my thesis was on, Evangelical Masculinity—touching on issues of sexuality and homosexuality. I really wanted to get at the heart of the question of why the gay thing is such a problem for some of the churches. I began to examine it through the gender lens of this insecurity with masculinity and I found this whole movement of masculine Christianity that had been revived through certain sects of Evangelicalism. So that became the final project that I graduated with.

I was predominantly looking at it from a cross-cultural perspective, particularly of Pentecostalism. Some non-denominational churches were also in there. I made an argument that the hyper-masculinity that exists in the Black church and in the Brown churches is in direct response to hyper-masculinity that was produced by White, Evangelical men. I was saying that this explains the Black church in terms of the inversion of the color line that existed coming out of the Civil Rights movement. I grounded that and I then used the Latino churches as a new model, asking in what ways am I seeing this equally replicated? In the Latino church communities, one thing that was remarkable to me was that there are no real strong Latino theologians that are demonstrating a strong masculinity in theology. Instead, they're reading the same books that are available for White churches. They've just been translated and distributed widely. The number one destination for mission trips happen to be in Africa and Latin America, so that was something I was re-examining; the colonialism of masculinity.

You seem to be fighting strongly to demolish boundaries in several groups, particularly regarding gender and sexuality. However, when you talk about the Latino church or Black church, do you feel that these communities or specifically oriented churches are still a necessity? Or are they relics of the past, where some segregated communities only celebrate religion amongst themselves?

Whether or not they are necessary categories is a good question. Something that seems unique about Black churches and Latino churches is the preservation of a racial history. I think that to lose that would be to lose part of their culture. There's a book that came out a few years ago called 'United by Faith' that talks about how we need to integrate the church but it was interesting that their idea of integration was, "Oh yes, Black churches should join White churches." My response is like, "Well, why can't it work out the other way? Why can't the White churches join the Black churches?" [Laughter] "Why is that the solution?" So I think that there needs to be this preservation of some of the indigenous religious practices that remains true to these specific communities. I think that you would lose the integrity of their theology.

You started thinking about options for graduate institutions about a year before graduating from your undergrad school in California, correct? Where and why did Harvard come up?

Harvard was not initially on my radar. Coming from a Latino background and from a lower socio-economic status, I thought that people like me just don't go to Harvard. I first started thinking about what I was going to do for graduate school and if I wanted to go to graduate school at all. All my advisors said, "Yes, you are going to apply to graduate school." They would have been boggled had I not gone on to grad school.

I became concerned with how I should approach religion from then on. I actually applied as an MDiv to divinity schools; I switched during my time here. At some point in college, and I still can't remember when, I decided I liked being a Christian. The term has been misused and abused, but you know—I like Jesus. He was a cool guy, I want to continue following him. I ended up joining a Methodist church that was very welcoming and affirming, go figure. I didn't know that there was a place that was like that. I decided that if I wanted to be a religious leader and to be the one that's going to create spaces … if I want to see change happen in the church, I have to be the one to do it myself. I still want to do that. I really enjoy doing research. I loved writing so I applied to MDiv programs that would give me the best of both worlds. Yes, it would prepare me for traditional ordained ministry if I decide to go down that route; or yes, it would still equally prepare me if I want to go on to doctoral work in the future. I was mainly looking for programs that would give me the best of both worlds.

I didn't realize at the time that the Methodist Church doesn't ordain openly gay and lesbian individuals, I later found that out. It's one of the reasons I chose to go MDiv.

So, I applied to Pacific School of Religion, because I knew they had a really strong reputation of having a lot of gay folk that went there. I applied there, I applied to Claremont School of Theology which is also United Methodist, so that was interesting. I applied to Union Theological Seminary and I applied to Princeton Theological Seminary. And then to Harvard. The founder of the Equality Ride, after he was done with the Equality Ride, came to Harvard for his own theological education.

When we were on the Equality Ride we stopped at Harvard Divinity School, because he was a student here. We came to see the school. I really didn't remember it thereafter, but I knew that I had visited. It was interesting that when I arrived here it just looked so different than the school that I had visited in 2006. It was on my radar, and then Jonathon Walton had asked how come I wasn't applying to Harvard. I said, "Well, what am I going to do at Harvard?" So, I looked at it, and I was like, "Okay, I'll apply to Harvard, everybody needs a reach school." I applied, thinking that it was just my reach school.

I had also applied to Yale for the Ph.D. program in Religious Studies, to UC Santa Barbara for the Ph.D. and Religious Studies, and to stay there at UC Riverside for the same program. I got into all my programs except for Yale, which was fine. I began visiting schools to get a feel for them. I wanted to know where I would fit in best, spiritually and academically. I started with Pacific School of Religion. I went on my tour, and the first question I asked was, "what is student life like for LGBT students?" The girl started laughing at me, and I was like, "Did I offend you? I don't understand!" She kindly replied that "A better question would be, 'What student life is like for our straight students!'" I said, "What does that mean?" She was like, "You'll begin to just assume that everybody is queer unless they tell you otherwise, because pretty much almost everybody here is LGBT, or at least flexible." I found that to be amazing! It was encouraging to find spaces where people could be themselves in their preparation for ministry.

I next visited the Claremont School of Theology. I got to know the school during a scholarship interview weekend, so I'm sure that they were definitely on their best behavior during that weekend. [Laugh] It was great! I got to meet with faculty. I felt like they were a little bit more moderate, which I liked. I didn't want too liberal or too conservative; I wanted somewhere in the middle, a way to challenge me and push back when I need to be pushed back against. I was very honest with them in my essays and everything about where I was coming from and what I wanted to study. They were very excited about that. I kept them in the running.

Union, I just didn't really—I felt like I would have gotten lost in the city and I didn't need that type of distraction in my education, so they were out. Even though I really enjoyed the social justice aspects of their curriculum, I just felt that I would be distracted. UC Riverside was interesting because they didn't really want me to stay at UC Riverside. They wanted to see me do work beyond the university. I got into the Ph.D. program at UC Santa Barbara, so at the end of the day I was torn between the Ph.D. program at UC Santa Barbara or the MDiv program here at Harvard. It was a very tough choice, going to a Master's program over a doctoral program. I visited both.

I came to visit Harvard Divinity School during the Admitted Students Open House here. It was definitely very different to the school I had visited in 2006 when I came to visit. I didn't recognize any of the buildings. I really enjoyed talking to the students, the Christians that were here, and hearing what their experiences were like. I didn't meet any gay students during my visit here, at least none that were out or told me that they were gay. I had asked straight people, "What is LGBT student life like here?" The standard response was, "I don't know much about it, but I know we have a student organization. It's a pretty progressive area; I don't think that's going to be an issue." The way that they presented it made me feel welcome.

I ended up meeting with Mark Jordan when I came to visit. Mark is the one that pretty much convinced me that this would be a good place to come, considering the questions that I was interested in. I was very excited about that, and then Jonathon Walton called me on the phone to also express his support for me to choose Harvard. In the end, I chose Harvard and I was very, very happy with my decision.

So you moved here in July, 2010. How did you find the Orientation days and the shopping period? What were your first thoughts about your classes and your fellow students?

It was overwhelming. I just didn't really know what I was signing up for. There was definitely a huge culture shock. At my undergraduate college it was a Hispanic oriented campus, so 85% of the students were Latino. It was weird to know that I was a minority student and to feel like I was a minority student. I wasn't really aware of that when I was at my Christian college, because at my Christian college it was 9% Latino, and that felt like 12 students, but race wasn't an issue for me at the time. For some reason, when I came here it was something I was very conscious of. I definitely looked around and did not see people that looked like me or sounded like me. It was rough.

How long did that take? Is it still rough?

Well, I am now the president of the Latin American student organization: Nuestra Voz. After a few months, I discovered where people were hiding. There are still not a lot of us, but we sustain each other.

That was helpful and I then realized that there a lot—at least in my cohort—there are a lot of gay people, and that was something that I was not expecting at all.

Is that not the price you pay to have diversity, because true diversity means that you will only have a few people from each community?

Yes, I acknowledge that now. It was just a little shocking. It was sort of like, "Wow, there's a lot of white folk here."

In regards to my classes, at the time there were a few courses that I had to take whether I wanted to or not. That made for an easier choice. I mean, I came here to study evangelical theology and examine this relationship between sex, sexuality and the evangelical tradition. That later changed when I switched my degree. What did I take my first semester? Oh, I took a class on Theologies of the Body. I also took Love and Money in the 20th Century Revival, with one of the visiting research fellows from the WSRP. I was very focused on Evangelicalism and sex and love and everything.

Two of them were seminars and two of them were the lecture sessions. It didn't feel that different to what I had done in undergrad. I definitely felt like I was prepared for the course load, that nothing caught me off guard when they were like, "You're going to read a whole book and four articles this week." I said, "Sure, lay it on me." None of that caught me off guard. I was definitely prepared for it. I was used to the speed that things were going. I didn't really feel overwhelmed. I definitely still felt like there was a lot on my plate, in the sense of, "Okay, I know I am a student, but I don't really know how to shift to the student life." I felt like I didn't have that when I transferred to my second college because I wasn't that connected. Everybody that was there already had friends, and groups that they were a part of. I would hang out at the LGBT center at my undergrad, I was connected that way but I never felt like I was truly part of the college. Here, I'm like, "Okay, this is new to me. I don't know how to get involved."

At the end, there was an announcement sent out for the first Queer Rites gathering. Naturally I went there and met a bunch of gay folk. That was great. I met new friends here and there was an announcement for the Latina/o Students first gathering. There weren't that many, but there were enough so that I felt that we could form a family community, and we really did. That's where my best friends are from—they came out of that group. After that I had friends, clubs, classes—I felt like a student. I feel like that came towards the latter end of my first semester, definitely more so than the beginning of my second semester.

Were you content with the intellectual level and content of the courses?

I definitely felt challenged by most of the courses. Some of them kicked my butt. Mayra Rivera's classes definitely introduced me to materials I had never encountered before, vocabulary I had never encountered before. I would stay up every single night frustrated that I did not understand what I just read at all. I would ask her to explain it to me, but she didn't explain it in a way that I could get to grips with. In some ways I almost felt like I was 60 steps behind some of the students that had backgrounds in philosophy or backgrounds in theology. I felt frustrated. I was like, "Does everybody else get it? Why are they all having this conversation about something I don't understand?" But yes, my experience with being able to talk to faculty about some of those concerns, about what I couldn't understand, was welcomed. That I appreciated a lot; it helped me grow. I think that because of that relationship, it produced an intellectual culture that I was happy to be a part of. It created a safe and welcoming space to learn in.

In terms of student life, were you part of any clubs? You mentioned Nuestra Voz. Did you go to Community Tea or Noon Service?

I never really attended Noon Service unless I was involved. I just never really made my way to the Noon Service. People have asked me why, I never really had a good answer. Thinking about it right now, recapping my life, I'm beginning to wonder if I have this animosity toward chapels because of the forced chapel that I had to go to in my Evangelical college, something worth exploring. I became very heavily involved in Queer Rites, and I helped them organize events. Queer Rites is about creating ritual spaces for queerness. I never took up a leadership position with them. I am the President of Nuestra Voz, which is the Latin American student organization. I'm also the Associate Executive Director for the Immigration Project, which is the immigration awareness group we have here at HDS.

I continuously went to Community Tea during my first year. I made a lot of appearances. This semester, not so much. I really loved Community Tea, and connecting with people in that capacity. I'm always bobbing around between groups. Sometimes the Anti-Oppression Coalition wants me to show up in drag for one of their events, and sometimes I'll do that for them. Or I'll attend some of the meetings that they have because they're dealing with issues that I'm involved in. This year, as part of my commitment as President for Nuestra Voz, I want to create connections between the different groups. Nuestra Voz teamed up with Queer Rites to offer a queer Día de los Muertos celebration. We're also working with the Catholic groups to offer a service in celebration of the Virgen de Guadalupe.

It can be tough to combine those groups.

I wanted to create those intersections and to build those relationships in order to offer some more opportunities and some more events for students. I wanted to see a richer environment, exposed to such multi-faith, multicultural moments.

Can we address your switch from the MDiv to the MTS? Most students take the MDiv because they feel they have a higher calling. Did you find that academia was the higher calling for you?

I can give you the exact numbers of the people who switched last year. The year that I switched, 11 people had switched from their degree programs to an opposite degree program. Two of which went from MDiv to MTS and nine went from MTS to MDiv. The reason why I had switched was because I very quickly realized that I was not going to become a pastor in the United Methodist Church. I could have, had I been willing to be silent about my sexual orientation, but really all they would have had to do is Google me and they would have found out in the first ten hits.

I decided that I was not willing to go down that route, so I knew I wouldn't need MDiv for that reason. I knew I could still get my Ph.D. [as] an MDiv but I just really didn't see the reason to stay in the MDiv, based on the structure of the degree. I didn't want to take scriptural interpretation courses. I don't have any interest in biblical interpretation. However, one of the most interesting courses I happened to take here was on the works of Saint Paul, so go figure. I didn't want to be required to take a language, because I already spoke Spanish. I was going to do Spanish anyway because at the time, I had taken one of my elective courses in The Yard. The course title was Sex and Power in Modern Latin American Literature. After taking that course I was just enthralled by Latin American literature.

I really found these novels that I was reading in class to be deeply theological. I wanted to focus then on Latin American religion, and think about the ways in which literature intersected with that. I was no longer interested in evangelicalism and sexuality. I knew that I would address both of those things through this [new focus].

In order to switch, you fill out a form and write a letter explaining why you want to change your degree. Then your adviser writes a little blurb too, explaining why they think this is the best decision for you. Technically it goes to a committee, some committee. I don't know which committee reads it, and they vote on whether or not they're going to allow you to make the switch. To my knowledge they've never turned down somebody for making that decision. I was eventually told that, yes, my request had been approved. Now I'm graduating as an MTS.

Regarding the Queer aspect of your social life at Harvard Divinity School, have you found the atmosphere to be open or closed? Has anything changed during your time here?

I feel like I got gayer being at Harvard. [Laughter] I don't know if it's just because I became more comfortable. I think it is in the same way that I became more aware of the fact that I was Latino, in the sense that both of them ended up being very elevated whilst being here. It was a very different environment to where I was in undergrad. It was great and I would hang out, but I felt like I was out at the LGBT center or out in my specific classes when it was relevant to be out. Whereas there are so many queer people here and so many people that are just really progressive and liberal and accepting of queer people, that I felt like that I could just, you know, be gay all the time. That was just how it felt, and that's how it needs to feel. I mean to the point that I will openly, just sometimes in class, be like, "Well I know that as a gay person," et cetera.

I've never felt uncomfortable; specifically at the HDS, I've never felt uncomfortable. I identify who those people are who have very conservative voices, and I am very cautious of the way that I carry myself and the things that I say. But at the same time I remain true to myself. I respect their position, and empathize with it; I used to come from a very similar background myself. I found that even with their conservative voices I can be in a very deep conversation with them and still learn from their experiences, and still offer my experiences in a way that they will find worthwhile. The greater Harvard? I feel equally connected; well, all my classes outside of HDS have been focused only on sexuality anyways.

My partner lives here with me. We've held hands in The Yard and some people stare, but we're just used to people staring sometimes. Some people do that. I've never felt unsafe; I don't try to act and behave in a different way than I would outside of here. I've never encountered direct homophobia whilst being at Harvard. I've encountered direct homophobia elsewhere in Boston, but not here.

Can you tell me about those events?

Something even as casual as, I happen to be talking and somebody will blurt out "faggot". Or there was one moment actually when I was leaving Harvard Square. It was late at night and one of my friends who is a lesbian, she and I were getting out of a cab. We had another friend that was going to stay in the cab and there were these three guys that were upset because they couldn't take the cab because our friend was still in it. So they made a big deal about it. My friend, the lesbian, had put them in their place. One of the guys looked at me as like, "You should shut your woman up." My friend explained to them that she was a lesbian and I was gay, and they decided to express their own thoughts on the subject. I was just like, "I am not having this. I am not going to deal with drunken stupidity." So, we just both walked away.

You also perform as a drag queen. Can you expand upon your experiences in performing drag here at Harvard? Is it kind of your ministry, a method of preaching?

Drag is definitely a huge passion of mine. I've been doing drag for five years. I preached last Sunday in drag, at an actual church. Yes, there is a connection! I first started doing drag on Halloween five years ago, when someone had "jokingly" suggested that I should dress up as Liza Minnelli. So I dressed up as Liza Minnelli! I looked nothing like Liza Minnelli after I was done! I had no idea what I was doing with make-up, but I had so much fun. I had a background in theater and in dance and in voice. I went to my first college on a music scholarship, that's how I paid for it. When I was going through sexuality therapy I was told I need to change certain behaviors about myself, to make myself more masculine. They said by making myself more masculine I would be able to become heterosexual. I did everything. I had to give up everything that was non-masculine behavior, such as theater singing and dancing, instead I should play more sports, learn how to change the oil in my car, very ridiculous things like that. I had really missed theater so much and I had missed performing so that when I was dressed up as Liza, even though I didn't look anything like Liza, I really felt like I was channeling a different type of theater performance to anything previous. It was exciting, it was thrilling. Soon thereafter there was an amateur drag night at my college.

One of my new friends that I had just met, because I had just transferred, asked me. One of the guys had asked, "Hey, do you do drag?" I was like, "Well, does it count that I dressed up as Liza Minnelli on Halloween?" He was like, "Yeah, that's close enough. We have a drag night coming up; you should sign up and perform something!" I was like, "I don't do *drag* drag." He was like, "Well, nobody who's in the show does *drag* drag, it's amateur." I was like, "Okay, why not?" I performed that night; everybody that was there describes me as the horse that came bucking at the gate, that I stole the show. I had a standing ovation. Of everybody that performed that night, I was the only one that got the standing ovation. I had never danced in heels before. I performed in front of hundreds of people, because it was such a huge event at the college.

I just went out and did it. I am a very high energy performer, so I danced with very high energy. I didn't break my ankle, which was great. There is just the adrenaline rush that came out of it. I just wanted to keep doing it. I was like, "this is exciting." I got in touch with the local club, they were going to be starting an amateur drag night. At first I was like, "I want to do drag." They were like, "Sweetie, everybody wants to do drag!" "No, but I *really* want to do drag." So they were like, "Okay, we're starting to do an amateur drag night on Wednesday nights. Why don't you start there?"

That's where I started. I needed a venue; I needed a stage and an audience. I just have progressively gotten better, and learned how to finally do make-up and really create a character for myself. I've been doing drag ever since.

I am beyond the amateur level now. I get paid to do it now, and perform in Boston. I came up through the club system, where you get paid to perform at certain clubs, for certain nights, and that's how it is. I have since moved on from that because I feel that drag queens are the ambassadors to the LGBT community. We're the most visual part of PRIDE. When we think back to the Stonewall riots, it was a drag queen that picked up the first brick. I feel like I have a duty to pay an homage to the queens that came before me, that made it possible and acceptable for a man to put on women's clothes and perform. I want to give back to the community, so I do a lot of benefit performances for fundraisers.

I think drag queens are pioneers. I think we're pushing the envelope on acceptable gender performances. I think that we carry a message of discovering beauty from all parts of your life and putting that on display. We really teach people to find the uniqueness and courage that is within them that makes them special, and to celebrate it. I almost see drag as a public theology of love, and of the body, and yes, I see drag as form of theology.

So how did you make the move towards ministry in drag?

I like educating people about drag. I get very excited about it and I love telling everybody about it. This semester, I've experienced a new kind of tokenizing here at HDS, where I got used to the sort of—"Vince, can you give us a Latino perspective?" Or "Vince is going to give us the Queer perspective." I've now been recently asked, "Vince, can you give us a drag queen perspective?" [Laughter] Because I guess I really put myself out there as a drag queen.

Do you feel that it's misleading to be asked for the 'Latino' perspective, or the 'Queer' perspective, or the 'drag queen' perspective, given the diverse array of perspectives? Does it bother you when people ask those questions?

Oh, I kind of throw it back at them. As a Mexican, I not going to tell you what people think in Peru. [Laughter] Or as a non-homo-normative male-identified queer person from California, I'm not going to tell you what a lesbian from Kentucky thinks. [Laughter] The same way with drag, I don't speak for all drag queens. But in terms of ministry ... I truly believe that it is a ministry, and here I come back to the traditional Latin understanding of ministry as the care of souls. I feel that drag queens are really caring for our souls; that there's just something so entertaining and so safe feeling, for a gay person, when you see drag queens. Even when I was recently out, I would see drag queens and I would know, "Oh, I'm near somewhere where there are people like me." I feel that I carry that message with me.

Is it the provocative element or the popularity element which attracts you most to that kind of performance?

Both. I like provoking people to imagine things beyond what should be happening. I said in my sermon last Sunday that drag makes the impossible possible. That's what I love about it. I could convince somebody that for 5 minutes Madonna is in the same room with them, and that's exciting to me. The drag queen, according to Ru Paul, possesses the charisma, uniqueness, nerve and talent to be a true queen. I think that those are categories that everybody can live by and I want to share that message with people and show them how I've used drag as a way to empower myself. To give me the courage that I need every day as a gay man, and the ways in which I learn from my drag persona as Carmen in the same way that I think that they can.

Can you tell us more about your preaching?

One of my best friends, his mother is a pastor. They have an open and affirming church. A problem she has identified in the church is that, "Well, we're open and affirming, but there are no gay people that come here, we should fix this." I was like, "Yes, darn right you should fix that!" She asked me to come and preach in drag. I wasn't sure if I was going to give her the right image, but I agreed! The church is in Lexington, right outside of Boston. It's the United Methodist Church. I remained United Methodist. I am now serving on the board of directors for the Reconciling Ministries Network, which is trying to create full LGBT inclusion in the Methodist church. But my preaching gig was a Sunday service during Lent, at 10am.

It was a huge surprise for the people who came. After this we decided [that we] need to do more than just throw a drag man at the pulpit, randomly. We were like, "Why don't we just queer all of Lent? Why don't we offer a sermon series and bring in different queer voices so that the church can hear this perspective. We wanted to challenge them to move beyond, "We're a welcoming church" to "How do we fix this issue?" Because the real issue is not being welcoming; the issue is that queer people don't think that this is a safe space to exist. So that was our approach, to queer all of Lent. However, we did not tell the congregation that we were queering Lent. We kicked things off with a transgender speaker. He shared his story, then we proceeded on, up until we built up to the drag queen moment. We didn't tell them that a drag queen was coming. I had been attending the church for four weeks at this point, so they'd got to know me as Vincent.

So I show up, nobody recognizes me, because I'm in drag. I have multiple looks, but I went with my standard look. I created my own character. She is always described as a stone cold ice queen.

I also had to think, "What would a drag queen wear when she's preaching?" So I decided to create my own drag pulpit robes. [Laughter] I had this long, flowing train that was white, and this huge white gown that was just gorgeous. It had a great silhouette that was very accessorized. Oh, and they also asked if I would do the children's moment too. So I was like, "Hey well, you know the children would be terrified!" So they responded, "Yeah, you should probably not sit behind the pulpit like we would usually do. How about you go up with the children?"

So I agreed! There are pictures of this on Facebook, and I'm looking at the picture afterward- there's me, this drag queen with all these children. I said, "It looks like a painting, like Madonna and children." [Laughter] I tried to explain drag to the children; that was my moment with them. The Christian Education director said, "Okay, we have a special guest with us this Sunday, we have Carmen," and everyone looks at me. We were like, "But you already know Carmen because you've gotten to know Vincent for the past four weeks, and sometimes Vincent dresses up like Carmen, but Vincent is actually Carmen, and Carmen is actually Vincent." We were trying to explain it to these young children, some of them got it, some just weren't having it.

The kids were aged six to nine. The nine year old got it, she was excited. She wanted make-up tips. [Laughter] So the rest of the congregation seemed to come on board. I gave my sermon; the title of my sermon was 'Onward Fierce'. The lectionary for that Sunday had me covering John 3:16, so I had no idea how in heck I was going to drag John 3:16. I gave the same message that I was just talking about, of learning to embrace the impossible, discovering the charisma you need to serve, and talent that is already within us, and how at the church we can move forward to accept that. It was very well received. Afterward, so many people came up to me in the receiving line. It was like, "Thank you so much for your message."

Is there a preaching class here at HDS?

Well, I don't have any experience in preaching other than the fact that I won a preaching competition when I was nine in the Pentecostal church. That's still my preaching style. I still preach like a Pentecostal even though I'm not in the tradition any more. I do find it interesting, how I still get called to preach and to be a preacher, even though I know that's not my calling.

Aside from these experiences, you've been doing admissions work here at HDS. Can you tell us about your work, and how you found it?

I definitely found it very fulfilling. I serve as a Student Admissions Representative. My role is to be a resource to prospective students on academic student life here at Harvard and to provide tours, information sessions and conversations with students about what my experience has been like as a current student. I had the unique opportunity to actually serve on the selection committee this year, it was great to read an application and see the full process all the way through. I've seen the recruiting end as an Admissions representative, to then see them in the application process, and now seeing the acceptances and working with the admitted students.

I learned that a lot of people think that being gay is a unique experience, which I thought was interesting because that's the way that I approached it; talking about my coming-out experience, about leaving institutions that did not welcome me. It's interesting reading several applications that had stories of leaving institutions that did not welcome them and just the ways in which we talk about it make it seem like we are so alone.

I met a lot of queer people! It's interesting though to see that connection that I had with them. It is interesting, the way that we write about how we felt so alone in this experience. If only they knew that forty other people wrote about the same thing in the same applicant pool. I've learned a lot about the different interests that people are bringing to HDS. I was interacting with somebody who went to a conservative Christian college, and coming to do Biblical Studies and the prophetic writings of the Old Testament. Then there was someone who wanted to specifically study some texts from the Hindu context, out of a specific city in India. Seeing that vast spectrum of interests was remarkable. People view HDS as this magical place where you can study just about anything. From an Admissions perspective, I know that sometimes I need to kind of push back against that and tell them that, "No. HDS is not the place to do everything for all people." I really had to talk with folks to see, "What is your interest?" and talk about the ways in which HDS can be compatible with those interests.

Did you participate in the Diversity and Explorations program?

I did not participate as a participant itself but I did assist as a volunteer once I was a student here. That was great just to meet people from diverse backgrounds. Many of them had never seen anyone major in Religion.

We encounter these students that somewhere in their career as a student, somebody has told them that, "You know, you should consider religious studies". When they would contact me at Admissions, I told them that Diversity and Explorations program would be a great opportunity to explore the ways in which religious studies and theology could help your work. I've been told today that they've received a lot of messages over the Admissions season. People saying that they applied because of a conversation they've had with me, particularly.

A young woman was in the office today and I know she had gotten in. I congratulated her and she was like, "Thank you, you're the reason I applied." I said, "Thank you. I'm flattered. You're the reason you got in!" So yes, the Admissions staff tell me, "We hear that a lot. I don't know what you're telling them but it's working." I'm just honest about my experiences. I'm honest with them with how I think HDS will fit their interests. I don't lie about anything. I don't sugarcoat anything. That has been my experience even through the Diversity and Explorations Program. I'd be sitting there talking to my students, "Tell me about your background. Where are you coming from?" A lot of people were like me, and I would tell them "For the longest time I thought, 'People like me don't go to Harvard.' But let me tell you how I overcame that and why I feel like I've been successful here." A lot of them are moved by that and apply. Some of them get in and some of them don't. At least somebody sat down with them, talked to them and made them see beyond just this place. My goal has always been to sort of demystify Harvard. It's always important in the process.

Has your personal spiritual life evolved at all here? Has anything changed since you came here two years ago?

I'm out preaching, so I guess so! [Laughter] Yes and no. I began to feel more comfortable talking about my religious life and the struggles I have with finding a personal religious life. That has been welcomed in the conversations I've had with people who I see have great spiritual lives. I've wondered how to get that. But I don't think I have a religious life specifically at HDS, though. I mean, I don't really connect with the Methodist students here. I don't go to Noon Service unless I'm in it. But I think that the courses that I've been in challenged and extended the ways in which I think about faith and the ways in which I interact with my own conceptualization of God. I haven't become more or less religious here, just more informed about it. [Laughter]

Knowing what you do now, what advice would you give to the Vincent of 2010, as he arrives in Boston?

You're not going to want do Evangelical Religion much longer! [Laughter] I would say break out of your shell a bit sooner. I came here with blinders on, "I'm focused. I'm here. I'm an academic. I'm here to study Evangelical Theology and nothing is going to get in my way." The greatest part of my HDS experience has been connecting with the larger community and connecting with other students. It's been being involved and allowing that to be part of my classroom experience that has made this an amazing place to be. During my first semester, I was just so focused on being a good student, and yeah I had a good time, but I wasn't really connecting. I would definitely tell myself to get out of your shell sooner. It's okay that you'll be the only Latino boy sometimes, but at least there is one.

After two years of graduate theological study here at Harvard, what will the future bring?

In the fall, I'm beginning my doctoral work in the University of Southern California in the Spanish and Latin American Studies program. My grand shift has now focused on finding an intersection between Liberation Theology and Queer Theology in a Latin American context. I think the intersection exists within literature. I learned so much about what theology is and what theology can do, that I want to try that in different disciplines now. When I went to meet with the different schools I applied to, that were in Spanish and Latin American Studies, I kind of explained how I think of theology at least for the sake of my work, as a reflective theoretical framework. I affirmed that that is the way I want to approach it. In different ways of constructing reality, different ways of constructing our relationship with the Divine and that's the way I want to approach literature. They seemed very receptive and excited to hear about it. My specific project is to look at the ways in which public sexuality and literature and culture serves as spiritual practice. We'll see if it does. [Laughter] I see myself still writing about theology and I am currently finishing up a book now. It examines the use of exorcisms as a spiritual treatment for homosexuality—as I have experienced, myself. I'm using my own personal experience as a springboard for critical engagement.

I think that the type of activism I've done has shifted from being arrested to taking up a voice and pushing back through my writing and through changing the voices that are involved in the discourses. Instead of going and confronting the heart of information, I want to be a part of that heart of education, to change the ways that people are learning and talking about sexuality.

To conclude: will you continue with your activities as a drag queen and could I ever invite you to come as a guest professor in my classes as a drag queen?

Definitely! I would very gladly accept. I do find I want to continue drag, I see drag as a valuable part of my work. I think I am going to explore drag as public homosexuality in my research. Why not participate in it? Why not take a practical approach? Yes. I personally believe that I am America's next drag superstar and I'm going to keep on going until I reach that point.

John Coggin

My name is John Coggin, and I graduated from Harvard Divinity School in 2011 with a degree in Religion, Ethics, and Politics. Some would say my route to Harvard was a straightforward one, since I entered my graduate program the semester after I graduated from my undergraduate university, but I would say my path to Harvard was anything but direct … or even intentional.

I was born in Greensboro, North Carolina, which is one of the largest cities in North Carolina, but in the grand scheme of things is a rather small city. I lived most of my childhood, though, in Sanford, a small town in North Carolina. My father's family is from this traditionally tobacco-growing town, and we moved there when I was in elementary school. So, while some of my formative years did happen in Greensboro, my most meaningful memories came from growing up amidst the slow pace and social intimacy of that quiet little town.

As far as my family life goes, I come from that prototypical, and often lampooned, traditional nuclear family. It was basically what 1950s American society idealized as the "American dream." A husband and wife who owned their own home, raised kids—well, I was an only child, but when you add in the dog and cats, I guess we totaled that "2.5" kids standard—and worked hard to prepare them to succeed in the world. I could try to add in some gritty fiction to make it more interesting, but I really did come from a happy home, with parents who loved each other. I would consider it almost an apolitical household and a neutral religious background. I was always raised to be a Christian and my parents are wonderfully devoted Christians who truly try in all aspects of their lives to live up to their faith and to love their God and other people, but they never wore their religion on their sleeves to condemn others or to make a political point.

My parents may have achieved that middle class existence, but they had to work to get there. My dad grew up on a tobacco farm as the youngest of seven siblings and was the first person in his family to go to university. He worked his way up through the Xerox Corporation, and after he retired from there and moved back to Sanford, he started a second career working for my uncle in real estate appraising, from which he retired just a couple of years ago. I think this time he means it! My mom is from Fayetteville, North Carolina, and began her career in Christian Education at Hay Street United Methodist Church in Fayetteville. She has spent most of her life working for Social Security, either directly for the US Government, or with firms who help people applying for Social Security disability.

I would say that my parents are my stronghold and my examples for all aspects of life. My dad has always worked hard to take care of his family and to provide and to be a good person during that; my mom has devoted herself especially in her marriage, and with me as a child to making sure that I had all the opportunities that I could have. They taught me to try my best in everything I set my mind to, to treat school and academics as a job and learn as much as I can—often just for the sake of learning, and to always think about how I could live my life in service to others. Those lessons were never intended to push their son from rural North Carolina into the Ivy League, but it was definitely their inspiration and support that taught me to live every day to the fullest and seek out every opportunity to improve myself and the world.

Those are some pretty strong family ties! Can you expand on what you meant by "a neutral religious environment"?

Wow, so you caught that. As soon as that came out of my mouth I thought, "Neutral is totally not the word for what I meant." What I meant was that religion for my parents takes the form of a deep, abiding faith that informs the way they live their lives and the way they treat other people, but is not used as a chastening rod or for one-upmanship. It wasn't something you talk about excessively, in that every life event was not verbally attributed to God; but there was also a keen and deep awareness of how God works in the world and through people to spread love and justice. Religion also wasn't politicized in my family. People talk so much today about religion being conservative or liberal, or being used to prove some political point, but in my family God wasn't characterized as either a Democrat or a Republican.

Where did your family go to church?

You'd think that would be a simple question, wouldn't you? When people ask me what denomination I am, I either say, "I'm everything" or I tell a very long story. I'll tell you a long story! I was baptized as an infant in the Presbyterian Church, USA, in Greensboro. My mom is Methodist, so when my family moved to Sanford, we began attending a Methodist church. I was confirmed there in middle school. Then, in high school, many of my friends attended the youth group at First Baptist Church in Sanford, which is jointly affiliated with the Southern Baptist Church and the Cooperative Baptist Fellowship. So once I joined, and was so happy in that youth group, my family started attending there. Now you may be beginning to understand a bit of the long road to Harvard! Though, I do want to point out, we never actually officially joined the church, since my mom and I did not have the "appropriate" baptism, and because none of us were ever completely comfortable with some of the theology. However, I can honestly say I've never been a part of a congregation of such earnest, devoted, and loving Christians—which proved to me that the body of Christ transcends theological squabbles.

In college, I was a member of the Presbyterian Campus Ministry, and while there I served on the leadership team for three years, and as president for one. In grad school I attended a United Church of Christ congregation, and I've even read Scripture in a Roman Catholic mass! So I say that all I need to do is handle some snakes, and I will have completed my tour of the Christian world!

How did you decide, as a high school student, to go on to college-level studies? What strategies did you use to decide what to study and which college to attend?

Strategy? I was supposed to have strategy going into college? These days, I look back at my discernment process going from high school into college, and I can only see God's hand, because I had no idea what I was doing!

My dad went to North Carolina State University in Raleigh, and in my mom's family there's a long tradition of going to NC State, so I had been raised a die-hard State fan. NC State is a land grant university, founded in the late 1800s to provide practical education and academic resources (at its founding that was primarily in agricultural and engineering technologies) that would increase education and foster opportunities to more citizens around the state. Because of that land grant heritage, and NC State's reputation for focusing on engineering and technology, I had never assumed I would go there, despite my being a diehard fan, because I'm a humanities buff; I love social sciences and history and communication, and I did not see myself in a laboratory. I did not see myself as an engineer. I had set my sights on other schools, but then I was nominated for the Park Scholarship (a full merit scholarship and leadership training program). In the process [of] going through that interview process, I fell in love with NC State and its people. I saw that even though the humanities programs were smaller, they were still of a high quality, [and I had] the opportunity to interact with tenure level professors from day one. So, I chose NC State, and it was one of the best decisions I ever made. My years there helped transform me into the person I am today, and the land grant mantra of learning for the good of one's community has become engrained into my career, my worldview, and my core personal values.

As for what I studied while at NC State, this is embarrassing, but I accidentally chose my major. When I applied to NC State, the application process included a gigantic list of all the available majors. I was looking through it, and I happened upon a Communication major with a concentration in Film and TV Production. Now, you should probably know that growing up I didn't have an imaginary friend—I had an imaginary television station, JOHN TV, where I was the star writer, creator, everything, of all the shows. As I saw that major on the list, my inner child kicked in, and I thought, "Cool! You can major in TV production? I'll check that box!" Now, I was thinking that checking a box indicated my interest in learning more about this major upon arrival on campus. I realized I had made a big mistake when I received my acceptance letter in the mail that said, "Congratulations! You have been accepted into the college of Humanities and Social Sciences with a major in Communication, Film and TV Production." I thought, "Whoa, how did that happen? I didn't mean to do that!" But, I went with the flow and showed up the next fall to NC State, took my Introduction to Communication class, and it just clicked. I had always been interested in many subject areas. I joked in college that I wanted to major in "Everything," and when they told me I couldn't do that, I decided to compromise by taking a class in every building. Learning fascinates me, and being exposed to new topics and interesting ideas gets me excited, but in the world of the academy we have to silo ourselves into particular disciplines and specializations. With a Communication major, I was able to bring together my disparate interests in one coherent frame of reference that touched them all. Whether you're examining biology or religion or astrophysics or queer theory, the way we communicate our ideas, our identities—and especially our complaints and confusions—can mean the difference between a scientific breakthrough or a declaration of war. That topic of study allowed me to use one interpretive framework to examine a host of interesting subjects, while remaining intellectually cohesive and rigorous.

When you were starting as an undergrad then, the academic study of religion wasn't an interest?

Not academically. Of course, religion was always central to who I was as a person, but I had never given much thought to studying it as a major. Remember, I was growing up as an only child to parents in this small town in North Carolina. As far back as elementary school, I remember my parents bringing me along with them to their weekly evening Bible studies at our Methodist church. They would go into one room, and I would hang out in the Sunday school room across the hall, supposedly doing my homework. Instead, I would stand in front of the room of empty chairs and preach sermons. So from very early on in my life, being a pastor was always on the list of possible professions. Sure, it wasn't always as high as killer whale trainer or archaeologist, but it was up there.

I'll never forget one conversation I had with a Methodist minister about my desire to be a preacher. He was one of my mom's best friends and mentors, and he has continued to provide guidance to me throughout my life but around that time, when I was giving those sermons to chairs, he sat me down and said, "John, when it comes to the ministry, try to do everything in your power not to be a pastor. Only when nothing else feels right should you go into the ministry." What he was trying to communicate to my childhood self was the idea of vocation, or calling, and I have taken those words very much to heart. Over the years, I have often felt called to some sort of ministry, and I actually aim to structure both my life and career to be in ministry to God in everything I do, but whenever I get pretty close to formally starting down the road of ordination, something holds me back. Either wise people advise me against it, or other opportunities arise that seem more interesting, or doors shut in my face. I still would never say that is a direction I would never take, but at this point I am confident in saying that my life of service will be lived vocationally outside of the ordained ministry.

Academically, my journey toward the study of religion came about during college. As I said, I loved taking classes in a variety of subjects. I knew I wanted to keep my communication major, and during my sophomore year I saw the opportunity to formalize some of my various interests. I had a meeting with my academic adviser and I told her, "I want to have three minors. I want them to be in Biology, History and Religious Studies". She said, "John, you're an idiot. Why don't you combine all those interests together and do an interdisciplinary studies major?"

NC State had offered an Interdisciplinary Studies major for years, but while I was there, the university was trying to rebrand this major as an opportunity to improve connections across the colleges. You know, in our academic system, we have drawn such stark lines around each subject area and subdiscipline that we often forget we are interconnected as an academic community. NC State saw an opportunity to bridge some of these intellectual gaps through students creating their own majors, incorporating courses from different colleges. You might, for example, take design courses, pair those with engineering courses, and throw in environmental studies and public administration courses to examine how to design sustainable urban development strategies. In my case, I took courses in ecology, philosophy, history, genetics, religious studies, and environmental technology and created a self-designed major focusing on Darwinism and religion in American society.

Not only did this major allow me to expand my academic lines of inquiry, but it also allowed me to examine, in much more detail, something which had occupied my thinking for years: the relationship between science and religion. It all started for me in high school biology class, where I heard lots of pushback from other Christians that science is irreconcilable with a Christian faith. I'll never forget a conversation I had with my dad that semester. My dad was driving me to school one day, and I was laughing about evolution. I said, "Dad, you'll never believe what they're teaching us in school. They say we came from monkeys … blah, blah, blah." I can't remember exactly what we were studying, but it was some particular piece of evolutionary theory that I was just scorning, and my dad said, "John, why don't you pay attention to what your teachers are telling you? Because whether at the end of the day it's right or wrong, you need to learn it." My perspective changed immediately. Evolution may or may not have been correct, but my dad was always right! I started listening and learning, and I started thinking about how that related to my faith. Before long I started reading more and more about it. By the end of high school—and two biology classes later—I had come to the conclusion that not only was evolution not irreconcilable with Christianity, but that the Christian story did not make sense outside of an evolutionary framework! We can talk about that if you want to, but the point is that this opportunity to examine religion from an academic perspective and analyze how religion impacts society opened up new horizons for my thinking. This second major paved the way for my thinking more deeply about the sociology of religion and the interplay of religion and politics, and ultimately played a large role in leading me to apply to Harvard.

Let's delve a little deeper into the tension you sensed between studying religion and biology at the same time. Were you confronted with a dichotomy in your thinking? Were the two classes difficult to combine?

As I said, after some in depth inquiry, all pretense of dichotomy had fallen apart. However, that dichotomy was there in the beginning. We like to think of science and religion, at best, as non-overlapping magisteria; at worst, as incompatible and competing conceptions of the nature of reality. I think this dichotomy is actually heightened in the university, because it often privileges empirical modes of reasoning, which are very different than many religious ways of approaching the world. However, once you start looking at the rise of the Enlightenment and how the paradigm of rational, evidence-based inquiry colors our perceptions of reality, it is not difficult to put other paradigms in an equal perspective. At that point, you can see how all ways of looking at the world—religious, scientific, economic, political, etc.—influence how we think, how we act, how we interact, and how we look at ourselves. And then you look at the way modern science and modern Christianity approach the "big questions" of existence—cause and effect, right and wrong—and you realize that they're not all that much in conflict. Modern science arose out of monks conducting experiments in churches. The way many modern Christians process the fall of humanity and our ultimate redemption is intimately connected with an idea of natural selection and survival of the fittest. The classes in my interdisciplinary studies major gave me the opportunity to delve into this supposed dichotomy, and eventually to emerge, calling the attention of my colleagues in various disciplines [to the fact] that there is not necessarily that firm of a dichotomy.

Tell me more about your religion classes, John. Were they theology focused classes, or did they take more of a comparative overview approach?

I was attending a public university, so we weren't getting into dogmatic theology or anything. I did have some classes that would fall within the theology sphere, though. One on Darwinism and Christianity was taught from a theological frame, where we looked at different conceptions of evolution and Christian theology and how various thinkers had tried to reconcile the two systems of thought. Most of the classes I took, though, were approached from a social sciences perspective.

What about your personal evolution during your undergraduate education? You came from a deeply Christian religious background. Did anything change during those four years at NC state?

Yes. My undergraduate years were extremely transformational for me. I do not think I "changed" that much, in that I did not necessarily adopt a new set of values, but the way I looked at my faith and the values I had always held changed for two reasons. First was simply the international perspective I gained. I grew up in rural—well, not rural but small-town—North Carolina, and neither I nor my parents had ever been out of the country. I had been to Epcot at Walt Disney World, if that counts, but I had never actually been out of the country. Then, I entered college at NC State, where I participated in programs like the University Scholars Program, which takes academically successful students and attempts to expose them to a wide variety of intellectual, cultural, and social experiences to broaden their horizons. We went to arts events and lectures around the university and region, traveled around the state and even nationally and internationally, and were constantly presented with new, diverse ways of looking at issues. Experiences like those I had with the Scholars program opened my eyes to the world, even though I rarely had to leave campus for them.

I was also fortunate to travel abroad on several occasions during my undergraduate years. The summer after my freshman year, I participated in a study abroad program at Oxford University, where I studied Shakespeare and modern British history under Oxford dons. I also got into France for a bit right after that experience. I also spent spring breaks studying in the Galapagos and Ecuador, Cuba, and the Peruvian Amazon. The summer after my junior year, I went to India with a group from the University of North Carolina at Chapel Hill. You have to understand that, as an NC State student and fan, it took a lot out of me to travel with that group, but I was motivated to get to India! The summer before I had completed an internship with New York 1 News in New York City, and on my days off I had spent hours in the Metropolitan Museum of Art, where the Indian art section particularly fascinated me. I told myself that I needed to spend some time where this beautiful artwork originated. This trip, more than any other, helped expand both my cultural and religious worldview. I spent the summer visiting Hindu and Jain temples, hanging out with Buddhist monks, and helping prepare langar at a Sikh Gurdwara. I prayed with my host father at his mosque, bathed in the Ganges River, and circumambulated holy shrines with Sufi mystics. We even found some empty Christian churches! Living in the midst of such incredible religious diversity really helped develop my respect for the breadth of human interaction with the divine, and it also helped me ground myself in my tradition and more clearly articulate what motivates my religious thought and practice.

Speaking of my own religious thought and practice, the second major factor in my collegiate transformation was the time I spent at Presbyterian Campus Ministry. When I arrived on NC State campus, a couple of friends and I decided that we would church shop together. I was Methodist (even though I was technically going to a Baptist Church back home), another friend was really Baptist, and the third friend was Presbyterian. The plan was we would, for three Sundays, go together to the closest church of each denomination to campus. The Presbyterian had gotten a letter in the mail saying that the first Sunday of the semester was college student Sunday at the Presbyterian church, and a free meal was included, so we all decided that would be a good place to start! Well, we went to church, met the campus minister and the student members of the ministry, and I fell in love. Our whole plan fell apart that week. We never went to another church, and my Presbyterian friend never returned to the campus ministry, but I was from that point basically a member for life.

As I started attending more regularly, I found a very different brand of Christianity than I had ever before experienced. Presbyterian Campus Ministry was the largest progressive campus ministry at NC State, and it introduced me to concepts of social justice, inclusivity, and intellectually driven faith that helped integrate my religion with the expanded worldview I had begun to acquire in college. Still, though, I was a bit uneasy for the first year or so, because it *was* a different message than I had heard most of my life. I couldn't help wondering, "Do I like this because it is the truth, or because it is what I want to hear?"

The turning point came at a retreat for Presbyterian Campus Ministries across North Carolina during my sophomore year. A professor from Elon University was the keynote speaker, and she was talking on the theme of "A Christian Response to Globalization." I actually think most students thought she was a painful bore to listen to, but for me she made progressive Christianity come alive. I had this moment where I broke down, evangelical Christian style, and realized that the love I was experiencing through this campus ministry, through the words of this woman and others like her, was the fullest incarnation of the Christian message I had ever heard. The love was big, like God. The vision was grand, like the kingdom of God. And the practice was peaceful, like the life of Christ. I knew I wanted to be a part of this Christianity. I knew I wanted to dedicate my life to this God and ever since that moment, I have tried to live into the faith I found that night. Sometimes I've done a decent job. Other times I've failed miserably. But if it hadn't been for my college experience, I may have known much less about the world for which Christ died, and I may never have found my particular entry point into Christ's kingdom that has so defined and ordered my life.

You spoke about the various places you visited during this period of your life. Were you studying or participating in academic programs on those trips, or were they a sort of in-depth tourism?

Yes, I only did summer or other short-term study abroad experiences. All except my Cuba experience were part of a university program. Oxford and India, as I described, were summer programs. At Oxford we studied under local professors, and in India we took language and literature courses from UNC professors traveling with us. The Galapagos Islands and the Peruvian Amazon trips were with the Environmental Technology program at NC State. We took semester-long courses on environmental and ecological issues facing the respective regions, and then for a week at Spring Break we would travel to those places and continue our studies, mixed with some eco-tourism, which was actually part of the study itself. The Cuba trip, while I define it as educational in nature, was a mission trip through the Presbyterian Campus Ministry focused on international relations and social justice.

At this point you were slowly coming towards the end of your undergraduate experience, and you were changing spiritually and intellectually as you traveled the world. How did you see your future developing? When did you start thinking about grad school, and specifically focusing on religion?

As I said, I had a long and winding road to Harvard. I was struck, when I finally arrived on campus, by the fact that many people had been setting their sites on this place for a long time. For me, that wasn't exactly the case. I was at NC State, as you said, with the world open to me. I was taking more religious studies classes and enjoying them a great deal, but what I was really enjoying were my film and television production classes. I would sit for hours in the production room, creating mockumentaries, or in the college's television studio, anchoring a startup student news program. I also had, as I mentioned, an amazing internship in New York City doing television news. I was working with New York 1, a 24-hour cable news station serving the greater New York metro area. My summer internship was with the Living Unit, which meant I was covering Broadway: music; restaurants; movies. Interestingly, money and economics reports were in there, so during 2007 I covered a story on subprime mortgages right before the housing crisis really hit, but for the most part, I spent the summer experiencing New York City by covering all of the most fun activities in it!

That summer was a decisive one for me in many ways, because while I had the time of my life covering some really fun stories, whenever I would turn on the television for some "hard news," all I saw that summer were stories about Britney Spears and Paris Hilton. Now, I love my Britney, but I really couldn't imagine spending my life following her every move. At the same time, I was going through the omnipresent discernment over vocation, and I really could not justify reporting on frivolity as fulfilling any higher calling. So, I began thinking about how I could take the skills and passion I had for communication and transferring them into something more productive, more meaningful.

One of the areas in which I found the greatest need for communication skills was in conflict resolution, especially at the nexus of religion and politics. Both domestically and internationally, we suffer so much because we are often not able to translate our motivations for our actions into terms that are identifiable by others from a different mindset. That may be a conservative Christian trying to persuade Congress to act on a particular measure, or it could be Hindus and Muslims arguing over contested land in the Kashmir. I thought, "As someone with the background in communication and with a passion for religion and society, I could find a niche at this intersection of religion and politics."

I found what I thought would be a perfect place for that study at Harvard. Not only do they have a degree title named after what I wanted to study: Religion, Ethics, and Politics, but they also approach that study from a perspective I found refreshing. I didn't want to go to a religious studies department where people took a cold stance toward religion, as if we were trying to better understand the bizarre behavior of flies in a Petri dish. I also didn't want to go to a cloistered seminary where a close study of faith ignored the world around it. At Harvard I found a place that took faith seriously—took many faiths seriously—while also deeply caring about how faith traditions interacted in a pluralistic, globalized, and sometimes secularized world. I knew that whatever career path I took, that I [would be] living in a diverse, interconnected world. As I try to do my work in the world I certainly will be working with Christians, I certainly will be working with other people of my own denomination, but I will also be working with people of other denominations and of other faiths and people with completely different worldviews, [or] people who don't subscribe to any faith at all, and it's imperative that we learn to work together.

So at that point as an undergrad, you were already aware of the pluralism and diversity here at Harvard Divinity School?

Yes. It was … Harvard makes that evident in their messaging, and as soon as you set foot on campus, you realize that the messaging is accurate.

Once you'd been admitted, did you come to the open students' day or any similar activities?

Well, I actually came to visit before I was accepted. One of my friends, whose name is Dawn, and I decided to take a second spring break senior year and visit divinity schools we were interested in attending. For my first spring break, I had my Amazon trip, so I got off the plane from Peru, where it was 80 degrees, and onto a plane to Boston, where it was 20 degrees and snowing. That factor did not immediately ingratiate this Southerner to Harvard! We landed in Boston, and decided to check out the Freedom Trail, since that's what everyone says to do. Well, we weren't prepared for snow, so we were out in what we would describe as a blizzard, with one layer of clothes and thin coats and one small umbrella between us to shield us from the snow. We decided after about the first sight that we would take advantage of our freedom as Americans and go inside! At Harvard, Dawn and I did not visit during any special event, but we were able to sit in on some classes, get a campus tour, and by the end of the tour I had fallen in love with the place. I'm a highly intuitive person—it's just the way my brain operates—and there was this moment, after I had met some students and gotten out of a class, where I was standing in front of Andover Hall, and I just knew this was the place for me.

I was not yet accepted, though. From Boston we flew to New York, where Dawn wanted to visit Union Theological Seminary. I had already visited there when I was living in the city, so I had a good idea of what it was like, but I will never turn down a trip to New York! While we were in the city, we were visiting a museum, and I received an email on my phone saying that I had a decision for Harvard. I checked that email and learned that I was accepted. Dawn and I started jumping up and down, screaming, right there in the gift shop. That was a fun moment. Once I learned I was admitted, I decided to return for the formal open house in April.

What were your first impressions?

My first impression was of Divinity Hall, which was originally built to be far away from main campus on the Yard, but these days is surrounded by biology buildings. I took that as a sign I was in the right place, after my work breaking down those dichotomies between religion and science, since here biologists and religious studies folks were able to coexist … and even play volleyball together in the space between the buildings! My first personal impressions were of really kind people. Growing up far away from Harvard itself, it's easy to get an impression of Harvard as an elite, snobbish place; filled with rich, vain people who only care about their studies. But at Harvard—across the board, not just at Divinity School—I've had the complete opposite experience. The people were genuine, the people seemed to care about other people, and the people actually knew how to be sociable and have some fun! What meant most [to me], though, was the kindness. Everyone at Harvard Divinity School was so warm and welcoming, and I felt as I entered the space that I had been received into a special community.

Then you came to Boston, and moved to Cambridge in August 2009. You registered, went to orientation, and started shopping for classes. How did that go—your first experiences, your first interactions with other students?

Class shopping is the best idea anyone's ever had in academia. Put that on paper. I love it that you are able to take the first week of classes to go to any that sound interesting, to experience what a professor is like, to look at a course syllabus and ask questions and get a sense of what the class will be like before you register and are committed for a semester. I loved it. I just reveled in that. Someone told us during orientation to be selective in the courses we shopped, since it is very easy to wear yourself out during shopping week. That is probably wise advice, since I would get a week into each semester and have about twelve classes I really wanted to take. However, one of my favorite parts of the shopping period was I could visit classes I knew I would never fit into my final schedule and experience a tidbit of something new and different.

How did you like the methodology of those first few classes? The content and the intellectual level—how did it contrast with your undergrad experience?

That's an interesting question. Because NC State is a land-grant institution where a great deal of the student population is focused on more scientific endeavors, a lot of the people there taking religious studies classes, or especially lower level under-grad classes, aren't necessarily invested in a deep study of religion. They are mainly there to fulfill a general education requirement, or to learn more about the Bible. I did have a couple of courses in religious studies that were higher level, for people who were majoring in the subject, where we tackled some of the biggest thinkers in religious studies. With those classes, mainly in small group conversations, I did have intellectually rigorous experiences.

Harvard, though, was on an entirely different level. That is mainly because of the size and esteem of the program. I was studying with people, most of whom already had a degree in religious studies, who were interested in delving even deeper into the academic study of religion. Many were aiming for a career in aca-demia, so their commitment and base of knowledge was astounding. In that envi-ronment, I at first felt a bit out of my league. Soon, though, I realized that most of the difference between some of my peers and me was in the use of jargon. I did not have the language—the vocabulary of religious studies—as ingrained in me as others did. As soon as I was able to take command of the words and phrases used to signify major thoughts and opinions, I felt much more comfortable engaging in fruitful and substantial conversation.

As far as methodology goes, I do not think there was any revolutionary peda-gogy or approach to religious studies in use at HDS that I had not discovered elsewhere. The difference, once again, was in the people. For example, my first semester I took a class in Christian-Muslim relations. Nowhere else in America—with the possible exception of Hartford Seminary—could you have a class that paralleled that exploration of the relations between Muslims and Christians. That is because we had an amazing grouping of Christians and Muslims from around the world, along with Jews and humanists who added their own points of view. Harvard Divinity is truly a microcosm of the world we live in, bringing in view-points from across the world, only the people it assembles are some of the smart-est, most insightful, most compassionate people the world has to offer. Having a conversation about a topic as contentious as Christian-Muslim relations suddenly becomes a joy and a community-building exercise at HDS, and it leaves you wanting to go out in the world and spread that type of conversation.

You've already touched a bit on your interactions with your fellow students. Tell me more about what the student population is like here at Harvard Divinity.

These are some of the best people I've ever met in my entire life. I'll say it again. These are some of the best people I've ever met in my life. I was here for two years, and I have never in that amount of time gotten so close to a group of people. It's redundant with Harvard Divinity School to say that it is diverse, but in addition to the classroom experience I just described, you are also sharing your life out of the classroom with Pentecostals from Georgia, Catholics from India, Muslims from Italy. You are interacting with people who are on fire for their academic interests and are actively seeking ways to cross bridges, make friends, and work together for increased understanding and social justice. Yes, there are some people who sit in the library all day—no matter where you go there is going to be that—but for the most part, the people at Harvard Divinity School are people who want to use their knowledge to make an impact on the world.

A wonderful surprise for me, arriving at HDS, was that these people were also folks who like to have fun! I'll give you an example, and it's really one of the reasons Harvard became so special for me. I arrived on campus on the first of September, and my birthday is September 4. I was a bit depressed, because I knew I wouldn't know many people by that time, and I wanted to celebrate my birthday with friends! But, I met a few people here and there at orientation, added them on Facebook, and then I decided, "Hey! I'll just throw myself a party!" I created an event on Facebook, and spread the word to people I met, and just let people know that if they were looking for something to do on the fourth, which happened to be a Friday, that they should come to dinner at John Harvard's, a restaurant on Harvard Square. I thought we may have five or six people show up, but we ended up with 30! We took that restaurant by storm! What I had not realized is that everyone else was also there alone, not knowing anyone, and everyone needed an excuse to come together outside of class to get to know each other. We had so much fun that we searched for someone who had a birthday the next week and did it again the next weekend! Realizing that we could not keep up the birthday game forever, someone had the bright idea to form a group on Facebook. We called it, irreverently, the Transubstantiation Club—and we used that as a social organization mechanism. Throughout our years at Harvard, if anyone wanted to go see a movie, or someone wanted to throw a party or take a trip or go to church, they would post it on our group's page, and they'd always have people show up! It was by no means a closed group or anything—we added people to it all the time—and it ended up being this organic yet constant means of organizing a community that gave a great balance to the intense coursework of graduate school.

It also gave me friends who will last a lifetime. I'm a very social person—I call myself hyper-extroverted—and so I normally like running in many social circles and keeping large networks of friends, but during my two years at Harvard I developed some of the closest and deepest relationships of my life with my fellow HDS-ers, and I feel as if that has made me a more complete person.

What about general student life at HDS? Were you part of any formal organizations?

As you can probably assume from that last answer, the students at HDS are keen to participate so student life is robust. My most significant contribution to student life was serving on the Noon Service Steering Committee. The HDS Noon Service is a weekly service, held on Wednesdays at noon—surprise!—and each week it features a different HDS student organization. It is a wonderful means of exploring the amazing diversity at HDS, and it is also a great time to detach yourself from the stresses of schoolwork and enter a worshipful space right in the middle of the week. Each service is also unique; you never know what you might be getting yourself into! If the Methodists are leading the service, they may focus on the hymns which are central to their tradition. Their choir may sing a few, you may be invited to join, and the speaker may focus on the meaning of worship music for the Wesleys. If the Muslim student group is leading, they may read from the Qur'an and the Hadith, play a call to prayer, explain the progression of daily prayers, and then serve some halal snacks for the group afterwards. (Oh, yeah, there is always food after the noon service, which is another reason that it's not to be missed.) We've even had some that are further out there. I was a part of EcoDiv, a group that promoted awareness of the environment and the importance of the natural world in various faith traditions, so we were challenged to do a noon service that highlighted how environmental concerns spanned many religions. In one particularly upbeat service, Queer Rites, the LGBT group on campus, ended theirs with a dance party in the center of the room to Cyndi Lauper's "True Colors." Now, in all of this, no one is ever compelled to participate in the sectarian rituals taking place a noon service, so if you're coming from a faith tradition other than the one leading the service and would rather sit in the back and experience the service rather than participate, you are welcomed and encouraged to do so. In fact, to facilitate the community nature of the service, each service is opened and closed by Noon Service Steering Committee members, who welcome the group, share prayer concerns, and lead a responsive reading that in a sense hands over the service to the host group and affirms the community's respect for that group and pledges to enter respectfully into the time led by that group in order to learn from them more about their tradition.

As part of the Steering Committee, my responsibilities were also to work with the host groups to make sure they were developing services that were appropriate for the occasion, accessible to outsiders, and, of course, fit within the hour allotted. We also made sure the lights were on, set out and cleaned up the food for the service, and helped open and close each week's service. The Noon Service is an event at the heart of HDS's identity, it's really special and it's really personal and I was very honored to be a part of the Steering Committee.

I was also a founding member of the Harvard Divinity School Initiative on Religion and Government. This was really the brainchild of my dear friend and patient interviewer, Werner de Saeger, but I immediately jumped on board when he threw the idea at me because it fit right in with my tradition of breaking down boundaries between disciplines. What I found true about NC State on that front also rang true at Harvard. Being a student in the definitionally multidisciplinary Religion, Ethics, and Politics program meant that I truly was a student of the entire university. REP-ers, as we called ourselves, took at least half of our classes at the Divinity School, but we also took classes in the Yard, or the Graduate School of Arts and Sciences, the Kennedy School of Government, the School of Education, the School of Law, and sometimes even the School of Public Health or Business School. What we found as we traversed the university was that many students and professors were studying the same things from their bases in different disciplines, and often they were not even aware of the related work going on elsewhere in the university!

Our student group tried to combat that through hosting events aimed at building bridges across these schools at Harvard. In the second year of the program's existence, Robert Putnam published his award-winning work, *American Grace*, which focused on the social capital of religion in America. I had studied under him at the Kennedy School, and his work on this topic had done much to inform the way I approached religious studies, but I was shocked when I walked across campus to the Divinity School and some people had never even heard of him. Rather than yelling, "Stop reading Foucault and read Putnam!" I decided it would be more productive to just bring Putnam over to the Divinity School. So, our group worked to schedule an event at the Divinity School where Bob would come and present on his new book. It ended up being one of the biggest events of the semester. We filled the largest room at the Divinity School; people came from many different Harvard colleges to hear him, and people were talking about his ideas in the halls of HDS for weeks. In fact, one of my good friends was introduced to Putnam's work on the "Nones"—not the habit-wearing sisters but those who say they have no religious tradition—and has used some of that work as a basis for his Ph.D. work on that topic. It was great to see the impact that group had in bringing together people approaching religion and public life from many different directions and seeing how something as simple as an evening lecture could serve as a catalyst for collaboration and new thought across campus.

Apart from the Noon Services and the HGS initiative you mentioned, did you participate in less formal events like Community Tea?

Yes, I tried to attend those community teas because as a Graduate student, you get a taste of what poverty is like, and you're always willing to go the extra mile for a taste of free food. With Community Tea, you come for the free food, and you stay for the community. In fact, tea on Tuesdays was so important to me that I ditched other commitments. I've played handbells at churches since I was in middle school, and I had joined a handbell choir at a church in Boston, but because the rehearsal time conflicted with Community Tea, I simply told the group I couldn't play with them anymore!

One of the reasons Community Tea is so important is because it is the one event that truly brings together the entire HDS community. You meet all these amazing people at orientation, and you hang out with some of them going forward, but the weekly tea gives you an opportunity to catch up with people you do not see in class or elsewhere. It also keeps you abreast of all the sundry events happening around campus. Student groups make announcements, noon service committee members tell you who is hosting each week, and the HDS administration alerts you to special lectures or events. Sure, you can get much of that via email, but it's much better to do so in person while eating some chicken … or pie.

Let's discuss your insights into communication and politics, and your ambitions in both fields. Did these evolve whilst you studied religion at Harvard, whilst studying the integration of religion and politics?

As I mentioned briefly earlier, when I arrived at Harvard, I intended to focus my studies in Religion, Ethics, and Politics on conflict resolution. I wanted to explore how religious communities factored into political conflict; how they sometimes perpetuated conflict and violence, and how they could also be agents for reconciliation. I thought that study, combined with my background in communication, would prepare me for negotiation work on an international level after graduation.

Did Harvard give you the tools and the resources to do that?

It certainly gave me the tools and resources—I took courses on negotiation, interfaith relations, religion in global politics—though I quickly learned that Harvard, even more than a place of tools and resources, is a place of transformation. What Harvard gave me was the opportunity to explore exactly where I best fit within the realm of religion, ethics, and politics, and so while I could have benefited greatly from its resources on international conflict resolution, in the end I decided to take a different path.

As I was taking those courses on international political conflict, negotiation, and development, I found that my idea of conflict resolution was getting the right people to the table to sign the right document. And my aspirations for bringing religious communities into that was making sure that the right rabbi or priest was in the room at the drafting and signing of that document. Quite bluntly, it doesn't work that way. I would even go so far as to say that true reconciliation could never work that way. Conflicts begin and end in communities and neighborhoods and in personal relationships. People come together or are torn apart in everyday life that is influenced by, but can never be controlled by, heads of state or religious leaders. That means, in order to solve conflict at any level, you have to be a fully engaged member of the community at hand. Now, I love my people in India, and I feel strong connections to them and the issues they face, but I will never be the person to go in and tell them how to solve the longstanding conflicts within their country. The whole idea of that, these days, gives me the postcolonial shivers. I don't want to be that guy.

I learned, through my time at Harvard, that in my position as an American, middle class, white man, that I will be most effective and most authentic by working in my community on the problems facing my community. Of course, in a globalized world I am still connected to communities in India and Cuba and Ecuador, and I will always want to work in solidarity with people around the world. But I have to begin at home, and work with my community to solve the enormous issues we face right here, before I can begin to even comment on another community, be it Delhi, Damascus, or Detroit!

Is that something you discovered here at HDS?

Yes, though of course that understanding began to develop in me through my travels at NC State. That is where I began to understand the interconnectedness of the world, but at Harvard I began to understand the situatedness of each person and community in the midst of the connected world.

Now I have to say, I don't think that what I said about basing my operations out of my home community is a universal point that applies to all people. I have friends who have visited Haiti, and returned again and again, and have felt more at home there than they ever did in the town in which they were born. For them, their community is Haiti, and it is authentic for them to work with Haitians and on behalf of Haitians. Likewise, I have friends from other countries who have found a home in the United States and are more comfortable working as a changemaker here than they ever did in their country of birth. What I learned is that for me, my community is in North Carolina. The conflicts and the problems and the issues that I want to dedicate my life to addressing, the people whom I want to serve and with whom I wish to be in conversation and communion, are in North Carolina. That doesn't sequester me in my home state by any means—I can learn from communities experimenting with new forms of democracy in Brazil, and I can team up with groups in Boston and Albequerque to address national issues that face us all—but I have found that I can do that work around the country and around the world most effectively by focusing firstly upon, and working with, my people in North Carolina.

I think what Harvard did for me was refine my understanding of my place in the world and show me how important it is to live in a holistic community. When I say community, I mean politically, socially, and religiously. In order to address some of the social issues I want to address, I'm going to have to work alongside other people in their totality and in their complexity; I'm going to have to understand the nitty-gritty of people's backgrounds, their situations, and their hopes and dreams. I caught a glimpse of that sort of community for the first time at HDS, and I wanted to carry that forward and develop it in my life and career back home, with people I love and cherish.

Of course, Harvard also presented me with a winter of historic snowfall, which made North Carolina look even better day-by-day!

Was your original study project transformed by the end of your time at HDS? Originally, you came here intending to apply your background in communication to the interdisciplinary field of religion and politics. In the end what did you end up doing?

My focus centered upon social capital. I first encountered social capital theory in a sociology class in college, and I really liked what Robert Putnam had to say about community in America. When I saw he was teaching a seminar my first year at Harvard, I jumped on the opportunity, and was fortunate enough to get into the class. That study of social capital helped me put words to what I had been wanting to study for a long time, and it also presented me with unique challenges that I wanted to tackle in both my academic and professional life, such as how to bring people together in meaningful ways in an age of digital connectivity.

While studying with Bob Putnam, I began research on the Tea Party, when it was first beginning to attract public attention. I reached out to the local group, the Greater Boston Tea Party, and the leader reluctantly allowed me to attend their meetings. Bob said that it was my short haircut and Southern accent that ingratiated me to them! Over the semester, Vanessa Williamson, my research partner, and I attended meetings, rallies, and protests, interviewed many members, and conducted a survey of the entire 1500-person organization. After we wrote our seminar paper for that class, we worked with my partner's Ph.D. adviser, Theda Skocpol, to put the paper into publishable form. It was published in an academic journal as one of the first studies of the Tea Party movement, and it remains the journal's most-downloaded article!

Theda and Vanessa went on to publish a book-length study on the Tea Party, and I went forward after graduating with a social capital lens that would help me in my work to bring people together, be they in religious or political communities, to make a real difference in their town or state. My study of social capital was one of the driving forces behind my shift from international to domestic focus, and it very much changed the way I wanted to go about solving the issues that concerned me. So did my general interest change? Not so much. But it was re-oriented in a way.

To be able to do that, did you venture outside of HDS? You cross-registered, and went to other schools, can you tell me about that?

One of the best parts about the structure of the degree programs at HDS is their flexibility. There was not a single course I was required to take while at Harvard, as long as six courses were classified as fitting in my area of focus, and three were completely outside of that area of focus. And only half of the courses had to be taught within the Divinity School, so I could take many courses at other Harvard schools, or even from a consortium of over ten other universities in the greater Boston area. That meant I took several courses at the Kennedy School of Government. Some of those were actually cross-listed with the Divinity School, so I got HDS credit for them, but others, such as the Putnam course, were purely Kennedy School. I also took some courses, and audited others, from the Graduate School of Arts and Sciences and the School of Education.

What I find interesting, looking back, is that the time spent at the Divinity School, versus other schools, varied. One semester I would take only HDS classes. The next semester I took most of my classes outside of the Divinity School, and by the end of the term I would think, "I want my Div School back!" So, the next semester I would be heavy into HDS once again, and so forth.

What kinds of different approaches existed in the different schools, as compared to HDS, on the topic of religion? What changed? What made you say, "I want to return."?

I think there's a greater understanding and respect for religious experience and expression at the Divinity School. I'll just say that.

What about your religious life? While you were here from 2009 to 2011, did some of your views change? Were they challenged at all?

I'm glad you asked that, because I have heard reports from some students that HDS "shook their faith," or concerns from conservative folks in the South that Harvard is a "godless place" that will destroy a person's faith. I felt nothing of the sort. I am sure that many people, if they grew up in a sheltered religious environment, may reel at first from some of the ideas flying around the Divinity School. I had already dealt in college with those sorts of questions and ideas, though, so it was nothing shocking or new to me. In fact, I would say that my time at Harvard strengthened my faith. Here, in the midst of such diversity, I was able to regain my sense of who I was as a Christian. Sometimes in the modern world it is easy to look at these ancient faiths and dismiss them as irrelevant. However, I was surrounded at Harvard by good people who thought deeply about their faith, struggled with the big questions, and clung fast to their faith in the midst of it all. That really served as a strong example to me and kept me dedicated to the Christian walk and to never giving up on God.

Also, I was supported by the most incredible church I have ever attended. Old South Church, a United Church of Christ congregation in downtown Boston, amazed me because of its integration of various forms of worship and tradition. The first time you walk into the sanctuary, it will blow your breath away, with its giant arch ceilings, gigantic stained glass, and magnificent organ. There are lots of pretty churches, but not nearly enough of them fill the pews with such a strong Christian community. Old South does this by remaining steadfastly committed to its Trinitarian theology and its broad sense of inclusivity. I'll never forget that the first Sunday I visited, there was a lunch after church, and I sat across from this older bald-headed man. I struck up a conversation with him, and asked what he did with the church. "I teach the fifth-grade Sunday School class," he replied. Then I asked what he did for work in Boston. He said, "Oh, I'm a drag queen." At that moment, I knew that church was the place for me.

Old South confirmed that feeling with a unique and beautiful worship tradition. Each Sunday would be different. One Sunday, all the music may be baroque style, with a string quartet providing accompaniment, or the hymns sung might be Benedictine chants. The next week, an Amy Grant song might be sung from the pulpit. The next Sunday, you could have the theological jazz of Thelonius Monk, and the next they could bring in their old timey Salvation Army drum to lead some gospel music. The pastors keep it all together with beautiful, poetic sermons and liturgy, in which every word appears to be intentionally and delicately crafted.

I really admire the way Old South brings generations—even centuries—of worship together seamlessly and without alienating members of the congregation. I have seen congregations literally torn apart by infusions of contemporary music, or disappear because of an inability to reach across generations. Now, I'm guilty of that a bit, since I love my traditional worship service with an organ and choir and hymns sung out of a hymnbook. However, at Old South I was able to experience in one setting various ways of worshiping God, and I think it put me into better touch with the traditions that shaped the style of worship I love so much, while also opening me a bit more to the continuities within newer forms of worship that are on the rise today.

Mainly, though, I loved the theology of the church. I think you also find, especially in progressive mainline Christian denominations, either very firmly committed Christians who are also very conservative and take a hard line on rational orthodoxy, or people who really like the ethics of Christianity and really like the community of a church but would rather not talk about God or Jesus. Old South got it right, in my opinion. They are deeply committed to Christianity, to Trinitarian orthodoxy, to the tenets of the Christian faith, whilst also recognizing that God calls us to transform our world, to open our arms wider than anyone would ever expect, to love people to a degree that is scary in our society. Those are two balances in theology and practice that fed me and inspired me in remarkable ways. The bad part is that my experience at Old South in Boston has actually made finding a comparable church back home very difficult!

If you compared John the alumnus and John-before-Harvard, how would you compare the two? How would you define your transformation?

I think the biggest change was probably coming to understand how to better engage diversity in a very wide sense. I came here ready to talk with Muslims and Jews and Buddhists and Atheists. I felt comfortable enough in my faith to engage with people who thought differently than I did, and I was excited about figuring out ways to work together across our differences. Interestingly, I think I left ready to engage people who *weren't* willing to talk to Muslims and Jews and Buddhists and Atheists. Now, I am back working in North Carolina, which has a fairly good degree of diversity, but social life there is still dominated by a traditional hegemony of Protestant Christianity, and many people there have yet to come into contact with the sort of diversity that I have been blessed to encounter. In short, it's a very different place than Harvard, where people are sort of self-selected to be open-minded, tolerant, and respectful of different points of view.

In fact, the whole time I was at Harvard, I felt as if I—and a couple of other friends who grew up in similar situations—constantly asked the question, "It's great that we're having this conversation across lines of diversity, but what about all the people out there who don't want to have this sort of conversation?" While that question was never exactly answered for me while at HDS, I believe that my being attuned to the question has helped me translate the lessons I've learned here to people who are not quite ready for interfaith dialogue. It has also helped me, as I've worked not just across religious difference, but across lines of economic, political, and social difference, to be able to productively engage many different types of people in sometimes uncomfortable situations. In a way, I guess it did prepare me for conflict resolution!

If you were able to talk to John Coggin two years back, knowing what you know now, what would you tell him?

Be at peace where you are. I came straight from undergrad. I had a passion for putting thought into action. I got to Harvard, and while I was impressed with people's commitment to making the world a better place, I was sometimes frustrated by all the conversations about how to do that. I had been in school since I was four years old. Twenty years later, I was ready to act and I was tired of studying. Now that I am out in the world trying to put thought into action, I've realized two things. First, all that studying was immensely important. Without those two additional years of thought, I would not have been prepared to do the work I'm doing now. Second, I didn't realize that by studying, I *was* doing work. The contributions of the academic community to the larger world are immense, and while they're not always readily apparent from within the Ivory Tower, they are apparent when you get out into the world. Where else are you going to be sitting in a room with America's top theologians and economists and political scientists whose words and opinions are respected across the world? Where else are you going to be working with such a diverse set of experts—when a religious studies person can work alongside an engineer, who can get advice from a public health expert? Even as a student, there is great power within the university for social change. I wish I had more fully realized then that in a college environment you are uniquely situated to make a difference in the world. So, I think that's what I would tell the 2009 version of John Coggin, "Be at peace where you are and work where you are to do good."

Let's talk about life as an alumnus. Where are you right now? What did you do after commencement and what does your future hold?

I am back in North Carolina working in public policy for an organization called the Institute for Emerging Issues. It was founded by former Governor Jim Hunt and is based, appropriately for me, at NC State University. Basically what we are is a convening organization that tries to bring people together from across regions, sectors, and perspectives to develop a consensus vision for long-term economic development in North Carolina. HDS cemented in me an idea that everybody needs to be at the table. HDS taught me that in a conversation about religion in a pluralist world you need to have as many points of view represented as possible, and now as I enter a policy world I take that same mentality. You have to have Democrats and Republicans, you have to have business and government and education and non-profit. You have to have the rich and the poor, the male and the female, the gay and the straight, the old and the young. You have to have everybody at that table committed to a common cause to make a difference. And so that's what I'm doing in North Carolina, trying to spark those conversations and help people navigate the process of making those conversations productive and inspire collective action as a result. I'm really excited about embarking on a career of public service, using what I gained at Harvard and combining that with the multiple skills and talents of the people with whom I am working in North Carolina to make a real difference for our community.

As for the future, I really cannot presume to know where life will take me. Like I said before, I ended up at Harvard via a long and winding road that I could not have predicted, and I am sure I will say the same about wherever I end up forty years from now. What I can say is that my experience at Harvard prepared me for whatever life throws my way, connected me more closely with God and my fellow humans, and taught me that there is always something more to learn, always something grander to do, and always someone better to be. I will never go a day without using a lesson learned at Harvard, and I will always thank God that my long and winding road took me through the gates of Harvard Yard.

Professor Diane Moore

Senior Lecturer on Religious Studies and Education and Senior Fellow at the Center for the Study of World Religions

In your work, you make a relatively clear distinction between teaching religion and teaching about religion. Could you explain that nuance and tell me how Harvard, and HDS in particular, fits into that difference?

It's a very good question, thank you. I would say that the distinction I make would be more explicitly articulated as the distinction between the devotional expression of religion and the teaching of religion.

Here in the U.S. and in many other parts of the world that I've had occasion to both visit and work in, people will recognize that difference but often conflate it in actual practice. For me, the importance of making that distinction explicit is very significant. So in any teaching I do here at Harvard, or in any of my other capacities, I am always very explicit about making that distinction for students and recognizing that what we do here in the university setting is teach about religion—teach about the diversity of religion. I don't know if you want me to elaborate on what those distinctions mean.

Yes, please.

For me, those distinctions are really important to recognize. The Religious Studies approach to teaching about religion recognizes three fundamental truths that are often misunderstood when we only associate religion with devotional expression. One is that religions are factually, internally diverse. They are not uniform. The second is that religions are evolving and changing, as opposed to static and ahistorical. The third is that religions are embedded, religious ideologies and distinctions are embedded, in all dimensions of human expression, in historical and contemporary ways, rather than the association of religion as somehow uniquely situated around ritual and practice and private faith communities or private faith practice. When you approach religion from a religious studies academic perspective, you recognize those understandings and you recognize that particular assertions about a belief are appropriate but they are theological assertions. Those theological assertions are not universal, they are particular, and recognizing that is the study of religion and the diversity within traditions in the evolutionary dimension as well as then their embeddedness in cultures.

So those are the important ways that we in religious studies across the academy understand the distinction. Here at Harvard, we have the incredible strength of being able to teach both aspects of religious expression. For those who are here training to be religious leaders in a particular faith tradition, they will have occasion to develop their own theological lens, but they will all be exposed to the study of religion including the diversity of religious expressions within our own tradition as well as among others. That is a real strength, I think, of what we have here and one that I believe enhances all aspects of what we do.

So here at Harvard you teach both MTS and MDiv students, right?

I do.

People tend to see that diversity and pluralism as one of HDS's greatest assets. Yet that diversity is not only religious but also intellectual. How do you handle this diversity in the classroom, where individuals come with different backgrounds? Is there a specific methodology to align students in your classes?

That's a really, really important question but I'm not sure if you mean diverse intellectual strengths or if you mean diverse in an intellectual or ideological sense?

Say you had a classroom here with ten students. One might be a Jewish rabbi, one might be somebody who studied Ancient Eastern philosophy, there might be a historian in there, and there might be people with life experience as well, but also a 22-year-old who just came out of undergrad. How is it possible to mingle all these people and cultivate a creative, intellectual atmosphere?

Yes, that is a really, really good question and you are right. It's a tremendous strength that we have, but it also causes particular kinds of challenges. I think it's just so critical for all of us to be really attentive to those differences and to assume those differences, and to have to create some framework within any class we teach that will help bring people into a common conversation, still recognizing the strengths of those diverse perspectives.

For my own teaching, I employ what I have identified as a cultural studies method that gives language to particular perspectives. I use Donna Haraway's language. She is a historian of science, who I have found to be tremendously insightful. Her language would be situated knowledges.

So pedagogically, you set up a classroom where you are allowing the uniqueness of each individual voice to come through; there is very little lecture in my classrooms. It's very focused on discussion and then shaping the nature of the inquiry, whatever the course is, to a common set of questions that lead people to bring their own unique perspectives into the conversation.

So it's a balance between honoring and recognizing and even soliciting that difference, but with a common focus for whatever the topic of the class happens to be. I found that to be one of the most incredibly rich experiences teaching here. Having that diversity and being able to pursue and engage that diversity is wonderful.

So your classes are partly lecture-based and partly interactive or …?

I do very little lecturing. That's part of an overarching initiative here at the university—not just the Divinity School, but throughout all the schools, the professional schools, and the college as a whole. There is an initiative that is really investigating what it means to teach and learn in the 21st Century. Lecture and the kind of monologue related conversation is very much challenged now in a contemporary way. The requirements for us to be engaged, collaborative and cooperative learners are much more profound, both in terms of what we know about learning theory and the implications for that, as well as what we know about the kinds of skills that we need now to address the challenges we face in the world. So for me, I've never felt that a lecture-based course has been as productive, educationally. I've always been very focused on a more problem-posing, discussion-based course even in what would normally be lecture courses. I prefer to set them up with more dialogical opportunities. So very little lecturing, I would say. Modest, if any.

So within the general pedagogical strategy at Harvard, religion is not seen as a topic apart, it's just seen as one of the many topics someone can study here? There is no special kind of strategy to deal with religion? It's just one of …?

Right. The only unique aspect of religion, and I think it becomes a real strength for other disciplines, is that we have to face the assumptions that students and many other colleagues outside of religious studies often bring to the table. They are often so profoundly problematic that the discipline requires you to give special attention to what we should always be giving attention to: the assumptions that students bring to our classes. Again, religion provides an opportunity for other disciplines to hone those skills. It's so required in religion. You have to be really good at it, otherwise if you don't anticipate the often misrepresentative assumptions regarding religion that students will bring into a class, then your conversations always get derailed very early on in whatever topic you are teaching.

I do think the uniqueness of religion is only in that we have such a profoundly illiterate society in terms of religion, in a way that is really pretty unprecedented in any of the other topics we teach at the university. So there are special skills that those of us who have the privilege of teaching religious studies have around pedagogy that I think could be beneficial to our colleagues in other disciplines.

You also teach at a high school and an academy. There you maybe follow students over the course of a full year? Is that so?

I don't. I just have students for one trimester.

Here it's semester-based and I was wondering if, in such a short period, you are able to transform the thoughts of students who basically, without them knowing, come to class with a set of notions already implemented. Is it possible in such a short timeframe to make people reflect upon their own notions of religion, and specifically I'm thinking here about Islam, because that seems to be the major challenge these days.

Absolutely. Again, another excellent question. I would say in both places, here at Harvard and also at the secondary level, a semester offers a very effective opportunity, when teachers are explicit with their students about the distinctions between devotional expression and the study of religion. When they are very explicit about helping students identify their preconceptions, to assume they have preconceived notions and to help them through a series of exercises and consistently throughout our course to give them language and tools to recognize those self assumptions, those preconceived notions and to then interrogate them.

They may decide that those are notions that they still want to embrace but to be more conscious about that embrace, rather than it being unconscious or subconscious. I have found tremendous success in that. It's not that the students aren't capable, we just rarely give them the opportunity, the language and the tools to help them reflect on that dimension of their assumption. Again, I've found that there's not so much deep transformation, but that what students are able to leave classes with—even in the short trimester at Phillips Academy or certainly those outside of religious studies here at the Divinity School, because we do teach people from across the university—that again, when you invite them to learn that language and give them those tools, then they are able to represent and utilize those methods. I have found that to be tremendously satisfying.

I have two questions about your specific work, which you talk about at great length in your book on religious literacy. First of all, the strategy of teaching religion in high school specifically. According to you, this strategy would be able to counter the media attention that has been given to Islam and other religious traditions which aren't necessarily the majority religions. You feel that the strength of religious education could be big enough to counter the kinds of tension engendered by media ties and what is, very often, one-sided journalism.

Absolutely. I think that ultimately, what we teach when we teach cultural studies with focus on religion, are critical thinking skills. So, what students are able to do very consistently is to at least recognize that there is a bias in those representations. We hope that they will not only feel that they have critical thinking skills, but the moral agency as citizens to respond to misrepresentation. So they certainly have the skills and capacity to do that. They recognize it. So we even talk about that, that we hope that they will start to recognize biased misrepresentation and just have a discomfort when they hear it, and that alone is a really critical first step. There are further steps that I hope they'll take. I sometimes hear back from students that say they are pursuing those but our expectation, our modest but true goal in a class, is to have them recognize those biases. I think that is key to beginning to transform that culture.

Professor Moore, your view of religious education as you explained it suggests that the teaching of religion is crucial when educating citizens who participate in a democratic process. However, one might argue that teaching children in an extremist religious environment about other world views is somehow taking away their opportunity of staying within a closed community. It is, in a sense, infringing upon their right 'not to know'. How would you counter such an argument? Could you say something about the family and state approach that you discussed in your book?

Yes. Good question. Complicated question. First of all, I think that the precondition for engaging the question is that, in whatever the educational setting that a student and family find themselves in, you have to be explicit about what the purpose of that educational setting is. What are the aims that the institution itself or that individual teachers hope to achieve? In a nonsectarian context, a really critical one here in the U.S. and I would say in many countries, the aim is to develop informed and responsible citizens through the host of the literacies that are required in our very multireligious, multicultural communities globally.

In more explicitly religious or conservative religious settings, I still think that question is a critical one and some may choose to create an educational environment that is going to be—I would like to use the word language, but I don't want it be pejorative—that specifically promotes their own theological world view. In the end, many of those—not all, but many—will also recognize the importance of exposing children at different ages (this will vary depending on the institution) to other world views in a responsible way, recognizing their legitimacy while still encouraging their own constituents to embrace the theological world view that they advocate. It would be a misrepresentation to assume that all conservative religious communities want to restrict exposure to other views, that's unfortunately one of the ways that religion is misrepresented. So it is very possible and there are many institutions that do this. They promote a particular world view but also expose students to diverse world views, and often those will be in different kinds of classes. So, many Roman Catholic schools for example will have the entire school focused on a particular Roman Catholic belief in framework, and they'll have theology classes that will promote that Roman Catholic understanding, but they will also often have then an introduction to world religions from another religious studies perspective in the religion department. Two different tracks; that's not uncommon. I would say that it's not uncommon, even for a more conservative Christian or evangelical groups. I do think that there certainly are communities that want to focus on a more exclusive representation. Even there, my modest hope would be that they would be explicit about this as one among many other representations, rather than only promoting the representation as though it's universal.

I think that approach would actually be a strength for them in the formation of the students that they're trying to serve because in the end, eventually they're going to be exposed to other traditions, and will need the language to be able to understand those differences. I think it serves everyone, in the interest of still wanting to promote a specific set of values within a religious community. When we don't expose students and give them the language to confront the complexities of whatever they're going to face, and religion becomes a significant one, I think we certainly do a disservice to them. I ultimately think we do a disservice to our larger democratic project that is inclusive of particular theological views. We need and want to cultivate opportunities for particular theological voices and communities to be able to exist.

So this is not a challenge to the particularity of theological voices. It is in fact a robust support of them, I think, and ultimately it is the aim of what those of us in religious studies are trying to help cultivate.

Here at Harvard there is no fixed Christian curriculum. It seems that students can be very eclectic in their way of getting an education in religion, and getting a taste of many of the world's religions, traditions, and issues. Such an approach has strengths and weaknesses. Would you say that this is the ideal way of becoming literate in religion in the 21st Century, or would you think it better to be more grounded in one religious tradition, and to have more of an in-depth knowledge of that tradition?

I think you're asking two different questions, so let me see if I can make sure I understand where you're really at. Let me talk about it at the secondary level. I don't promote a required course, for example. Some people would say that part of the way we can increase religious literacy in America would be to require an introduction to world religions course for all high school students. I totally disagree with that because I think ultimately, that will inevitably be just a very superficial and very problematic, supposedly content-based curriculum.

What I advocate for is a method for how to think about religion, and that method can then be applied in particular case studies that can go in-depth into a particular tradition, or a particular historical region, rather than try to be comprehensive in coverage of religion. It's a fool's task to try to be comprehensive in an introduction into religion, even to be comprehensive in an introduction to a particular religious tradition. So what I advocate for is teaching a method which would be a cultural studies method, and then giving students the opportunity to apply that method with particular case studies about religion and then give them the tools to pursue further inquiry if they're interested.

So here at Harvard, I think we actually do that. I think it's a powerful and positive way that we have restructured particularly our Master of Theological Studies program. We require that there be an area of concentration, and then we require that students also experience courses outside of that area, so that they still have the capacity to employ the methods they're learning within different contexts, rather than what their area of expertise is going to be grounded in. We do not in any way require that students cover all religious traditions here. That would be a terrible misunderstanding of what the study of religion can offer, so we don't.

Some HDS alumni go on to teach about religion, and go to high schools and colleges and universities. How would one be able to relatively objectively teach about religion, knowing that one can never attain that fully external view on religion? For a high school teacher for example, would a four year teachers' curriculum be sufficient, or a two-year Master's? Knowing that it might take a scholar a lifetime, knowing that a scholar of theology would take decades to just grasp the issues of Catholic doctrine? In other words, as you've said already, wouldn't it be a very superficial way of teaching religion?

In that sense, could you talk a little bit more about that cultural studies method?

Yes. Really, really good questions. The method for cultural studies is really to give students the language for understanding religion in a way that can normally counter their very common preconceptions of religion. We have identified several assumptions that people often bring to a classroom about religion. They're not universal, not all students bring them, but there are cultural assumptions that are embedded that we recognize and can counter.

So first of all, it helps students recognize they have those assumptions as one dimension. Secondly, to recognize and give them exposure to experiential dimensions of learning that challenges those assumptions. When I say experiential, I don't mean experiential in terms of going out into communities, which I also disagree with, going to visit mosques or places of worship for example, for experiences in learning about religion.

Could you expand on that please?

When I say experiential learning, my aim is to give them, for example, case studies—specific case studies—and diverse expressions of Islam, as an example. So in courses that I teach, I will introduce the cultural studies method. Of course with Islam, explicitly for seniors … I also do it in an Introduction to Asian Religions course for tenth graders, but in the advanced course for seniors I'll teach them about the Sisters in Islam in Indonesia, which is a feminist Muslim group that recognize and challenge the patriarchal interpretation of the Koran from a Muslim lens. So it's within the tradition, yet they are looking at the structural dimensions of power that have shaped a particular ascendancy of understanding of the Koran, both in terms of its Sharia law application as well as its cultural assumption. They challenge it, and they say, "this is one voice, it's a voice that's risen to ascendancy because of the dynamic of patriarchal power. It's not the only voice, and we would like to recognize that there are multiple interpretations."

So that's a group that most people have never heard of. It's an important representation, and it's not unique in Islam, that just becomes a case study again. So I expose students to that, and then I expose students to the diversity of expressions of the Muslim Brotherhood in Egypt—the historical representation of that community as well as its contemporary manifestations—which are diverse and complicated. So even within a community, we have diverse representations, some that would mirror the "fundamentalist assumptions" that people bring to that, and many that challenge it within the organization, and the tensions within that.

Then we will study, for example, the Aga Khan—the spiritual leader of the Ismaili Muslims, who is involved very deeply in philanthropic efforts in education and medicine, through his belief and his own understanding, and it's not exclusive to just Muslims. Right there you get incredible diversity and they have to get exposed to it. They incorporate that rather than just having me point out this diversity with only one experience. They are embedded into papers and research and projects in understanding those diversities, so they have an exposure to it in a deep way. That's the difference, I hope that it will translate.

So, the cultural studies method is really about method. We're not trying to cover all of Islam, we're not trying to cover all the historical Islamic dimensions, but only to the extent that I hope the students will have their appetite sparked. They'll always have an occasion, at the end of the term, to do an independent research project on something that captured their interest so they have an opportunity to explore something of their own. You engage them to something that is exciting to them—that's important. That's a part of the cultural study method, giving students the opportunity to explore things that are of interest to them particularly. Then they will know the kinds of questions to ask as they pursue their own life-long learning.

Even if they choose to be a scholar of Islam, they will never know it comprehensively. No scholar of Islam can *comprehensively* understand their tradition. It's too rich. It's a fool's errand to try to expect that any of us become experts in a given tradition. We become experts in particular dimensions of a tradition, so that's the distinction between the cultural studies method. It's really that we teach a method of understanding, rather than trying to engage in content coverage. In fact, method is more important that content, because the content becomes the vehicle to express and represent the method and that is about giving students tools and skills to learn, rather than giving them information to absorb. That distinction is a critical one for educators across the board, across all disciplines.

That is an amazing insight. You were talking earlier on about visiting mosques, visiting religious communities and you were a bit critical of that kind of approach?

Yes.

However, I must say that I've seen it in Europe—it is very popular. Basically the way teachers do it in Europe is: they hire a bus, they put the students inside, they go for an afternoon to a mosque and they may even eat some food from some kind of particular Islamic country. They take their shoes off, they go inside and that's it!

It's an incredibly popular way to teach about religion here as well, and with the best intentions. I don't want to be in any way disrespectful or critical of educators who employ those methods. I understand their reasoning. I'm very critical of it as a method and we in the American Academy of Religion are critical of it. You can say to your students until you're green that this mosque is one among many different representations of Islam, but the power of experiential learning is so profound that that's what the students are going to remember. So what you've then done is exposed them deeply to this one representation of Islam and that will enforce their preconceived notion that Islam is, or any religion is, uniform. You enforce that it is all about ritual and practice, rather than embedded in culture. It is stuck.

So, the power of that one exposure will be pervasive and is often pervasive for students. Rarely do educators have this opportunity, but what we do say is that if you can visit three mosques, maybe that would help. Three very different representations within—obviously, it would have to be within a geographical region, because it would be impossible otherwise—but if you then can really represent diversity within a tradition in a very experiential way, and then also look at the dimensions of the ways that that mosque is only one dimension of the parishioners or community's life.

If you take these three assertions that I said at the beginning: that religions are internally diverse, that they are evolving and changing, and that their religious understanding and expression of ideology are embedded in all dimensions of human agency and experience; if you can assume those and teach those through an experiential dimension and recognize that unless you counter the assumptions, you can often end up reinforcing them in really problematic ways. Typically, what we do when we have field trips to religions, it's easy for those from the US and Europe to say, "Okay, well, let's go to a mosque," or here in the US, "Let's go to a Hindu temple." So, what are we going to do when we're going to say, "Let's go to a Christian something?" Where are you going to go? Are you going to go to a Roman Catholic Church? Are you going to go to the Quaker meeting? Are you going to go to the Southern Baptist Church of the African AME Church?

So, we recognize that we're caught within this dilemma that none of those are going to represent Christianity. We can recognize the problem in, basically, privileging one interpretation, but we tend not to recognize that it's "traditions that are not culturally normative for us." That becomes, I think, one way for us to recognize the challenge.

I must say, as a comment to your statements, that the strategy you advocate is extremely challenging. Here at HDS, a lot of students come with very good intentions, relatively open minded, they know they come to a liberal environment, they're open to critique. However, I interviewed one student [Maytal], who is Jewish and she told me that, consistently, students would ask her in classes, "What does Judaism say about this?"

Absolutely. We're not immune to that at Harvard, and these assumptions are so embedded that the horror of other students expecting that a single student could represent his or her own theological expression is real. That's why they're here, partly to study and formulate, but to then say what is all of Judaism or Islam? We do that all the time.

Yeah, you're the Jew, can you please enlighten us?

Exactly, we did it and we continue to do it, so with African Americans, "Well, what's the African American perspective?" "What's the female perspective on stuff?" I mean, these are things that, at least in other arenas, we at least recognize or are starting to recognize—I shouldn't say we do because we still, unfortunately, don't—we at least have some potential critical lens, to say that we shouldn't be asking that, we shouldn't do that anymore. We used to do that more frequently, but we won't do it with religion yet, because those assumptions are still so ubiquitous.

I believe you started teaching in '93, am I correct?

I did.

How has the concept of religious education evolved over these last ten, fifteen, almost twenty years? Did you see major changes in methodology? Do we have new insights, academically?

I wish we did. You in Europe are actually far and away more sophisticated about your understanding of religious education than we are here in the US. Partly because we're still—and I would say that we also share this with France—we have a very skewed and problematic common interpretation of the separation of church and state. Many people here in the US still think that it's illegal to teach about religion in schools.

So, we're fundamentally aware that in many parts of Europe, and in historically colonized communities outside of Europe, religious education is a standard part of the curriculum. I can speak about the international trends better than I can speak about ours here because we pretty much haven't moved very far … maybe even backwards. International trends used to have opportunities, usually once a week, we have a relatively modest amount of time, but embedded in the curriculum, where students of different religious traditions would then go for religious education in their tradition. So you would have, depending on the population, you would have a fair amounts of Protestants and a fair amount of Roman Catholics, a fair amount of Muslims, a fair amount of Jews, and you'd have a teacher who would teach Judaism, which is itself still problematic. But what's happened now is that we've changed and shifted to moving toward more of a religious studies, cultural studies approach to what it means to embed religion in the curriculum, not uniformly known across the board and depending on the purpose of education in any given setting, so that questions will arise.

Quebec has done something incredibly bold, in the sense that they have made it required and they did this in one fell swoop, from K through—well, pre-K to—I think it's standard—I can't remember the particular language in the Quebec educational system, but throughout the pre-college curriculum they've required a curriculum all the way through—that's religion and culture; religion, culture, and belief, something along those lines. It is basically religious studies and ethical approaches to religion and they require that. They did it all at once, two or three years ago, and it was really challenging. It's getting challenged in courts by some independent school communities that are sectarian, but it's a really bold move and a very ethically visionary one too. Their rationality is a sound one because it means having to recognize this dimension of multiculturalism in a democracy, and that we need to enhance understanding of the dimension of our cultural lives in a better way, because the illiteracy around religion is causing so much strife, misrepresentation and misunderstanding.

I haven't followed it in the last year or so, but in fact, now that you're asking me, thinking about it makes me want to go back to see how they're doing. I thought that was quite a bold move and that other colleagues who are studying this internationally are seeing these kinds of trends in their own settings, but they'll be unique to each, not only to each country, but each region within a country.

How do you see that interdisciplinary education at Harvard, first of all? And secondly, how is the teaching of religion carried out in schools other than HDS? Is it different? Do students act differently? So there are two questions.

First of all, religious studies is by definition interdisciplinary, and that's the real strength of the field, as well as a challenge. It is difficult to then locate us and for a host of reasons, it can add to the misunderstanding of religion. By definition is has to be interdisciplinary. I think that what happened, in terms of the study of religion itself, is that we have evolved in a very exciting way from a more phenomenological approach to religion, which was how religion used to be taught, to recognizing that strength, but nuancing it more. This is because it made presumptions about uniformity across religions that were highly problematic in the postmodern age.

So, the postmodern understanding of religion is really fascinating and a really important field, because it represents in a pure form some of what other fields have to wrestle with. They struggle with what it means to recognize the interdisciplinary nature of old fields, but religion is already that by definition, in a way that is purer and clearer than older disciplines are. Religious Studies is a relatively new discipline—so there's that. I don't actually formally teach at the Education School, but hopefully, eventually, I will be doing cross-listed courses there. That's our hope, but I do teach a lot of Education school students and I do teach at the Extension School, as you know.

I would say that the experience is very similar for me in any context, whether in secondary schools or the Extension School or what I teach to students at HDS or other schools, so I just always assumed—and even actually assumed here at HDS—a particular illiteracy about religion that I don't assume any longer. You just made me realize that I don't actually discern or teach differently in any of these settings. I'm always, always teaching about the method and always making the method very explicit. First of all, I might get first year students, so they are coming from whatever contexts. Secondly, even if I have MTS students or MDiv students—if I have MDiv students, it's most likely, to the extent that they will have had studied religion previously, that they will often be coming out of their own religious tradition and through their own experience and their devotional setting. So they are just as uncertain or illiterate about the methods of religion that they're coming here to study as anyone else is. I think the only potential difference—I don't even think there's a difference, because again, students would choose my courses—is in recognizing that religion is part of what they are going to learn, so I don't make a distinction. When I used to assume that I could make one, it was to my peril, because students were bringing the same assumptions about religion, even if they're here, because most of these students are new to the discipline.

If we look over time, do you see a shift there, from pre 9/11 to post 9/11, in the way students approach religion in your class?

I think that 9/11 and I would say the George W. Bush presidency, and the way that our experience of 9/11 was represented, unfortunately, has set us back. In one way, that can be a blessing and a curse. The curse is the consequences of that representation, which are devastating globally, to the consequence of two war zones, countless tragedies and casualties. But the other side of that is that now there is a very clear case study about what's problematic about the way we deal with religion and numerous examples, including our deeply inadequate understanding of the complexities of both Afghan and Iraqi societies, because we didn't understand the religious dimensions of those societies. Madeleine Albright has been especially articulate about these foreign policy blunders and lack of understanding about fundamental, fundamental things that we should have known, prior to whatever we think about those engagements or if we should or we shouldn't have gone to war. We absolutely needed to have better understanding of what the consequences of our involvement would be and we just didn't, and we still don't, to my great sadness.

I think we still don't understand the consequence of the illiteracy, but there's more out there now that helps people recognize the importance of that understanding. Not as much as I wish, but I do feel like now it has given us a very pure, unambiguous, clear representation of a case study around those consequences and it's unfolding. Having said that, it's not just 9/11. We see the Park 51 mosque controversy, we see the Koran burning that was done in Florida, I mean, we see a whole host of ways that tragedies get interpreted or they get promoted through these misunderstandings, so it unfolds constantly, every day you pick up the news.

Would you, as a scholar, tend to lose hope when you see the political discourse here, for example, during these Republican primaries? Many Europeans look with very wide eyes to the kind of political discourse some of these candidates are having, especially on religion.

Oh, well I would say this: first of all, it's devastating and it is incredibly disarming. You and Europe have many colleagues here who share your horror. Actually, one of the reasons that I decided to turn to secondary school teaching, after taking a brief sabbatical for three years, was that I felt like critical thinking and media literacy are the most important skills we can give to the next generation, because we cannot abide what is the hoax of free press, the hoax of responsible discourse that is normative here. We will completely unravel any foundation of real, true democracy. We are unraveling it and it is to my great horror and great concern. Of course it's not just our little efforts at our school, but the educators need to focus on this to the extent that they are able, although there are many obstacles for them, to be able to do so, not unrelated to the same kind of values that are fueling the current political, cultural ...

Those values, the special interest values, that have given sanction to this level of conversation, have given credibility to this normativity. Our effect in the nature of how we educate, or in effect in the nature of how we build our healthcare, it's consistently across the board—to the extent that we can help students understand the role that special interests are playing in the neoliberal context. If we can give them language around neoliberalism itself, and give them language to recognize this is one set of values that are being promoted, and to have some critical thought about that. Again, maybe embrace it, so it's not against it but it's to recognize that it's one among many options. To recognize the deeply embedded ideological values that are being promoted throughout these policies—that's where I have hope, I still continue to have hope that if we have a language of recognition and critical thinking, that we will still emerge with a strong democracy. But without that, I do worry.

Just to make sure I understood well, you didn't really see a rise in racist discourse within the classroom these last few years. That didn't happen, did it?

I would say yes, but not intentionally. I think part of what is so powerful about this is that there are embedded assumptions that people bring without having ever recognized them as racist or elitist in any way. But they are profoundly so. That again is my hope and deep belief in strong education. Not just any education, but education through a critical capacity. In my very consistent experience, no matter what the ideological belief systems are across the range, that students are horrified when they realize that they hold and reproduce certain kinds of assumptions that do perpetuate the kind of discord that, whatever their belief systems are, they would never voluntarily recognize and promote. So I would say that it is embedded assumptions that are deeply problematic. I have seen a rise in that. Therefore there is all the more urgency to help give them a language to understand and be more self conscious of those assumptions.

If you look at the future of religious education here at Harvard, what would you change right now in the teaching of religion here, if there is anything you would change? Also, how do you see these next few years, maybe even decades, evolving?

That's an interesting and important question. I think a weakness we have here at Harvard, at the university, is that those of us who are most well trained in religious studies are not involved in teaching about understanding religion in other parts of university. That's partly self-generating. We tend to be a school that values historical inquiry and we have tremendous scholars that do that work without parallel and without equal. But the contemporary questions about religion that are so captivating and so urgent are ones that people outside of religion are tending to lead the education around.

So, we have people in all of the schools of the university teaching about religion in ways that I don't want to challenge across the board, but that are somewhat problematic, to the extent that I have hopes, modest hopes, because I think the history of this professional school, the university, is such that it would take a lot to challenge or change. But I do hope there would be better connections across the schools in an interdisciplinary way, whereby specifically the teaching of religion is more informed and sophisticated. I'm not blaming colleagues outside of here—we have tended to be pretty isolationist. Not in any explicit articulation of that, but just in terms of the nature of our interest. I think that's been a problem.

So, you would push for more collaboration?

Yes, collaborations and projects. There are opportunities now that are opening up and some of us are pursuing those. I hope for those gains, but I do feel like this whole conversation is about religion that has been outside of the ... it's as crazy as having conversations about the law, or teaching about law, that don't include our remarkable Law Faculty. But again, religion does that. Because people think that most of what we do here is train religious leaders, so that's irrelevant to them. It's a representation of the very illiteracies that I am so concerned to try and overcome.

Kat Milligan

I was born in Knoxville, Tennessee. I grew up dancing. In fact, I started dancing when I was four and a half years old. At that point my older sister was in dance, and so of course I wanted to dance too. It's funny … looking back, two of my loves—dance and shoes—entered the narrative of my life from a very early age. When I was about four or so, my mom used to line the hallway with her shoes so that I could walk back and forth past them and admire them. Then, there's this other story from when I was very little, before I could speak. My sister was at a birthday party at Showbiz Pizza, which was the precursor to ChuckE Cheese, and my mom and I attended too. So, while my sister and her friends were on the various rides and in the ball pits, my mom and I sat with the other parents in the room where an animatronic band was playing. There in my highchair I apparently was getting down to the music, causing a nearby boyscout to remark, "Boy, that baby sure can boogie." Interestingly enough, the first sentence my mom ever heard me say, when I was about one and a half was, "Get me down out of this highchair." So I think being free to move was always really important to me.

Anyways, I never became a cobbler (although I still love shoes) but I did become a dancer and choreographer. Dance has been my first love, my saving grace, my connection to the divine, my confirmation of the divine, a constant companion, a safe place, the place in which I am most myself, a space of being deeply heard and seen.

I had this really wonderful opportunity in high school to go to a magnet high school, where I could dance during the course of the day, choreograph, learn stage technology, costume design and dance history, and participate in the dance company. It was a public school, only in its second year as a magnet high school when I attended, and located in the inner city. I learned a lot about my own privilege there, and I also learned a lot about how to have difficult conversations concerning race, prejudice, family issues, relationships, and more, and my primary site of learning was the dance company. Through conversations in rehearsals, through improvisation, through the actual choreography, through the bonding that occurs backstage during performances and dress rehearsals, we talked about, processed, and reflected upon really difficult things. Of course at the time, being high schoolers, these "difficult things" felt less like "issues" to discuss and more just … life.

There's something about dance that makes going into these difficult places seem doable, possible, necessary, and safe. It brings people together, not on a surface level. I mean, sure, we're all there in the same studio or stage, but it brings us together in breath, in exertion, in creation, in vulnerability. When you dance, you can't hide. There you are: there is your body, there is everything you are in your movement.

Did religion play much of a role at high school or at home?

My parents divorced when I was five years old and a lot of my religious under-standing and background has been shaped by Mom, who in many ways began her own religious journey after the divorce. She went to college to become a Baptist missionary, but by the time that she met my Dad they were going to Presbyterian church. In fact, they met at a Bible study, a fact I just found out about a couple of years ago and honestly, have a hard time comprehending. When I was very young—before the divorce—we attended a huge United Methodist church in the area. I don't remember much, aside from some color-your-own Bible story sheets and how beautiful the sanctuary was.

Yet, when my parents divorced, my dad quit going to church, and my mom began her own, more personal spiritual journey. She began studying tarot and astrology. She also had a great love for American transcendentalism. So, this meant that there were always lots of very interesting books in the house. At night, when I couldn't sleep, I used to sneak into her office and read sections of all sorts of reli-gion books, from Mary Baker Eddy's *Science and Health* to the Jeffersonian Bible and Emerson's essays.

Interestingly enough, my mom had a poster of Walt Whitman on our kitchen wall, directly across from where I sat. So, everyday, I had some time with Walt, star-ing at his portrait, and reading part of the preface of *Leaves of Grass* written beneath, the part that begins with "This is what you shall do …" In many ways, this was the religious foundation of my upbringing. My mom always encouraged my sister and I to develop our own understandings and beliefs concerning God; but treating others well, respecting the earth, continually educating and questioning oneself: these were just expectations of, well, what we should do. I was a very pre-cocious child (my sister often complained that I was "born 40") and often asked my mom questions like, "What is the purpose of life?" Her answers often didn't satisfy me, but I realize now that I asked questions that don't have a concrete answer, and I appreciate that she never gave me one.

I also had this other exposure to the New Age and New Age religions growing up. I remember some instances—probably late elementary school, middle school—where my Mom would work a couple of different psychic fairs. What my Mom did never seemed all that "out there" to me, mainly based on her approach. She disliked doing readings that predicted the future, as that is never concrete. Instead, she focused on tarot as a tool for self-discovery and reflection. It never seemed like something that was highly mysterious to me.

I remember being a kid and going around the psychic fair, just imagining an energetic shield around me because I was so scared that the fellow psychics there would read my mind and tell my mom about all these thoughts that I had. [Laughter] There was also this sense that, especially being in Tennessee, that that was something that I had to be very careful about telling to people. I didn't want to say, "Oh, my mom works at psychic fairs and she reads tarot cards!" When I was in college she was actually a published writer within that community and well-respected, but there was a sense that this was not something that I could freely share with people.

Considering your geographical area, that could be considered a very alternative lifestyle.

Yes.

Was there no church attendance at all?

We went to a Unitarian Universalist church for a few years, but I didn't really like that. Well, I should clarify: it was the religious education program I didn't like. For some kids, I think it worked great, but here I was, pouring over my mom's various books on religion at night after she went to bed and then going to church on Sunday and being asked to bang a drum and sing a song about the earth. It just felt so trivializing: I wanted to talk about the big issues. It was like, "What am I doing here? I'm not learning anything. This isn't exciting." The times where I would go to the actual service instead of the RE class, I found much more exciting and energizing. I liked listening to the sermon, and that to me was better than sitting around eating goldfish crackers.

Then, I don't know, for whatever reason our attendance dropped off. Well, I think my sister continued to go, she liked the youth group she was in (unlike me, she connected much more to her peers). Then, when I was in high school, 17 maybe, I saw an ad in the alternative paper of Knoxville that was like, "Hey, are you interested in the spiritual teachings of Deepak Chopra and Oprah Winfrey?" I don't even remember the other people, Marianne Williamson perhaps, and I was like, "Yes, I am!" So there was a new Religious Science church that was forming. My senior year of high school I started going there. Then when I went to California I saw Religious Science churches all over the place. So I was actually involved in New Thought for about seven years.

How did you decide where to go to college and what to study once you got there?

It was pretty blindingly obvious to me what I was going to do. I had gone to a dance intensive called Pacific Coast Dance Fest during the summer that I was seventeen. It was at Long Beach State, which I later attended as an undergraduate. The facilities were amazing, as was the weather and everything around. They have a whole dance building with six or seven dance studios, a dance clinic, dance classrooms, a Pilates' studio, a dance theater, a costume workshop, a music studio—just incredible. It was also so close to LA and I wanted to be a professional choreographer for music videos, to have my own company and tour as a master teacher on dance convention circuits. So I thought, "OK, I'm going to go out to Long Beach and I'm going to start going to college." I wasn't sure that I was going to be a dance major. I thought I might do something like Kinesiology, but halfway through my first semester there I auditioned for the dance program and got in.

You did that for three years?

Three years.

Did you enjoy it?

I did, especially at first. I was probably doing about six to eight dance classes a week. In addition to this, I was working out about three or four times a week and I had yoga and Pilates a few times a week. This really took a toll on my body and I developed severe Achilles Tendonitis. After every dance class I was having to ice my Achilles tendons and then having back spasms. I had this physical pain that was becoming increasingly more intense. Then simultaneously my spiritual life was increasing. I was meditating more, I was writing in my journal more, I was really becoming involved with the Religious Science community out there and considering becoming a Religious Science minister. The more that I focused on that spirituality, the more that I became dissatisfied with much of what I was seeing in the culture of the dance world.

I remember going through a hallway one day and a friend of mine was crying about not being able to do a double pirouette and it was so normal, so typical. I realized I didn't want to be in a world where that's something that's understood as normal. The other thing was that I never had a traditional dancer's body. The people there were, for the most part, great. But there was still the sense of "If your body is not making you happy, then perhaps you should change it." That's how it was presented to me: we don't have a problem but we can see it's making you unhappy. I remember a teacher giving me the number of a nutritionist and that became troubling for me as well. Instead of saying, "There's no reason why you shouldn't be happy the way you are," the focus was, "well, if you're not happy with your body, you should change." I didn't realize it at the time, but that's just not the way it works: happiness has to come first. Then, whatever changes happen in your body become side effects and, if you're happy, you don't really even care about those side effects, you're too busy loving your life.

Within my own choreography, I began to become less interested in the traditional choreographic structures that I was learning in the composition classes, and more interested in choreographing as a spiritual process which, to me, is interesting because if you look at the writings of some of the early modern choreographers, you will find that, for them, dance and choreography was intensely spiritual.

So choreographing became something very intuitive: I'd close my eyes and say, "Alright, God, what needs to be danced?" Choreographing became this deep process of listening for the holy, and I began to find much of my choreographic inspiration bubbling to the surface while meditating. So I would then find myself in the situation where a Professor would then say, "Well, that part seems cheesy or hokey" and I didn't know what to say to that. I was at a public, secular university. I couldn't have a spiritual discussion concerning the movement, which was what I wanted and needed. I felt I couldn't engage with them if I was coming from a spiritual perspective while they were concerned with only the aesthetic or metaphoric dimensions.

So, as you were bridging that physical experience to a more spiritual experience, you were also transitioning slowly towards religious studies?

Yes, because religion had always interested me a lot due to my upbringing. So for part of my Gen Ed's I took some religion classes. I remember taking this one class, I don't even remember the title of it anymore, but it was American religions that began in America—so alternative religions and new religious movements. It was so fascinating to me because we looked at the UFO cults, Mormonism, the Serpent Handlers, New Age Religion, New Thought and so on. I had no idea that this was something that was covered under religious studies. I always connected religious studies to the Bible, which is something I never connected to growing up. I wrote a paper, looking back now I think it was probably a really bad paper, but at the time I was like, "This is great and this is fascinating." Fortunately, I had a professor who was really supportive of my enthusiasm. I wrote on the Serpent Handlers, and somehow throughout the course of writing that paper on something that so many people are bemused by, I saw the ways in which they were transforming their reality. I got a deeper understanding of what God and faith are.

It began to click for me that a lot of my thirst for dance and thirst for choreography were part of the same thing that drive many people to religion. So this need to transform one's current reality or to feel something beyond oneself, to feel connected to something bigger than oneself, which dance gave me in so many ways— I recognized that this is what religion did for some people. Once I saw that similarity, I began to think about religious studies as the place I could go to in order to engage with these questions that I wanted to take back to dance.

I was in my third year, I was 21. I had decided to switch my majors that second semester of my third year. I just felt like I needed to get out of the dance program. I still had many friends and definitely didn't want to give up dancing but it became clear to me that I needed to change my surroundings so that I could be in a place where I could freely engage with those questions that I had.

I dropped a Choreography class I was in and then the professor told the rest of the class that it was good that I had changed my major because, "So many people are too weak to be in this profession." Public university and he tells the class this. In fact, a professor here asked me if I sued him. I told her that I never even thought about that. She said, "Yeah, you could have done that." It's not that I necessarily would have wanted to do that, but it was completely indicative of the kind of thought in the dance world that is so prevalent that I didn't even question it. It's one of the things I find really disturbing now. So, that was hanging over my head.

Also, around this time, some pretty significant events were occurring with my family back in Tennessee. I knew that University of Tennessee had an excellent religious studies program and, as a bonus, I would qualify for in-state tuition. So, in the summer after my third year at Long Beach, I moved back to Tennessee. It happened really quickly and, looking back, I did not do it well. I've come to really hold closure and transitions as important and worth taking the time to honor but, at that point in time, I was 21, and I was a bit heartbroken. I thought I was going to live in California my whole life, and although I knew life, the Universe, or God, was leading me elsewhere, a part of me felt like a huge failure: I gave up on my dreams. That's tough. It's funny, because I was thinking about this the other day. Someone asked me, "Did you ever imagine that you'd be graduating from Harvard Divinity School?" The answer, of course, was no. Then I just thought about my 18-year-old self, who would probably see me graduating from Harvard with a Master of Divinity as a failure. She would ask, "But what about being a famous choreographer?" I still carry that with me, this mourning for the loss of that dream, even though I know it's not my calling and even though I love my life and am humbled by this ministry I'm called to do.

Anyways, so I moved back to Knoxville, and I transferred into UT, where I actually ended up double majoring in Religious Studies and History. The History program there is really incredible. A huge part of the reason why I double majored was because of one professor, Lynn Sacco. It was funny because when I told her I was applying to graduate programs in my final year and I was naming them to her, she said, "Have you thought about Harvard and Yale and Duke?" I was like, "What, no, I can't go to those places!" and she's like, "I'm telling you, your work is that good." It's just that I couldn't see it.

I applied to a couple of other programs that were not Harvard or Yale or Duke. Actually, I wasn't sure I wanted to do a Ph.D. and so I applied to places that would offer a Terminal Master's. I applied to University of South Florida and University of Missouri and because of funding, I ended up going to Missouri which was a terrific experience.

For a Master's in Religious Studies?

Master's in Religious Studies, yeah.

And that was a two year program? Did you focus on a specific topic?

My focus area was religion in America and it was interesting that when I entered the program I thought I was going to do something with New Thought. My first semester, I was in a West African Religions and Religions of the Diaspora class. We were assigned a paper and I wasn't sure what to do. I ended up writing it on the African-American dancer and choreographer Katharine Dunham in early 20th century about how her experiences of Vodou shaped her approach to choreography and the creation of her own dance technique. Her dance technique is in a lot of ways Vodou ritual made manifest in the human body. This fascinated me and nobody else was talking about that, nobody else was talking about these blindingly obvious similarities. I think a lot of the creators of modern dance came from a religious background and perspective. It's become so secular now that you can't go into a public university and say that dance is like a pillar from the heavens to the gods going through your body. You can't have that discussion. Also, for anyone running a dance studio for kids, I can guarantee you, the majority of the dance moms aren't going to pay you to say that either. So that really planted the seed in my mind.

The other thing that happened was that they have a Department of Women's and Gender Studies at the University of Missouri. They offer a graduate minor, and so I decided to become a graduate minor in Women's and Gender Studies. The first class that you have to take for that minor is Problems and Issues in Feminist Scholarship and then the final paper involves taking the course materials and class discussions and applying them to anything that we wanted to: one's research, one's life, an incident, whatever. I ended up writing this paper that took different stories from my life and dance and criticized them from a feminist perspective, highlighting what really needed to change. By the end of the paper I realized that I had this understanding of how to teach dance and how to approach dance that was vastly different from anything that I had been taught growing up. I asked myself—who am I if I just sit on this? I think that was probably when the idea that perhaps academia is not something I need to be in for the rest of my life emerged. I realized that I needed to be doing something more hands-on and in the field.

So it became clear to me that I couldn't escape dance. Also, within the graduate program I began to reject New Thought as my religious foundation, due to several different issues. My new feminist perspective weighed in on that and the thing that I could never get around was this idea that if our thoughts create our reality and we are victimized in some way, then we have to accept that in some ways we cause our own victimization. I would ask minister after minister about that and they said, "Oh, we never blame the victim" but the issue was that the theological framework requires that the victim must accept some sort of responsibility; you can't get around this. If thoughts create our realities, then this is something that happens all the time: it doesn't get turned on or turned off. That became deeply troubling and upsetting to me and I said, "I can't believe in this anymore."

Did you become a 'None', someone without a religion, or did you switch religions? Or perhaps you would define yourself as a seeker?

A seeker is probably what I felt like my whole life. So I began to question whether I was a UU. I went to the UU church in Columbia, Missouri a couple of times. I had a friend that goes there. It was nice, but it just was not my thing. There were lots of different types of UU services and this one felt very much like the sermon was designed as a lecture. I was used to being in a New Thought church, where for seven years things were more celebratory and energetic. That has its problems too, but it just didn't feel like something I wanted to spend my Sunday mornings doing.

But that didn't mean that I wasn't questioning if I was UU or not. I did begin to think more seriously about whether I had an earth-based spirituality. My Mom is a Neopagan High Priestess, a Neodruid as well. I rejected that frame of thought or that system of belief for a while because my Mom was just so high up within it and I felt like I needed to have my own religious identity. But I felt like I was distanced enough from it that I could kind of do my own explorations. I think earth-based spirituality was something that was very important to me. I wouldn't call myself a Neopagan but I, with a friend of mine, would do some small ritual celebrations of the pagan holidays. So that was something that I began to add.

The other thing was that the summer before I moved to Missouri and a little bit before that, my Mom started working at the local Unitarian church, the same one that I went to as a kid. She was the administrative assistant there. My mom knew I was at this point of feeling called to ministry but not necessarily having a denomination, so she said, "Have you considered Unitarian Universalism? They treat their ministers very well." By that point, she had this inside view. The point was also valid because they do treat their ministers well in many ways. I'm sure some of my friends heading into a UU parish ministry might have some other thoughts about this, but compared to a lot of the other denominations and types of religious organizations that I've seen, the ministers are, for the most part, treated very well. They are given regular sabbaticals and a wage they can live on and usually housing assistance as well. Also, there is great respect for continuing education, not only a respect but also encouragement and enthusiasm for it. I asked myself if this was an organization I could see myself working within and began to do some preliminary research. I think what initially attracted me was that it provides a religious community for those who are deeply committed to being of service to this world without requiring one to subscribe to a creed. Based on my own religious journey, I couldn't imagine finding a creed that I could subscribe to for life because what I'll know in ten years will be different from what I know now.

What happened there during that last year in Missouri and how did that phase of discernment of your future manifest itself?

Well, it's interesting. I wrote my Master's thesis on 'Where The Dancer Meets Her Divine: Dance As Religious Experience In The Lives of Isadora Duncan And Loie Fuller.' They were two of what we would call 'modern' dancers, but they were really proto-modern dancers at the turn of the 20th century. I was so fascinated by everything that had to do with that project. Not only the research into their own lives but engaging with these questions of what is dance and what is religion and the idea that these two questions are impossible to answer. Somehow in this impossibility of being able to define them, there's something that makes it so that they can work incredibly well together, each illuminating the other.

I found that this whole line of thinking was really inspiring to me and I had a wonderful thesis adviser who was so great because he saw the value and the merit in what I was talking about long before I did which I think is so rare. I was incredibly lucky with that and he really encouraged me to think about further programs. But he also knew that I had a different interest than perhaps someone who would be working in academia their whole life.

Were you still dancing at that point?

I had stopped dancing for a number of years (which led to a bit of an identity crisis, interestingly enough), and then it was actually writing that paper for the Women's and Gender Studies course that made me return to dance. I not only returned to dance but started to teach dance too. When I started to teach dance it was, I don't know, my world just opened up and this joy came rushing in to me. I hadn't realized that it had been missing from my life—I only knew when I started to teach it.

You felt it.

Yes, yes! So I started to teach in my second year of my Master's program in Missouri. Chip Callahan, my adviser, saw all these changes and certainly was in conversation with me. I talked with him and I said, "I'm really not sure, I feel like there are these different pulses and I don't know where to go." So I applied to two Ph.D. programs in Performance Studies. Then I thought, well I might want to do something ministry-related but I don't know if I want to give a sermon every day. He suggested Harvard Divinity School. He told me: "There are some people there that are doing really interesting things, so you might want to check that out." So I applied here, this is the only place I applied to for an MDiv. I applied to three places: two for Ph.D. in Performance Studies and one for Master of Divinity here. I did not get into either of the Ph.D programs which made things pretty obvious when I got into here with a full scholarship. I thought, "Ok, I guess I know where I'm going!"

You had never been here?

I had never been here—I came here without ever visiting.

Did you know anything about the school?

I knew it was the place where Emerson gave his Divinity School Address. I knew that it was non-denominational, which was really important to me. I knew the works of several of the professors. I respected several of the professors and looked forward to the opportunity to take classes with them. I looked through the course catalogs and the courses seemed exciting. I went to Missouri without visiting it first, and it ended up being a really great place for me, and I went because it felt—in my heart—like the right thing to do. I had that same feeling with HDS, and so, I thought, "Get out of your head and just go. It will be hard work, but you need to go."

Were the Religious Studies classes you took at Missouri a general overview of religion, or more of an in-depth study? What did you study there?

I took a variety of graduate courses and classes including Medieval Christian Mystics, Healing and Medicine, Asian Religions and Modernity and Indigeneity. So all of those courses, and all of these classes.

So you were actually relatively free to pick your own course?

Well, the issue is that there are about eight or nine graduate students at any time there. So you basically take what you are given regarding graduate courses. Fortunately, what was offered was usually really interesting. But then the other thing was that because it was so small, the professors knew each of the graduate students—what our interests were and what our backgrounds were. So all of them were very open to meeting you where your interests were. So for that Medieval Christian Mystics class, I wrote a paper about this woman who danced on the liturgical hour and brought in dance and performance theory for that, and these were theories I was able to bring to my thesis.

You were admitted to Harvard in March 2010 on a full scholarship. Then you moved here in August 2010.

Yes.

You met your adviser, and experienced Orientation. Can you talk a bit about that?

Yes, oh goodness. Orientation. My biggest fear about Orientation was getting here because I had never lived anywhere where I would have to rely on public transport before. I was really scared of public transport because I didn't even like the school bus growing up. So I got here that first day of Orientation, which was a major victory! I made my way on the bus and on the red line and so that was the battle halfway over. One of the things that they say—I'm told now that they say this at nearly every Orientation—is that you might think that you're here by mistake but you're not. It was just like, "Oh, I'm glad they said that because I kind of thought I might have been here by mistake and they accidentally let me through!" So that was good to hear.

I became aware that everybody has such different backgrounds here in as far as what they did between the time of their undergraduate and when they came here. Some people were here straight from undergrad, some people had done mission work and some people had done things like establish their own non-profit organizations. There is this feeling that everybody here is really amazing in some way. I remember when we had a lunch on the first day with our advisers. My adviser my first year was Leigh Eric Schmidt, who I was really excited about because I had used some of his work in my MA thesis.

I realized though that having someone who is more oriented in historical research and in pure academia does not necessarily make the best adviser for an MDiv. He said to me, "I'm excited about what you're excited about. I will sign your form, I will help make sure you're on track, but I don't know anything about the Master of Divinity." So there was that element. I had just come out of this program where I was very much in a religious studies phase, historically and culturally. I was kind of still in that mode and I didn't really know quite what the difference between doing that and being in Master of Divinity was and how this other element of ministry came in.

There was never a slight hesitation between the MTS and MDiv programs for you?

No. Doing an MTS seemed like it would be repetitive and there was also a sense of feeling like I needed to do something where I was creating something independently. Not that you can't be creative with research, but for me it needed to be something that was dance related.

OK. So then you started shopping for your first classes. How did that go? Did you like your first classes? Were they very different for you?

Well, I don't think I actually got to do a lot in the way of shopping because that first semester we had to take two required classes. They were History, Theologies and

Practices of Christianity and then Introduction to Ministry Studies. I also did German, my first semester, so then I just had one class left to shop. I ended up taking Michael Jackson's Ritualization, Play, and Transitional Phenomena.

What about the content and the methodology? Did you like it? Was it interactive enough or too interactive? What was the contact with your fellow students and professors like?

I felt a little odd in most of the classes. I began to ask myself, "What am I doing here?" In the Introduction to Ministry Studies class, a lot of it is very much oriented towards pastoral ministry, especially in the Protestant setting. They DO have a couple of other books. But one of the first things that you have to do is write a spiritual autobiography and then in your sections you share these autobiographies with people. I remember saying, "I'm going to become a Unitarian Universalist parish minister". My section leader said, "Well, if you didn't have to think of ordination, what would you do?" and I was like, "Oh, I'd have my own dance studio where I could give my own classes." Then it was like … I just knew it.

The question triggered something?

Yes, it did. My response was just so instantaneous. But I think the biggest thing that I was dealing with during my first semester was this idea where I felt that a lot of people around me had a great deal of enthusiasm for entering the ministry. I thought that I would have that same enthusiasm for entering the ministry, but what happened was that the impact of a shooting at my mom's church in 2008 never really hit me until I came here. I felt like you think that you're operating within a safe space but you can never know or be certain. A safe space can be taken away so easily.

While I'm sure that this is not the case, it really felt like I was so alone in having that perspective of churches: that they are not necessarily always the happy, life-giving places that they can be. I remember sitting in the Sperry Room thinking about the fact that something could happen in here. I really wasn't prepared for it to affect me in that way, but all these questions just started coming at me. I spent much of my first semester really feeling quite distanced from people because I felt like there was this trauma tinting my understanding of ministry that no one else shared.

Did that severely distance you from other students?

I don't think I would say severely. I had a couple of friends that I reached out to. I had these dear friends, but there was certainly a sense of feeling that even though

I was often surrounded by people and with groups of people, there was a feeling of not being together with them, of being external.

What caused that?

I think this trauma response was part of it. I think the other thing was the sense that I was trying to put myself into some sort of ministry that just wasn't exciting to me. The UU students here are some of my dearest friends but they're very much oriented towards the different steps that you have to do with the end (i.e. ordination) clearly in sight. They are very focused on that and very enthusiastic about the process, and I love that about them, but it also leaves me a bit of a loner at times. We'd go out to dinner and the ordination process and parish ministry would inevitably become topics of conversation, and I realized that I just had no enthusiasm for these conversations. All of a sudden, I'd find my eyes wandering to a basketball game on TV while they talked—and I am not a big sports fan. So there's this distance that comes from not feeling that way, which made me feel not part of the group. I think that was part of it—just trying to put myself in a box that just did not feel good to me.

Now we've been talking a little bit already about your interactions with other students. What about outside of classes? Did you participate in any social kind of activity like Community Tea or some kind of club or organization?

I went to Community Tea sometimes. I started going to Ministry in Motion during my first semester. The first semester I didn't go to HUUMS student worship, actually. I didn't go that often because it didn't feel very welcoming to me. So, of course, I had this brilliant idea during my second semester that I would run for the board of HUUMS: Harvard Divinity School Unitarian Universalists Ministry for Students. The way the board is elected is for a calendar year and not an academic year. So I ran for the board in my second semester and then for the first semester of this year as worship coordinator for HUUMS. I thought—you know what? I don't feel welcome in this space so now I'm going to create a new space and hopefully other people will feel welcome there.

The board meetings for HUUMS happened every couple of weeks and so I got to know those people quite well, there are six of us. So that happened in my first year. Also WomenCircle—actually I cannot talk enough about WomenCircle.

WomenCircle, as I understand it, began about six years ago here. It started as WomenChurch but they decided to change it to WomenCircle so as to make it more approachable for those not from a Protestant background. WomenCircle is open to all that self-identify as women and we meet monthly. It's a non-denominational ritual service and usually there's a different theme each month. There are a couple of components that are always the same, such as prayers of the community like a welcome, a passing of the peace. WomenCircle convinced me that I was in the right place.

What was it about WomenCircle that made you feel welcome here?

Well, it was a community. Not only did we share deeply in ritual, but we shared food and drink afterward. So, we never shared these deep and heavy or even cele-bratory things and then just abruptly left. This community space after ritual allowed us to feel like we didn't share in a vacuum, that those who we shared with will also be those who we walk with. The leaders my first year were so extremely welcoming and so open and honest with their experiences here. I could say that I felt like I didn't belong and that no one gets me and they all said, "I felt the same way too." It was so great to hear that. Then what happened was that the first semes-ter, I think in October, we went on a retreat. WomenCircle has a retreat every year in Maine. So we went on the retreat and a lot of deep sharing occurred between all of us. Then what this sharing and the safe space led to was that when I came back here and I saw all these women in the hallways, I knew that there were people here who really knew who I was and who saw me and that knew I was having a tough time. They knew I was genuinely having difficulties, and they could listen to that. In lots of ways it became like a lifeline.

Did you continue dancing while here at Harvard?

Yes.

Did you do that in the framework of HDS or just outside?

Well, I started sharing some of my dance curriculum within the Ministry in Motion setting and so that has been a big component. In my first year my head was spinning from being in such a new place. I wasn't really doing a lot of dancing outside of HDS. Then this past summer, I taught a "Love Your Body" dance work-shop at the Dance Complex and was introduced to the fact that pretty much every place to teach dance here requires rent, which is not the case in other places that I've been at. They put you on a schedule and so then they pay you. For a graduate student, putting up $55 a week is just not something that is feasible, unfortunately But it creeps into everything I do here.

Can you expand upon that a little bit?

Yes. I'm taking a Sacramental Theology course right now and I just wrote the mid-term paper discussing notions of the body and its potential for movement. I wrote about dancing and then dancing within a worship setting as a way to eliminate our understandings of thin places, sacramentality and sacraments. So that's an example. Also, a worship service that I recently led for HUUMS involved a dance. For the Sacrament class, I'm doing this final project where I'm creating a dance workshop that explores how to build or create more of a sacramental worldview through movement. At the WomenCircle Noon Service, I led a dance that even the Dean was doing! These days, it's pretty much like if I'm there, usually dancing is involved somehow.

Did your way of dancing evolve here? Did you change anything or did you continue with the same thing?

I don't know if my way of dancing evolved, but what I did become aware of was that my style of teaching was evolving. I realized that I'm not so much interested in making sure that everybody can do a perfect *plié* or land a triple pirouette; rather, I'm interested in helping people to feel safe in their bodies, to feel empowered by moving and to feel that their bodies are worthy of speaking through dance. That realization has really changed my approach to teaching dance as well as the types of classes that I'm interested in offering. I can teach modern dance, I can teach jazz dance and I can teach these different forms of dance. But I've also started to develop curriculum for some I call "love your body" dance. So it blends all these different dance forms that I know from a perspective of mindfulness and taking care of oneself. There's a sacramental dance workshop that I'm creating currently. This class I call "Sanctuary of Sweat" which is basically like—dance your heart out for an hour and just feel great. I think that dance classes can be like low church and high church; sometimes you have to have that high church, very holy approach to everything because it feels very meditative and tensional, and sometimes you need that low church approach to get straight to the spirit and straight to just letting everything go.

So I think it's really been within this curriculum that I'm building for dance offerings that I've seen the shift in my relationship with dance.

I think that's very well said. As you discover different kinds of spirituality you're integrating them into different forms of bodily expressions. Did your feminism evolve and grow here? Did it change direction? Did you deepen your understanding of feminism?

The feminism that I was engaged with at Missouri has not continued here—not intentionally, just because I've just been focusing more on dance. A course on Feminism in Islam versus a course like the Sacraments class, that I felt like could help develop more of an articulation with what I do with dance, just seemed like a no-brainer.

So you're saying you prefer classes on dance or bodily expression instead of feminist classes?

I don't think that there are classes so much of dance, but rather of expression. Well, hopefully they will bridge. I haven't quite found that to be the case yet.

How do you bridge the poles of dancing on one side and feminism on the other? Do you see a contradiction between both? Dances are often performed in a very anti-feminist way.

Something that really is pressing on my mind at the moment is my belief that it takes all sorts of movement to get people moving and feeling great and safe in their bodies. This has become more apparent to me since I've become a certified Zumba instructor. I actually offer a weekly Zumba class here in Andover Chapel.

In the chapel?

We do Zumba in the chapel. It's great! You see the stained glass of Jesus just looking down at us; I like to think he approves of us—all there, dancing together, choosing health, choosing joy. But one of the ways that feminism influences me as a Zumba instructor is in the language that I use when instructing. Many times I'll go to class at the gym or elsewhere, and the instructor will be like, "Make this sexy," or you know like, "Imagine that there is a hot guy in there that you want to impress," or "We want to get our bodies ready for bikini season." So I am very intentional about the idea that I can't tell anybody what sexy is and I can't assume that anyone wants to claim the concept of 'sexiness'. I try very hard not to be like, "Let's be sexy now!" because I don't want to impose that on anybody else and I certainly don't want to assume that what I think of as sexy is what they think of. So that's one thing.

The other thing is that I never suggest that there's an ideal body type that we should want to look like. That's really important to me. In any center or studio or curriculum I own or design, one of the requirements that I intend on having is that instructors never insinuate that there's some ideal body type. So, there are two points to this: first, there's the refusal to engage in complaining about one's own body in front of students because shame teaches shame. Second, there's a refusal to talk about 'bikini bodies', 'hardcore abs', 'small waists', and so on. This is buying into an ideal body type that has been constructed by popular culture and those who hold power. So, in many ways, teaching dance and fitness without lauding an 'ideal' body type is a subversive act; it's saying, we all have a right to dance, we all have a right to move, and we all have a right to celebrate ourselves and be celebrated exactly as we are now.

You know, there's this saying that people often quote, "Dance like nobody's watching." This saying actually really annoys me, because it suggests that the most expressive, most life-nourishing, most transformative, most real, and most joyous occasions of dance can only occur when one feels like nobody can see it: that if nobody's watching, then there's no reason to hold on to one's fears and worries about oneself. This reinforces the idea that there are people and ways of being that are acceptable and valid and worthy ... and then there are ways that are not. For this reason, my motto, the driving force of my approach to dance, and it's hard, is: "Dance like everyone is watching, and you've got something to say." We all have stories to tell, and I believe that movement offers the boldest, truest, most raw ways to tell those stories, so, if we're afraid to dance in front of others, then, on some level, there's a fear about the validity of our stories, our lives, ourselves. So, this is one of the main reasons I absolutely feel as if teaching dance is part of my ministry. One of the principles of Unitarian Universalism is a belief in the 'inherent worth and dignity of all beings' and, through teaching dance, I hope to help people recognize their own inherent worth and dignity. This is my justice work.

So you came here with the intent of becoming a UU minister. That radically changed, however, within your own regular practice of religion. What role did your studies and interactions with students and professors here play in that change for you?

I'll share perhaps one of the most surprising changes for me: I now consider myself a Unitarian Christian. I never thought I would call myself a Christian, it seemed counter intuitive to everything I grew up with, because my mom's narrative was about moving away from it. So, this new identity was shaped by a couple of different things. First, I took a Worship & the Arts class during winter session at Andover-Newton. For the final project, the class collaborated on a mixed media arts presentation of lines from various Psalms. One of the lines was Psalm 23:5: "You anoint my head with oil; my cup overflows." So, as part of that we did a photo shoot. I wore this white dress; my hair was down. I sat on a stool. There was a bright light centered right on me, so I felt the heat from that, and spots formed in my eyes. The instructor for the course stood behind me, she cradled my head in one of her hands as she poured oil right onto the center of my forehead.

I felt the oil running down my face; into my eyes, which I had to shut, into my nose, into my mouth, into my ears, and I couldn't wipe it away because these photos were being taken. So here I am, in the midst of this very uncomfortable experience, yet feeling deeply supported by the instructor, the photographer, and our other classmates.

The following Sunday, I was at the Family Service at King's Chapel, a Unitarian Christian church where I teach Sunday School, and we read aloud together Psalm 23. This was not unusual, the Church School reads one Psalm per year so that the children can learn it, so Psalm 23 was that year's Psalm. What amazed me, however, was that I had been reading this Psalm over and over again throughout the year and didn't even realize that we were using one of its lines in my class project. Yet, that Sunday, as we read Psalm 23, I found myself crying. I felt just … overcome, I felt God … because that Psalm had become deeply embodied for me through that experience at the photoshoot.

I also began to preach more at King's Chapel—at both their family and mid-week services. KC uses the Lectionary, which meant my sermons had to be Biblically-based according to that day's readings. This means that I got the opportunity to engage in the creative process with Scripture. I approach sermon writing in much the same way as I approach choreography: I pay attention to my body, to the feelings and sensations that rise to the surface. Then, once something rises to the surface, I listen to that as it moves through me. Scripture, then, became something that moved through me.

So, I think back to my previous experiences with Christianity, and it was all about listening and reading and talking … never about moving. So, of course, I could never connect with it. I wasn't approaching it and experiencing it through my own language.

Could you take specific classes on Unitarian Universalism here at Harvard?

There are specifically UU classes offered each semester, but I was unable to take one until this semester, actually. I'm in Dan McKanan's UU Thought in the 19th Century course right now. But I wasn't sure. I was a little worried about sitting in classes with all of these people who were so enthusiastic about going into UU ministry. Like I'd be sitting there feeling dejected or lonely while people broke out into spirited discussions of congregational life. [Laughter] So I waited and when I took the class it was really due to a longing to create a bridge between Unitarian Universalist thought and what I'm doing.

I'm glad that I waited because now I know there are people in the class who are very enthusiastic about UU parish ministry or chaplaincy, but I'm enthusiastic about what I'm doing, so it works.

So did Harvard or HDS change your religious practice? Did it change any aspect of it, specifically? Obviously, you feel more comfortable now in saying that you are a true member of UU, but what about your practice in day-to-day life?

It's interesting because Dudley Rose in our Introduction to Ministry Studies said something the first semester here, something that stuck with a lot of people. It was that the spiritual practices that you do now, you're not going to do more than this when you become a minster, whatever that means to you. It's not like all of a sudden you're going to have more time for your spirituality. So that's something that I thought about a lot. I think too that my understanding of spiritual practice has shifted, in that I used to be very much like, "OK, I'm going to write in my journal every morning, I've got to do this dance movement practice that I created, and I need to get all of this in." Then I burned out trying to get all of that in.

Now I find that I ask myself what gives me life, what plugs me back into this world, what gives me hope, what connects me to something more than myself, and what feels like it can just fit into my day to help me answer those questions. I go to the gym a lot, I love working out and one of my core beliefs or values is the idea that I have a body, and I can feel horrible but then I can work out or dance and be reminded that I'm a strong person. It helps me remember that I have strength, that I can create, that I can speak. Martha Graham once said that dance is the hidden language of the soul of the body. So this idea that when we dance we speak with the deepest part of ourselves really resonates with me.

I try to dance every day. Sometimes there's just a pop song and that's enough. That acknowledgment that it's enough is something that's changed for me because before I'd be like, "Oh, that's not enough." Now, I just have such a sense of it, an awareness of the fact that it plugs me back into this world and that's enough. That's something that's really evolved with me.

The other thing is a spiritual practice of getting sleep. I know it does not seem to go with graduate school, but I realized that if I wanted to embrace wellness as my ministry, if I wanted to practice wellness—one of the pillars of wellness is sleep. [Laughter] I realized that I was going to have to change things and try to get sleep every night. What happened before was that it would be 2 or 3am and I would just like fall over, exhausted. So then when I would go to sleep at 11PM deliberately, it felt very odd to me. I'd think, "What now? The lights are off, I'm lying in the dark, what do I do?" It was just so weird—I didn't know how to go to sleep. So I thought, "I guess I can pray, do something else." So what that evolved into is that I have a bracelet with smooth round gemstones on it and I just hold it in my hand and touch the different stones. I say my hopes for the day. I talk to God and sometimes it's just like a "Hey!" and then I fall asleep, and sometimes it's a longer discussion. That wouldn't have ever come about unless I had changed my sleep thing. So I think what really has been evolving for me here has been this spirituality of sleep, which of course touches all aspects of life.

It's both physical and mental.

Yes, right. Yes.

With the wealth of wisdom you now have, what would you tell Kat from two years ago?

[Laughter] You know, it's really interesting because actually one of the women from WomenCircle told me that between this year's retreat and last year's retreat I seem like a completely different person, which I can see. Obviously, I know I'm the same person but I totally understand what she's talking about.

Can you elaborate on this?

I think what changed was that I became loud about who I am and what I have to give—not screaming it, but just really embracing it and living it. That in turn gives me so much light and energy and happiness.

In a way, Harvard has helped you find yourself.

Yes, yes. It's funny because I thought I knew myself. Then I came here and I felt like I really didn't know myself. Now I feel like I know myself a whole lot deeper than I ever did before, which has been a really interesting journey. It's interesting—Ministry, I believe, asks us to go to the deepest, most vulnerable, most raw places within ourselves, and to give to the world from this place that most people try to keep hidden. So, here I am, deeply engaged in the work of helping others develop a healthy and compassionate body image when for so many years I struggled with intense depression in relation to how much I disliked my body. To share that which I once perceived as my innate ugliness with the world would once have seemed terrifying and now … now it seems necessary because, you realize, after some time here, all that I do here, as transforming as it is, it's not just for me: it's for all those that I serve. I do feel like a completely different person. So I feel like if I were to see myself, the self that was admitted, and I told her what I'm doing and I'm interested in, I don't think I would have believed myself. I don't think that I would have believed that I could love myself and my life to this degree. I spent a lot of time wishing I was someone else, and to now actually be the only person I want to be, well, that would be inconceivable to a me of the past.

So the experience was truly transformative?

Yes. My adviser, because Leigh Schmidt left, is now Emily Click. I took her education class, her teaching class last semester and I'm in her leadership class this semester. She has been such a support and somebody who really encourages me in this interest that I have. She not only encourages me but suggests, "Have you thought about this, have you thought about that?" and really expands my approach to what I have to offer.

One of the things that has developed from being in her classes is the absolute knowledge that I have something unique to give that is worthy of being given and that I can help people through giving. I think that when I entered I hoped that that was true, but my big fear was that it was not and that perhaps divinity school would be show me that I didn't have anything to give. I think that there's that recognition, that belief in myself, that belief in the worth that I have. The certainty of that belief is something that I've never had before, ever. I think that's why I cannot communicate with myself from August 2010 because to really think that, "Oh there's a time and a place in which I will fully believe in the work that I have to do and in myself," would seem beyond comprehension.

Soon, you'll graduate as a Master of Divinity, what next?

That's the big question. I think the interesting thing is that I certainly have an idea of a project that I'm going towards. I would like to have my own center for dance—for wellness really—which would include dance and movement and fitness at the beginning, and then hopefully even grow and offer massage services, salon services, all from this perspective of compassion and self-care and that you are worthy of love.

The spiritual dimension.

Yes, yes, yes, absolutely! So that's kind of the big thing. I hope to also within that be someone who writes about dance and can give workshops in different areas of the world with dance and how dance can help us to grow our own spirituality and to heal our relationships with our bodies. So, that's the big picture.

What happens right after I graduate is shakier because obviously, this is a project that will take some time to get underway. There are questions of location, funds, business plans, and more.

I think that the big thing for me is to keep hold of this vision and so whatever next step I take, ask myself how it is going to get me towards that. I want to write a book: part memoir, part reflections on spirituality, the body, dance, fitness, and body image. I want to continue to teach classes—actually teach more. It's interesting; I've never been a person good with uncertainty. When I was a kid, I demanded to know an itinerary of each day from my mom, which I think drove her a little crazy, but, these days, when I think about my life and those spaces of uncertainty, there's something deep within me that is unafraid, that says, to quote Julian of Norwich, "All will be well." This is new for me—to feel that—and I have conversations with myself, in which I try to talk myself out of this lack of fear, but, when something is deeply felt, I can't argue with it. Dance has taught me that.

Professor Charles Adams

William and Lucille Nickerson Professor of the Practice of Ethics and Ministry

Professor Adams, one of your focus points in education here at Harvard is preaching—what kind of students come to your classes and how do they operate?

Well, naturally one would expect people to come to a preaching course who are going to be preachers, or are already preachers. So you get that crowd. But then you get another crowd of people who really hadn't planned to preach, they just want to know, "What is this thing called preaching, and how is it done?" Then you get people who are not even interested in the church, not even interested in Christianity, but they end up in my course because they're absolutely fascinated by the power of religion to produce some pretty eloquent people who are very impressive and end up in conspicuous places. So, even though they don't believe, even though they don't worship, they still want to know, "Well, how do you account for things? How do you get into certain issues? Why are you concerned about this, and that, and war, and the H-bomb, and the plastic suffocation of the human race." Or whatever it is.

They come for that. Then they find out that they are preachers and that they do have faith. But we don't force it on them, we just say, "Well, just come and see how you like it." They end up enjoying speaking to the class about whatever it is they can affirm and can agree to, or agree with. And I tell them, I say, "Your Bible can be anything you choose. But be able to account for your interest in it and your willingness to share it with others." I find that sometimes they are the best preachers because they don't take faith for granted. It's almost that they stumble upon the faith trying to make sense out of the puzzle of life.

In the preaching class we talk about the methodologies. I have ten or eleven steps towards the production of a sermon. I teach two classes of preaching, one is on the uniqueness of black preaching, the other is Preaching for Social Change.

I'd like to talk about both, if possible. But first, let's discuss the ten or eleven steps methodology.

Yes, how you develop a sermon. The first step is that you have to write your first impressions of your topic. What is your topic going to be? Why did you choose that rather than some other topic? Where did you get that from? What inspired that? That's when you use the Bible or whatever you use and you make a quotation. You let the audience know what it is that you intend to tell them and why it is important. But you have to go through the first step, and that is to empty it out on paper. If you don't start with you, you will end up copying someone else. So, in order for you to have control over all the material you're going to encounter, you have to first encounter your own mind, your own spirit, your own commitments, and your own alertness. Something's going on in that text that you want to share with the world. Now, why? What is that?

I think that's the most important part of the sermon because if you don't do that, number one, you may not have a sermon. You just may have a few scattered ideas but it won't cohere. But secondly, it won't be you. You would certainly be the ventriloquist, but you would not be the person bringing the message. You would just be an instrument of Paul Tillich or Rudolf Bultmann, or somebody, but you don't have anything. You don't feel anything. You don't know anything. That's step number one.

Step number two is to—if you're talking about a Bible verse—you want to translate that verse into English in as many different ways as is possible. So if there are 26 translations of a New Testament text, then you want to go and buy them all. You're not going to preach it, but you've got to ... it's part of the information that you need to get as close as you can to the biblical sources of this mighty message that you're about to preach. So, I say work on translations. If you do Hebrew, pull out your lexicon and be your own translator. If you do Greek, provide your own. If you have a nuance, if you see a nuance, some ambiguity, put all of that on paper. So that's another step.

Then the third step could be, after putting down your ideas, after translating your text, then the third thing you want to do is to study a scholarly commentary, like Anchor Bible. It's got to be very technical and scholarly, something that you cannot take into the pulpit, but something that you need to undergird your understanding of this text. So I say, do that and make notes on it. Get the toughest, most difficult book you can find, highly technical, how many ways it's understood in, how it has developed through the centuries to come to where it is now and so forth. Very important. Then you relax a day. On your next day you look at some homiletical commentary material. That gives you an idea of how others have seen a sermon here, and how they have been able to deliver it so that it actually reaches the audience. So you want to read particularly their illustrations because these are the things that make the sermon light up. So that's the next step. After that step, you're ready to try your own. When you try your own you will not copy from any of the authors that you have read, whether they were scholarly or homiletical. You just want to write the message with the background of having read these other thoughts. You will refer to some of them, but whenever you refer to them, make sure, I say, that you cite your sources. If it wasn't your idea, if it was Bultrick's idea, then say, "Dr. Bultrick taught me," or, "Dr. Bultrick said," or "Dr. Bultrick wrote these words," and so forth. It does not take anything from you to give credit to someone else, but it will take away your integrity if you get caught, or even if you do it without getting caught. if you just copy a sermon and pass it off as your own, you are robbing yourself of the integrity and the confidence of being honest.

Nothing is worse in the pulpit than to stand there knowing that you have stolen something and given no credit to the true sources of your thoughts. You want to make sure you do that. Then you try it, and then you lay it down, and then you try it again. You write a second draft, and that should be sufficient. By then you're ready to soak it in your own prayer life, in your own deep motivations, trying to find out who you are, why you are, how this might help someone, how it might redirect someone's life, why it might keep someone from committing suicide, why it might save a marriage, save a home, why it might save a whole community that's in turmoil over some racial issue or financial issue or ethical issue or doctrinal issue.

You continue to pray, and that will change some things. It will make you leave out some things and put some things in because the last thing you want to do is to insult or offend anyone in the audience. If you have a joke anywhere in the sermon, make sure that the joke is on you, not at somebody else's expense. That way, Jesus Christ can be glorified. But if you're there simply to haughtily build yourself up, then you're preaching you, you're not preaching Him.

When you do that, make sure that you familiarize yourself with it so that it's okay to have your notes at the pulpit. I always have my notes right in front of me and sometimes, at the same time, I read. But then you've got to have freedom from that. So even in the presence of that help, you're able to go on without that when you really want to level with the people. If you have familiarized yourself with it, you can preach without it. So you will not show that off by going up on the pulpit with nothing. You have everything with you. Lay it out before you but then exercise the utmost freedom and the ability to leave it and still preach and still create and still find ways of answering the doubts and the questions that you see on the faces of the audience.

With your enormous experience and preaching power, do you still use that kind of ten-step methodology?

Yes, I do. It's for me. I think there's a way to do this thing and I just keep doing it that way.

That definitely is a way to bridge theory and practice.

Yes.

Do you do this in both of your classes? You were talking about one class specifically about black preaching.

Yes. Well, that was a subject of that class because that class attempts to almost define the indefinable, and that is, "what is it about preaching that everybody thinks is so good?" When I think about it, it has to deal with passion. It is [in] a sermon where one feels [a truth], [and it's] in the midst of feeling it that you are grasped by the depth of its power and its truth and its insight and its reality. As you study God's word, you think about God's word, you find yourself overwhelmed by God's word. You may cry, you may emote, go ahead and do that. But once you go to the pulpit, you must not be all wrapped up in your own emotion because you've got a message to deliver and you've got to deliver it. You can't deliver it if you don't control yourself. We had a student today that became overwhelmed, even in just reading the text and she was unable to continue. She didn't have a handkerchief so I gave her my handkerchief, and we encouraged her to continue and, gradually, she got hold of herself. So when I see her in private, I will say, "You have to pray very hard to make sure that you're used by the message but not so overwhelmed by the message that you can't deliver it. After all, if these people need bread, then you've got to feed them. So don't make yourself a barrier to someone else's understanding and appropriation of what you're saying." To me, I think that's very, very important.

But for students, the black preaching class can get very intense.

It can get very intense. Very intense.

What about the other class?

Well, the other class deals more with the social and political transformation that we want preaching to have, so it's called "Preaching and Social Change." So you will take an issue—for example, war—and preach.

One of the questions I wanted to ask you is about ministry and activism and how they mix. I guess this fits in there. Can you elaborate a bit on that?

Well, Jesus said there are those who will say, "Lord, Lord," but they will not enter the kingdom of heaven because it isn't sincere. So it isn't enough just to preach. You've got to represent what you preach—you've got to practice it.

If you're preaching peace, you cannot practice violence. You've got to be a peaceful person, a peace-loving person, a peace-granting person. You've got to pass the peace, pass all understanding. You can't talk about integrity and then spawn unworthy behaviors. If you're preaching honesty, you have to be honest. If you're preaching accountability, you've got to be accountable. If you're preaching transparency, then you have to be transparent. You have to practice what you preach or you won't be preaching much. Martin Luther King, Jr. said that the means must match the end, or if the means do not match the end, the end will be overwhelmed by the negativity of the unworthy means. I think that is very true in preaching.

You've got to be honest about it. You've got to want to see problems solved, burdens lifted, and needs supplied.

So it's not a question of standing up just saying beautiful things; then it becomes a wonderful tea party sermon. But you don't want a tea party sermon. You want a kind of sermon that sends people back into society determined to make a difference for the good. Because they've improved their own lives, now they want to improve their surroundings because surroundings become the context for lives that are developing and growing and being changed into the likeness of an ideal conception.

Why do you think that in Europe we have so few talents in preaching, as compared to the US? Why don't we ever see preachers with the kind of fire we see here in America.

I think that in America, there may be—now, there are notable examples to the contrary—but it may be that religion is more important here because the experiment, the political and social experiment of equality, became much more urgent here. You had that great openness, that wide wilderness well-populated with people who were there when you got here. You had to get it from them in order to have a way of carving out something for yourself. So it became very urgent for us to have a religion that we felt deeply enough to cleanse us from the stain of our own selfishness and our own inhumanity and our own violence. You haven't seen as much of that in Europe. Europe has belonged to Europeans pretty much for many, many millennia. That's one thing, I think. The other thing is that religion has had to function to give us a history and a sense of belonging that the culture could not give us. We were immigrants into the culture, and so pluralism and relativism prevailed. Religion gives you an absolute certainty that you are living in the grace of God, acting on the word of God, and involved in the work of Christ in the world. So I think that's another reason.

I think the other reason is, if you're black, you've suffered, you need something other than what the world will provide for you. It's religion that gives you the confidence that the world denies. Gives you peace that the world denies, gives you a joy that the world—there is a joy—in just being connected with the source of all life, and all hope, and all joy, and that makes rejoicing possible, even in the midst of imprisonment, and embarrassment, and dehumanization. But there's a joy that the world cannot give and the world cannot destroy, and I think that it's out of that [joy] that black preaching spills over the boundary from speech into singing. I'm almost sure that human speech is transformed into music because of the overwhelming joy that one feels when one knows that he has achieved, has been affirmed by God, accepted by God, cleansed by God, enriched by God, even though you didn't have any money, and that's what I think is the difference between black preaching and white preaching. They don't need it, if you've got everything else …

That might change with how the economy is going ... Are there any limits to what you can say in a good sermon? Where do you draw those lines? How do you know, "I'm going too far here?" Or, "I'm not going far enough?"

Yes. If you go too far in one direction, you become totally irrelevant. So you have proven the Virgin birth, but how is that going to help me get through this night? So how is that going to keep me from smoking that crack pipe? Or from opening that beer can, or drinking that scotch or whatever it is? I need more than that to get a wonderful exposition on who, or whatever happened to the Jebusites. That's an example I used to use a lot, you know.

So sometimes preaching can become so academic, so stilted and irrelevant, that one has gone too far. Or if I'm just doctrinal and ... I met a man once, he was of the persuasion that if in your preaching you didn't spend most of your time on Calvary, then your preaching was not so good. I said, "Well, what do you like about that sermon?" And he said, "Well, he didn't say a thing about Calvary." I said, "He wasn't talking about Calvary but, you know, he didn't say a thing about the creation either, and he didn't say anything about the proverbs, but they're real. He didn't say anything about the revelation, but it's there, and I believe it's true. But why is it that you've got to always make these stylized excursions into these crucial doctrines that sort of dominate everything? Are we not deifying doctrine, and dethroning God?" So I think that you can go too far.

I think you can go too far into trying to make sure that every sermon becomes one or two or three simple statements. I've had people that say, "Well, why aren't you preaching against homosexuality?" I said, "Because it's not the Gospel." You're preaching against something that people may not be able to help. You don't preach against things, you preach for people, and then they can make their own applications, "I can apply this to my sexual freedom, I can apply this to my freedom, from taking the enemy into my soul to steal away my brain," like Shakespeare said. Let people make their own applications. If sin becomes the center of my preaching, if the faults of the people, and the prejudices of the people, and the injustice—if that becomes my whole sermon, where is the therapy? A bunch of people say, "Where's the good news? Give me some good news, you know." I think we've got to keep it good news. We've got to keep it joyful, affirmative, not ... you can go the other way where you're so affirmative, and you're so happy, and you're so joyful that you forget there's some hungry people that haven't eaten in a week, there's some sick people that have no healthcare, there's some people who want an education, but it's not provided for them. So you think about those that have been expelled from their homes and ... what do they call it? I'm dealing here now with a family whose mortgage is foreclosed. They just weren't able to keep up the payments after the property values went down, and the jobs went down and everything. We have to deal with certain things that are real, but we don't want to ride on a political or an ethical hobbyhorse, so that they know that. Now Martin Luther King to the contrary notwithstanding, because he would tend to preach against four evils in all of his sermons, three to make sure: race prejudice, war, poverty and violence. Well, war is violence so it's still three, and he would always mention those things, but you never got the idea that the sermon was for the sake of those four things. I think he was still trying to preach his text in the context of social struggle, so we understand that.

It seems to be a rather delicate balance. I wonder then if preaching is an innate talent that you can develop a little more, or is it a skill that just about anyone can learn?

I think it's a skill that anyone can learn, as long as they listen to other people as their natural critics. I have friends that will tell me, "You spent a little too long today on history, and you didn't leave us with much hope," and I like that. Then I have others saying that, "You let me down today because you didn't say anything about this kid who got killed down in Florida, and we're hurt over that, we're troubled over that, we're disturbed, and you should've offered us some relief." I mean, you have people that will do that, and that keeps you from falling so much in love with your own ability that you're not willing to listen. I think anyone can preach if you listen well. You've got to hear the "Amen's", you've got to listen to the silence. The silence is not always rejection, but it is a deep way of receiving, and that's what my Canadian friends taught me. They said, "Charles, we know that you're used to this call and response of the congregation, but you're not going to get that in Canada, because when we are deeply moved, we are stone silent, so that we don't miss what is being offered to us. By making noise, we make it impossible for ourselves and for others to receive."

In your classes students come from very different backgrounds, with various levels of experience and also various kinds of personal faiths and religious convictions. How do you align them? Is there a uniform way of preaching for all these people, even if they've never preached before? Obviously they're all following that ten or twelve-step methodology, but could you describe a little bit about the different preaching styles of students as they develop? Within their different religious traditions, do you see great differences there?

Oh, absolutely. I think every preacher in my classes—and I usually have sixteen, or up to twenty in a class—they all differ. They're all alike because they have an urge to preach.

Even the non-Christians?

Even the non-Christians have an urge to communicate what it is that to them is the Gospel, is the Good News. I think the Good News is, "I have self-consciousness,

I have a social consciousness, and I have some kind of an ultimate consciousness. I don't want to call it God, but there's something else out there, that claims me and uses me." So every sermon is different and yet every sermon is the same. "There is a balm in Gilead to make the wounded whole; To heal the sin sick soul." That there's an answer to this question. There's a cure for the illness of humanity. There is a way of peace. There is a way of transformation. We can and we will all be changed. I think that every sermon leaves me with a little more hope, that as I step into my Red Sea and I begin to move toward the Promised Land, that even if the water comes up to my neck, that there is a force in the universe that will see that I can keep going and keep from drowning in the process of going forward.

That's what I think it is. It might be said in a different language, it might be said in a different faith, it might be said in the declaration that, "I don't have any faith." It isn't necessary for me to have faith if faith has me. And that's what we preach. We know that there are people that are letting us know they don't have any. It's not that it's hard, it's just that they can't see it and they can't feel it. We have to know that you may not have any faith, but you have faithfulness and that faithfulness which comes from another reality, will lead you to a faith that you can proclaim and share with others. That's why they're all different, yet they're all the same.

Do you see an evolution over the past few years in the way students approach preaching?

I've been teaching it since I've been here—five years. I've found that there is an ultimate that participates in everything that is penultimate. Anything that isn't ultimate, anything that falls short of ultimacy, has to be explained. And I can't explain it without drawing near to that which is ultimate, however one wants to understand it. So there have been people in my classes that have felt it, and experienced it in the act of preaching about something. Knowing that—you know, Reinhold Niebuhr has a marvelous sermon in his book, *Beyond Tragedy*. He has all these wonderful sermons. Somewhere near the end of it, he talks about the content of the ultimate. He tries all the answers. He says, "Take democracy. But democracy can become a lynch mob. Take civil rights. But civil rights can become a total abandonment of principle and responsibility. Take youth. But youth can give a silly idea and ratchet it up to a pretense of ultimacy, which is absolutely shallow and silly. What about age? Age can make one complacent and unfulfilled and satisfied with being unfulfilled." He talked about intellectuals. But what about the intellect? The intellect can be wrong-headed, and yet it sounds so plausible. He tries every god that we make for ourselves and finds every god guilty of falling short of that which is ultimate. And I learned that sometimes we can worship our own ideas, sometimes we can worship our own traditions, sometimes we can worship our own raciality, and we have to be careful of being what John Calvin said when he said that, "The human mind is a constant manufactury of idols." He said, "We have to be set free from the idols that we make," particularly in the realm of religion.

Very few people are as gifted in rhetoric as you are, so you might have students in your class who aren't able to speak as well. I remember a story of a Greek philosopher who couldn't speak well, I think it was Demosthenes, and he put stones in his mouth and that's the way he learned to speak. So if he could speak with stones, when the stones were taken out, he could speak more fluently and more easily. That was kind of his training. Is there some way you can push students to become more verbal? Say you have someone who's really shy in your class but he still wants to take a preaching class, for example.

Well, there's a way to build up your confidence. You have to cultivate it. Don't worry about speaking, just worry about being. Worry about being the kind of person that is sensitive to human struggles, human problems, human needs, environmental deterioration, or the beauty of nature, the gorgeous garniture of the universe, to use a poetic phrase. Gardner Taylor said three things about preaching. Gardner Calvin Taylor, he's considered the best among black preachers, he said, "You've got to see the truth, before you can say the truth. Then you've got to sense the truth, its power, and its beauty, its functionality. And then thirdly, if you see it, if you feel it, you will say it, " even if you can't speak.

I've seen people who came and said, "I was going to take the MTS, I'm now taking the MDiv." "I never thought I could preach, but now I seem to be a pastor." "I worked in Biology, I'm now in Theology."

So both of your classes are transformative.

They are. It's not me doing the transformation. There is a higher power, I point it up, but it's not only up, it's out. It's not only up, it's also down. As one of my students said today, that she was calling somebody and she said, "Sometimes you're looking for Jesus up in the sky and he's in the basement waiting for you to come down and have a talk with him." [Laughter]

I think that's very well said!

Could we discuss the recurring themes in preaching? Is suffering always a start for a good sermon?

Not always. It could be a joy. You can start with joy. You can start with coming to what Peter Gomes called "a thin place." Through the veil of that place you're able to see a beauty that can never be duplicated. And you're grasped by the ultimacy of natural beauty. It can start with the day you "got saved". Or it can start with the day your mother died, or the day your spouse died, or the day you lost your job, and yet found your joy. I think sermons may start with a question, you know, "What does it mean to be human?" "What does it mean to encounter God when you don't even know God?" and "What does it mean to fall and not stay on the ground?" You see what I'm trying to say? It has a lot to do with feeling.

How do you see the future of preaching, and the future of the teaching of preaching? Are there any changes happening?

I see it becoming more and more crucial, particularly as the Western world falls apart. We can't balance our budget, we can't solve our problems, we can't make the future generations feel more secure than the past generations. We're just failing and flapping all over the place. I think it's opened the door for these existential questions about who, why, where, what, when. I think that we depended upon prudential and prudential forgot about us. We had a piece of the rock, and now the rock has turned to sand. I think as long as we're living in a world like this, somebody's got to have some good news. Somebody's got to tell a story. Somebody's got to offer a hope beyond this world. Maybe the best way to do that is to pick up these ancient words and bring them into our present dilemma and look for some glimpse of light to take us to the next place, the next step.

So, given the kind of world in which we live, it mandates preaching, and it mandates hearers, and it mandates religious institutions like divinity schools, that will prepare people, that will give people the time and the support to think, to pray, to plan, and to participate in the solution, and not be a part of the problem. That's a cliché, but—it's the best way I can say it.

Elliot Niblock

I was born and raised in Appleton, Wisconsin, which I think was very formative. I spent a year in Madison, if that, when I was very, very young, but in general, I feel that growing up in Wisconsin grounded me in certain fundamental ways. When I was eighteen, I moved to St. Paul, Minnesota to attend Macalester College where I did my undergraduate degree.

I double majored in History and Religious Studies. I initially intended to do East Asian studies, but even then I wanted to double major in History and East Asian Studies. I started out doing the History track and slowly kind of pulled away from. My first year I took a course on Indian Philosophies and that's what really got me interested in studying religion academically.

I guess I was always interested in religion in general though. I was raised UCC, which is the United Church of Christ. It was a Congregationalist denomination, a very liberal Protestant church. My pastor—the senior minister at our church who has since retired—used to joke that it stands for Unitarians Considering in Christ, which I think is pretty apt. I had to write an essay when I was 13 for my confirmation class and it's funny, I had completely forgotten about it, but my mom reminded me of it and showed me the essay when I was much older. I wrote about how God transcends gender for my middle school church confirmation. So I did spend a lot of time, you know, thinking about religious issues when I was young, but I never thought it would become a serious path of study or a career.

Is your family's historical, religious background similar to your personal upbringing?

Yes, more or less. I guess, that is to say it's just generally hyper-WASPy, you know, various denominations of Protestantism—although I would say that on both sides my paternal and maternal grandparents were far more deeply Christian than my parents are and I would consider myself, in terms of being confessional doctrinally Christian, even less so than my parents.

That first year at Macalester College was really when you became interested in religion—what happened in the three years that followed?

So, I took this Indian Philosophy course which I found really fascinating and admittedly, in hindsight, in a somewhat Orientalist way, so, 'wow'—there's all this great wisdom out there. But it went beyond just discovering an Orientalist gaze, although that was part of it. A lot of it stemmed from the fact that I had gone to a public high school. I mean, it was really a fantastic education. I can't fault it in the least. I really lucked out. It was a good quality school but we didn't have philosophy or religion classes and so it struck me as, "Holy shit, you can talk about issues of truth and meaning and the nature of being in the world in class? I didn't think that this happened in school!" I thought this had to be on my "own time" so that was really exciting for me. As I also started to take more history classes, I got interested in Medieval history, which is something I barely even touched on as a high school student. So then my interest in religion and Medieval history merged to the point that I did both of my capstone projects on medieval religion. I did two theses as an undergraduate and they were both on High Medieval religion in Europe.

Did you travel during your undergraduate studies?

Yes, I spent one semester at King's College in London studying history. I had two seminars in which religion featured prominently. I took a kind of survey Medieval history, Late Medieval History 1200–1500 class which was fantastic because I also had a tutorial with a professor named Serena Ferente, who I think is still there. We talked about the rise of the Dominican orders and the rise of heresy and whether the inquisition didn't in fact actually create heresy. This served as kind of a touchstone, or perhaps a lynchpin in the course of my education, in which I was like "Wow, some of these theoretical issues or paradigms, a Foucaultian perspective in particular, can actually be put to real use in a historical archive." That doesn't mean that invariably every application of Foucault in academia is particularly helpful—often, it isn't. But that being said it was exciting for me.

When did you begin to think about divinity school?

I think that as I was working through my undergraduate degree, the notion that I wanted to become a professor really sank in. But you know, throughout my entire educational career this had been a trend. When I was six years old I wanted to be a kindergarten teacher. When I was twelve I wanted to be a seventh grade teacher and you know, when I was in high school I wanted to teach high school and then when I got to college I thought, "Hey, I want to continue having conversations at this level." I've always felt passionate about the idea of teaching and so the graduate study percolated as the natural consequence of that. Somewhere along the line I slowly hit the tipping point toward religious studies and away from history. I always had the idea, which is now dwindling (though not necessarily dead) that I'd ultimately do a Ph.D. in history or religious studies.

Did you apply for graduate school whilst you were still an undergrad?

No, I took a year off. I spent a year living in St. Paul, Minnesota, where my under-graduate degree was, working at a small wine shop there. I had lived across the street from the shop and built up a relationship with the owner, and ended up working part-time there throughout my senior year. Well actually, I started right after I got back from London, when the Dollar-to-Sterling exchange rate had dec-imated my bank account and I needed cash. So I worked there through my senior year and got a couple odd jobs to help pay rent. I inflated, you know, bouncy cas-tles for kids' birthday parties and also worked as a street team member advocating for cell phone recycling for a materials processing company that's based outside the twin cities. So yeah, I just spent a year working while also working on Master's applications.

Were you familiar with Harvard at this point?

Yeah, I mean, to be perfectly honest, I don't know if I would have even put it on my radar by myself, but I was really blessed at Macalester to have a fantastic religious studies faculty. It's truly a remarkable department. At this point, I think that almost everyone, barring Erik Davis, who has his Master's from Washington U and his Ph.D. from U of Chicago, everyone else has a degree from the Harvard Divinity School in the department. Jim Laine and Paula Cooey both did Master's and Ph.D.s here. Susanna Drake did her Master's here before going to Duke. Oh, though I'm not sure about our most recent hire Bret Wilson. I know he finished his Ph.D. at Duke. Anyway, so I had all of these advisers and professors with con-nections to Harvard who were encouraging me to apply there and that helped a lot. Without them, I certainly wouldn't be here talking to you right now.

When you applied to Harvard Divinity, did you already know that you would apply for an MTS?

Yes. I knew I didn't want to do the MDiv. A lot of my friends are MDivs and my conversations with them, I feel, are near and dear to the heart of what the Divinity School is, or at least should be, and so I'm very sympathetic with that. I flirted with the idea of switching a couple times my first year, but never very seriously. I always wanted to take the academic track and get through in two years. I started with History of Christianity and ultimately switched to Philosophy of Religion.

Can you tell us something about that switch? What triggered it?

There was a confluence of reasons. Not least of which, unfortunately, has been a dearth in the opportunities of study that I was hoping to be afforded here. Through a combination of sabbaticals and medical leaves of absence, three professors with whom I really wanted to study have been unavailable for much of my time here. They were Kevin Madigan, Mark Jordan and Amy Hollywood. There's not been one semester in which all three were teaching, which is kind of the nature of the two year degree I suppose. That said, of the four semesters I've been here at least one of the three has been teaching in any given semester, but that core of faculty whom I'd hoped to study under was never totally present.

So were you able to take classes with any of those professors?

Yes, barring Kevin Madigan. He didn't come back to teach until after I had already switched my area of focus, partly because this dearth forced my hand, but also in part because I just decided to get my general distribution credits out of the way. When I realized I was taking mostly philosophy of religion courses, then it seemed appropriate to just switch my focus, because who knew whether the constellation of professors under whom I wanted to study would actually come together in time.

Do you remember your first few days on campus?

Actually, my first days on campus were in February during a miserable week in which it rained literally every day I was here. It was not, as you would say, the most romantic introduction to Boston and the Divinity School possible, but one of my old friends from Macalester, Sonia Hazard, finished her Master's degree here two years ago, and she was kind enough to show me around and introduce me to the place. Sonia's now at Duke doing doctoral work, but I stayed with her and she gave me a fine introduction to the school and the city. This was actually before I was admitted, because I was a moving to Berlin that following April, so I couldn't have come to the Admitted Students' Day.

So just before going to Harvard you stayed in Berlin for a couple of weeks?

Yes, I lived there for around two months.

Can you tell us something about meeting your adviser and your fellow students? What was it like in the beginning?

Thrilling, intimidating, and with an undercurrent of 'imposter syndrome' where it's like, "Can I really be at Harvard, dude? Is there some mistake?" I've actually talked to a lot of people about this, having the ghost on your shoulder whispering, "This can't be." That lingered certainly over the first few days, even the first few weeks.

Who was your adviser during this time?

Beverly Kienzle.

Let's talk about your very first semester. What was it like? Was it very different from your previous educational experiences?

Yes. Certainly. I'm used to—I went to a very small liberal arts college and I was blessed with small class sizes, almost every Humanities class was a seminar. There was hardly a lecture. Even the lectures were a kind of lectured seminar format. So having come from somewhere with just a handful, maybe a dozen religious studies majors to Harvard where there are dozens—over 50 people, who want to hear a lecture just on Foucault and religion, was shocking. But the switch to the lecture/discussion section format was probably the most jarring change. I found the difference between three one-hour seminars a week versus a two hour lecture and a one hour discussion section difficult. That hardly seemed like the same amount of time, you know?

Can you tell us a little about your experiences with your peers, particularly in terms of your intellectual interactions?

The constellation of people who are not only interested in, but also very well prepared for the academic study of religion is amazing. My peers here are incredible, which isn't to say I didn't have fantastic peers previously, but it was a much smaller mass of people who were not only bright and motivated, but motivated towards similar goals to those that I held myself.

Were you and your peers able to enter into regular dialogue? Was it possible to have deep and stimulating conversations?

Oh yes, it was definitely possible. I think that the somewhat fractal nature of the community at the Divinity School sometimes made it difficult. Which isn't to say that there's not community at the Divinity School because I think there is, but the kind of nebulous formations in which it coalesces didn't really cultivate that in the same way that I was used to. With that being said, a lot of that has to do with the fact that when I went to Macalester, everyone lived in the dorms for the first two years, which provided a crucible for community, and also for intellectual conversations. The format of our first year course was structured such that everybody within the same first year course lived on the same floor, in the same dormitory, so I was having conversations all the time then. So that's perhaps an unfair comparison. I certainly had intellectual discussions outside of the classroom right off the bat here at Harvard, but it didn't seem as continuous and sustained a discussion as I had experienced at Macalester College.

Did you find the debates that took place during the discussion sections helpful?

Not particularly, to be quite frank.

Could you explain why? Was it due to the students not being sufficiently open?

The intellectual acumen that each student brings to the table is remarkable for sure, but the personal leadership of a lot of the teaching assistants leading the seminars—who are Ph.D. students, not actually professors—more often than not left something to be desired. Beyond the personal shortcomings of the handful of T.A's, you know, all credit to them. It's not easy to lead a seminar when everyone's really bright and engaged, and it's even harder when all these people are your peers—but that leads me to the fact that beyond the personal shortcomings I think it was a big structural problem. I think it's a gross pedagogical oversight, maybe just frank blindness, to the fact that structuring a 50 minute discussion section doesn't foster effective dialogue. Because classes you know start on 'Harvard time', seven to ten minutes after the hour, so a discussion section led by a Ph.D. student who is still working out a dissertation in a related field, not even necessarily exactly this field, for just 50 minutes a week, that's nothing! When it's week to week as opposed to every couple of days, it's difficult. Again, all credit to a lot of these Ph.D. students. I'm sure that if the structure of classes was that they led a discussion section three times a week for an hour each day, it would provide for a much better discussion. So I think that it's as much of a structural as it is a personal problem having discussion sections led by T.A.s, if not more so. That's what led me to be disappointed in the sections.

Would longer sections improve the system?

I think so. If you're just sprinting and stopping and sprinting and stopping, meeting only fifty minutes once a week, you're never going to hit your stride.

What about the student body at Harvard Divinity School, have you met a lot of people who share the same goals and background as you?

Yes, I was really flabbergasted by how run of the mill my set of interests were around here. "You're also interested in applying post-structural theoretical paradigms to Medieval history? Cool, me too!" That was certainly something new to me, which, again, speaks in favor of the Divinity School. But also, one of the reasons that I was drawn to Harvard Divinity School to begin with was the religious presence on campus, which is perhaps slightly more muted than I'd expected, but still present. This is opposed to a place like the University of Chicago where their divinity school is primarily academic. There's nobody who's planning on discerning, nobody really going into ordination other than maybe a handful of people. The general tenor is clearly, "We're academic, that's what we're doing." That difference was something that drew me to Harvard to be honest. Although, like I said, the on-the-ground reality is not quite as integrated between MDivs and MTSs as one would hope. I mean there's a certain effort thrusting towards that, but I don't know that it's particularly manifest at this point.

Have you been able to establish a social life here by attending Community Tea, or some other kind of student organization, or perhaps engaging in religious activities off-campus?

Yes. I did so less at first actually, which in hindsight is probably part of the reason why I struggled to really find community at the Divinity School. I would go to tea during the first semester about every week and I became fast friends with a group of second year students, you included of course, but then also the nature of the program is that those students leave. This year I have taken over as President of the Wick, the Divinity School literary magazine, which has been great. It's been a nice way to stay plugged in to at least a micro-community within the larger HDS community. I think this is the way that a lot of people here find a sense of community, by finding the smaller niches within the Divinity School at large. Maybe that's just the nature of it, maybe having so many hyper-specialized interests and really bright people can cause the community to atomize by virtue of those similar interest pools. But the micro-community I've found with the Wick has certainly been an enjoyable thing for me.

How would you describe your religious beliefs when you arrived? Is your family religious?

Religiously liberal, that's for sure. I would frequently refer to myself as something like a polyglot, harboring pantheism, panentheism, and Walt Whitman at the core of my religion. There's an Israeli author named Eva Illouz who wrote this book called *Cold Intimacies*. It's about how the filling out of profiles online has caused us to create this ideal, digitized self and how that has become the mirror for the construction of identity in the 21st century, through websites like dating websites and Facebook. A couple of years ago, probably the year that I was applying at HDS, 2010, I switched my Facebook religious status to 'Kierkegaard, Sartre, and Whitman walk into a bar.' With all 'critical distance' about the construction of the ideal self via the internet, I nevertheless think that's still pretty apt.

How have your beliefs and mindset changed since then and what's triggered any changes you've experienced?

It's certainly evolving. I mean, one of the foremost reasons that I got interested in the study of religion is so that I could study things that will meaningfully shape who I am and what I believe about the world. You know, it's not just what I believe about what really happened as though we could write the thirteenth century *wie es eigentlich gewesen war*. It's about what I think is the right way to view the world. I've certainly been influenced since coming here. If pressed, my general viewpoint is kind of a transcendental reverence, but I have nuanced it and given it various degrees of spin in different directions based on the philosophers and theologians I've had the pleasure of reading over the last two years.

It seems to me that your religious perspective is pretty intellectual. Have you engaged in any formal religious practice, like ceremonies, rituals, church, or synagogue?

I do not go to church. If I go to church it's because a friend is going or a friend is preaching. Over the course of the last year, my liturgical presence in any kind of sacred space has been as limited as it has been polyglot. I was in Philadelphia and I went with my friend Matt Arck, who is now at University of Chicago Divinity School, to a Catholic Mass there. I went to hear our former colleague, Alison Redfearn, preach just down the street at the Methodist Church here. A year or two ago, I went to a Unitarian Universalist service with a very close friend of mine who's planning on being a UU minister in New York. I haven't been frequently, and more often than not, I'm drawn into a community because someone I know and love is part of that community and they've led me into it. I'm a participant and observer but not a member.

The way I view my religious practice is non-liturgical, shall we say. If you want to put it into the terms of liturgy then, you know, the liturgy is in the leaves, as it were. I was that way as an undergraduate as well. I felt the presence of the divine, if you want to call it that, at large. I felt the kind of unity in experience and the world more often when I was sitting under a tree and reading a book, writing under a tree, riding my bicycle through the sunshine, than I did in a traditionally circumscribed liturgical space. Those have always been core religious practices for me.

Which is basically finding the divine in everyday practice?

Yes.

Let's move on to your true passion, Elliott, which is writing, if I'm correct.

Well, one of them. If I had to pick one that would probably be it.

During your two years here at Harvard were you able to develop new insights into the practice of writing and literature? Not just in an academic sense, but in your own practice?

Yes, absolutely. In some ways I feel that I've taken two opposite trajectories while here. My prose has gotten objectively worse. It's hard to be constantly reading authors like Foucault and Lacan and not come to write in the hyper dense prose style that is so often critiqued for being practically impenetrable. I hope that I'm not quite so bad as an Adorno or something, but you know, I reflect on my own writing and I think, "God, I really sound like an academic horse's ass." It's partly playing the game, it's partly having the game play me. On the other side of it, for that second trajectory, I think I've really grown as a poet while here.

Were you a poet before you came to Harvard, or did you just write prose?

Well, what is the litmus test that makes a man a poet? Boy, I couldn't begin to answer that in twice as much time as we have here, but I was writing poetry before I came certainly. It was something I did off and on throughout middle school and high school. I took a creative writing class here and there all through high school and then during my final semester at Macalester as an undergraduate, I had one elective left and I used it on a creative writing course, which is one of the best decisions I ever made.

Are you only writing poetry now?

I toy with the idea of doing non-fiction things, but whilst at the Divinity School the entirety of my non-fiction energy is put towards course work. It isn't to say that I haven't had ideas for, you know, creative non-fiction essays, but I kind of punt those ideas for the time being while I'm still in school. I've just never felt like I had the talent for fiction. I feel like the things that I want to say and feel need to be said personally, and the medium through which I can speak them is poetry rather than fiction.

Or non-fiction.

Or non-fiction.

So if we looked at one of your pre-Harvard poems and a poem written at this very moment, would we see a different kind of poem?

Yes. It would certainly be different, or at least I hope so. God, I hope I've grown as a poet in the two years I've been here! It would be a shame if I hadn't. I would say my style has changed to some extent. I hope that I can look back at the poetry that I was writing two years ago and reach back and grab something with that style. I'd like to think that I've gotten a slightly keener eye since arriving here, and have been able to create a certain critical distance between myself and my poetry that is on the page—that's a difficult distance to obtain, but I've started to obtain it here, I feel.

I think it's possible to see writing as a kind of religious experience. Do you think you can describe your poetic practice as an expression of your own personal ministry?

Absolutely. I think that in a lot of ways my turn towards poetry has been inspired by a frustration with the ability of academic discourse to get at what's most real and important about the human experience. That's really the core motivating factor. Writing poetry is definitely a religious practice for me. Although it's hard to simply call it that and leave it there. I mean, it depends on how we define practice, which is tricky. I don't know, I don't think even Pierre Bourdieu has done that, even though he's spent a whole hell of a lot of time trying to figure it out. More time than we have anyway. But for me, the act of writing poetry has so much to do with fashioning a space in which it can come. You know, it's like Emerson said, perhaps not in this very building, although he certainly was in this very building many times: all poetry was written before time, and you just have to access it, to pierce into that space where the air is music. I don't think that has any metaphysical credibility, but I think he's still absolutely right with the practice of writing poetry. It just depends on how you want to couch it.

One of your goals when you came here was to continue your academic career. You're on the path to a professorship somewhere in the future, and yet you're a poet. Do the two pursuits conflict, or do they balance one another out?

I guess I would have to say that my academic experience influences my poetry. There would be no point in reading philosophy if you didn't allow it to somehow shift the deepest and most important place within yourself. But I think I'd have to say that my poetry doesn't influence my academic work so much as highlight its comparative triviality for the most part. Yes, I can read academic philosophy and be interested in it, get a lot from it, write a paper on it; but I think that the more I write poetry, the more I realize that that which can be polysyllabically expressed very slowly and convolutedly in an academic journal can often be expressed with the beautiful utterance—perhaps not as completely, but perhaps more compellingly. It's not easy. I wish it was, but maybe that would impoverish it. I think the poetic utterance as opposed to academic discourse does benefit from a certain simplicity, but simplistic in a certain sense, simplistic in the Thomist sense that God is not more grand than we can think, but God is so simple that we cannot conceive of God in God's utter simplicity. In a similar sense, I would say that the distillation of poetry is a sort of honing down to that which can be both profound, and yet expressed with as tight of an economy of language as possible. In part it is, I think, a particularly apt analogy because it's when you get down to the heart of it that it becomes ineffable. Personally, I find the quiet haiku a much better way of running up against the limits of language than writing a thousand page treatise on the limits of cognition.

So your poetic practice, your writing, and your intellectual life in general has developed a lot since you've been here. Is it safe to say that these two years have changed you profoundly—on a philosophical, intellectual, and academic level?

They certainly have, but with the distinction that you drew previously. I would be wary of putting too much pressure on that kind of intellectual/academic cultivation because this degree has certainly not forwarded my trajectory towards a professorship. Perhaps it will open doors for me in the future, although it hasn't helped as much to open them at this point as I would have hoped, but that's probably true for anyone at this point.

This is just kind of a bridge which will be crossed when I come to it, if I come to it—the doctoral applications. But the diaphanous nature of the Divinity School MTS program allows one, even compels one, to pick and choose from various different interests, which can be fantastic. To be honest, the flexibility and diversity of coursework within the program is one of the things that drew me to the program in the first place, but at the same time, it also derailed the single mindedness of my academic trajectory. This diversity of subject matter then was coupled with the absence of the faculty with whom I wanted to work—you know, all these professors I wanted to study under, it's sabbatical after sabbatical, and that chops up the availability of the faculty with whom I wanted to study. Those two things combined to really undermine my trajectory to the Ph.D. but that might be a good thing to be quite honest.

It might give you some time to grow?

Yes, and if I ultimately decide to do a Ph.D. I think that it will be a better experience because I'll have taken that time away, gained some critical distance, but it has not been the springboard I thought it would be. That's for certain.

Given everything that we've discussed, what would you say to young Elliot as he arrived on campus two years ago? Would you have changed anything knowing what you know now?

You know, it's hard for me to say because it has been a less than perfect experience, although I suppose no experience ever is perfect. I think that the one thing that I would have encouraged myself to do would have been to be more proactive about making niches of community and intentionally seeking them out, because I think that based on my previous experience, part of me expected the community to descend as though the mother-ship had just kind of created a nice colony of friends and that didn't happen. I guess I had some unrealistic expectations about that, which were themselves forged by my previous experiences. Yes, I think intentionally finding community would be the biggest thing, because the problems with my course of study which aren't in themselves problems so much as derailments of my previous plan—seem to me to be systemic of the way the Divinity School was structured, and they might be for the best. So I don't know how I could have made different choices academically. I suppose the one academic thing I would have changed is that maybe I should have been a little more pigheaded and aggressive about making sure I got into the professor's discussion section, rather than being in a T.A. led section, because I've only had, in the course of my four semesters here, two discussion sections with professors over the entire two years. Other than that, I don't know how I would have done things differently, wrestling with the plurality of the program of study and the dearth of advisors and mentors that I'd hoped to find came with the territory I guess.

Does your original plan to go on to do a Ph.D. still stand?

Yes, and hindsight will hopefully be as close to twenty-twenty as possible when I look back on how my interests have been shifted, but not necessarily impoverished. I did think for a long time that, at this moment, I would be waiting to hear back from Ph.D. programs and, for a variety of reasons, I'm not. I would say the largest of which is that as much as the Divinity School has kind of derailed my previous plans, Harvard as a whole and the Divinity School's structure of allowing a lot of electives has allowed me to branch out and grow. It's a double edged sword because as much as the program's plurality let the bottom fall out of my single mindedness in my academic trajectory, it also allowed me to find what was underneath the bottom of that bucket, as it were. Being able to take these great classes in The Yard has fostered an interest in critical theory beyond what I previously had, which was minimal. In addition, it fostered a far more central interest in poetry which was previously existent, but definitely grew to the fore of my focus here. I certainly feel lucky to have been able to attend Harvard Divinity School in spite of all its flaws, even if those may be myriad. I wouldn't take these two years back.

With this intellectual background of yours, two years at Harvard, two years in theology, what's next?

That's a very good question. Who knows? I will ideally be applying to teaching positions, but a Harvard Master's degree, despite how high fallutin' it may sound, is hardly a guarantee of even an interview, much less a job. So it could be anywhere, from teaching to trying to spend a year improving my German in Berlin, to spending a year or two working in another wine shop somewhere. I think that my time at Harvard has brought me to appreciate what can be great about academia, what can be fantastic about having academic discussions. On the other hand, it has also led me to recognize a certain poverty amidst the seeming richness in a lot of academic discourse.

Professor Dudley Rose

Associate Dean for Ministry Studies and Lecturer on Ministry

Professor Rose, you are a Professor here at Harvard and the head of the Mdiv program. Can you say something about that role?

Sure, and maybe just set it in a little bit of context. I began working here in 1987 on a part-time basis. I graduated from here in '83, I took a church in the area and was asked to come back to do some teaching for field education supervisors principally, in order to train the people who supervise our students in the field sites. As life often unfolds, this one did sort of serendipitously and I just stayed and took on other responsibilities.

I became head of the Field Education program, which I held many years. Then, when Stephanie Paulsell was in the role that I'm currently in, as the associate deacon for ministry which oversees the Mdiv, when she took the Houghton Professor of Ministry Studies, then I was advanced to the Associate Dean position. So, I came to it through a number of years working in this office and we'll probably want to talk a little bit about just how that's changed over time, but principally, my work is to oversee a lot of faculty members, a standing committee of the faculty—the Mdiv committee—and then a variety of colleagues from Academic Affairs to whatever. So, it's not a one man job, not a one person show, by any means. But the main project of someone in my position, in working with others, is to oversee the three year program that is for professional ministry and to oversee the field education part of it. I have a director, Emily Click, who does that on a day to day basis with Laura Tuach, but that's under my umbrella. I would say that's probably the largest project that we have, just in terms of resources.

Every student in the Mdiv program has to do two years of field education, which is essentially like an internship. Many of them do more than that and it comes with a stipend so there's a whole infrastructure managing that. It's also a requirement of the curriculum that intersects with their academic work around the rubrics of Arts and Ministry. So, those all have to be adjudicated, cataloged and become part of their record as requirements for graduation.

Where do they go, Professor Rose?

Probably about half, or maybe fewer now, of our placements are church placements. So they would typically go into those placements—about half of our Mdivs are still going in toward a ministry. They would take on various roles within local churches, preaching, teaching, pastoral care, committee work. A variety of work to expose them to the role of minister and ask them to actually take responsibility so it's not a shadowy experience. They really are taking on minister authority doing things like pastoral care, like preaching and being treated like ministers, albeit ministers that are students, by the congregations. For many of us who went through that, it's a pretty significant shift when people began to look at you as someone who has ministerial authority because a lot of folks, myself included when I went through this, were learning how to wear that kind of mantel. So, it's often just learning how to do that with any kind of grace and ease, not just, "Is this a mantel I have any kind of comfort with?" What's always wonderful to me is to watch students who aren't sure of that role and see them find that they very often have both comfort and a lot of talent. So, it's really a great privilege to see that.

OK. About half go to church settings, I suppose that's a variety of Protestant denominations?

Yep.

What do the other half do?

Well, they go to a number of different things. Probably the next largest group would be people who go into healthcare chaplaincies, who go into public services kinds of work. Sometimes that's direct service work that looks very much like chaplaincy. Sometimes it may be administrative work, overseeing or being an executive director of a nonprofit organization, something like that. We have a number that go into teaching at the secondary level. So they go in and often those folks, if they're working in a secondary school, they'll works as—not always as schools are all different—but as someone who teaches religious courses and also functions as a chaplain. As I say, it varies a lot from school to school, it's kind of a changing landscape. A number go into college or university type of chaplaincies. Though that's a role that's also changing very quickly in the United States, and I'd say also campus ministers. Over in the Yard, there's a whole set of campus ministers. Most of them are not full time, but some are, if you were to look at Brown University for instance.

Brown?

Brown had Janet Cooper Nelson, one of our graduates, as campus minister. So that's a role in one way or another that still exists. It's beginning because of the diversity and plurality of religious confessions and traditions on campuses. Often a full time person will also be kind of the clearing house and will be organizing all of the other folks in one fashion or another. Then you have a very large group actually, or at least a significant minority, who want to do doctoral work out of the Mdiv program. In fact, if you look at the admissions to our own Th.D. and Ph.D. this year, several of those very few slots were Mdiv graduates of the Divinity School. So, it's a pretty broad reach, in terms of the ways in which folks leave here and work.

Now, what about the other Master's programs? There's a very small ThM program, and there is a substantial MTS program. Can these two also participate in field education?

They can. The ThM, as you suggested, is a small program. It's also a program that doesn't come with financial aid and because it doesn't come with financial aid, often stipends in field education—particularly out of the church realm—are funded through college work-study funds and then it doesn't work very easily for them to be funded. Many of them, particularly if they're coming to study a particular thing or if they're coming as ministers and want to do some work on a project, they've already got a whole life of ministry that they're working in. So they don't see it probably quite as urgently. Our MTS students, on the other hand, very often do field education and I'm not positive of what percentage now, but generally a significant percentage of the MTS. When I say significant, I mean maybe ten or fifteen percent of our students in field education would be MTS students at any given time.

Are there any MTS students going into ministry?

There are. From the Protestant world that's more unusual because many of the protestant denominations require an Mdiv as a qualifier for ordination. But some denominations don't. Some of the Baptist denominations come to mind. So, reasonably often we'll have students who are already ordained and so they can decide where they are in or whether their development requires two years or three years of work because they're not using them as a degree for qualification of credentialing. So, sometimes you'll have people going into ministry that way. Very often we have MTS students who come in as MTS students and change to the Mdiv program. We've been seeing ten or twelve, I would say, although Maggie Welsh [the registrar] can give you a better number—but a significant number every year who are changing onto the Mdiv program.

Is that always allowed?

It's not always allowed because even given that broad-spectrum of things that students are going into out of Mdiv program, we see that and we ask them to see it as some form of ministry. So, if somebody says to me, "I see teaching in a seminary as a ministry and I want to have the practical orientation, I want to have the rubric of thinking about the work I do as ministry" then they are likely to be welcomed in. If somebody were to say, "I just need another year to study some languages and I've got a good financial aid package, so I would like to move into the MDiv" then we don't encourage that. Actually the curriculum, because of the various places one has to focus course work and other things on ministry, it doesn't work very well for somebody who's trying to manipulate the program that way.

So, we don't try to put artificial barriers if it's warranted. Students generally can change. They have to do it before they're really into their second year and so it can't be something they can do halfway through or at the last minute.

And vice versa?

It used to be more than it is now. It's actually quite infrequent. We do occasionally have some that go from MDiv to MTS, but not very many.

Professor Rose, have you seen an evolution in field education and the student population over the past twenty five years that you've been here?

Yes, I've seen an evolution in a variety of ways. I think that certainly there has been an evolution in the area of field education. It really began as anything very formal sometime in the middle of the last century. So when I first came here, even though it was well established, it was a relatively recent area. It was still, I think, in many ways, sorting itself out and trying to understand from a theoretical point of view exactly what it was and what it's standing was. At this point there is a better integration of not just field education, but lots of ways of thinking about ministry across the whole of the faculty and the whole of the curriculum, even for people who aren't in our faculty ministerially trained themselves, that their interaction and support working with the ministry program is quite high. So, that means that they begin to see field education as simply another venue of learning.

When it first began, it was seen as a way of maybe giving some credit for what students were doing as part-time ministries in small congregations as part time work. Now it's a much more coherently integrated part. You have to do course work, but you also have to do field education and so they're seen as very integral and mutually inclusive. I think that points to a significant difference in the way that ministry sits within the culture of the Divinity School and faculty. In part, that's related to the fact that when I first came here in 1987, I'm not sure that the Director of Ministry Studies even sat on the faculty. He certainly didn't sit on what was then the Professorial Committee. Now we have any number of faculty members who do significant work in the industry who are part of the faculty discourse. Whoever is sitting at the table makes just such a big difference. So, we used to do a lot more adjuncts and had local ministers and other teachers; they did a fabulous job. There was nothing wrong with their teaching and in almost every case they were excellent, but they came and went and they weren't a part of the day-to-day faculty meeting conversation. That has changed, from my perspective, for the better. The way in which ministry is integrated across the curriculum and across the thoughts.

So, we've been talking about field education. Yet if we look at the spiritual or religious life here inside Harvard, specifically inside the Divinity School—can you say something about how that is structured?

Because we are, depending on who you talk to, an interreligious or interdenominational or non-denominational divinity school, we don't have any sense of, "this how the main worship is done here" and so on. In one sense or another, each group bears some responsibility and has an opportunity to develop spiritual life as they see fit. So, as we have had more Muslim students, you develop ways in which Muslim students gather for prayer or other conversations or a variety of things. The same thing with Jewish students. Then the Protestant domination, the Catholic students. Where we have a critical mass, that's always a little bit slippery, but where we have a critical mass of students in our MDiv program, we've had denominational counselors.

Those denominational counselors serve several functions. One is often, though not always, to help students organize the spiritual life that they're experiencing, but our students are very good at that so it doesn't really necessarily require denominational counselors. If you were to look at the Unitarian Universalists, for example, who have a very robust kind of infrastructure, they nominate their offices every year, part way through the year, so that there is continuity going into the Fall and their programming. Their denominational counselors have come to their services, but it would not be right to say that they actually materially guide them or implement anything that would be important in terms of that happening.

Now, their support, of course, is extraordinarily important. What denominational counselors are principally involved with is helping students navigate their own development toward ministry. So in that sense, if you think of spiritual formation, institutional formation, going informed into the institutional life of one's denomination or tradition, having guidance in that through the thicket of judicatories and gate keeping processes, those kinds of things—they are very much a part of that. That's really a very principal part of their focus. Because again, Stephanie and I teach a course on Intro to Ministry Studies to the entering class, thirty five to fifty five students, and there's no way that we could have simultaneous instruction in a variety of specific denominations or traditions. We cover a lot of those, but for that kind of deep process of formation we do depend on the denominational counselors.

Are they employed full-time by the Divinity sSchool?

No, not at all. We're grateful that, I suspect, some of them put in more time than we ask them, but they are about a half a day a week and that's the denominational counselor part. Some of those same people are hired to teach a course in Denominational Polity and History and that will vary a little bit again by denomination or tradition as to what the expectations are for students, but that's also a process of formation into the governance and the history of the traditions that many of our denominational counselors provide. One course in some cases and half a day a week.

There seems to be an unlimited variety of religious backgrounds here in the student population, however, there are a limited number of denominational counselors. How do you select the denominational counselors? Which faiths or which student groups or religious beliefs get the privilege of having a denominational counselor? How does that really work? Does that depend on the number of students?

It does. It's an imperfect situation, but over the last few years we've added a Pentecostal denominational counselor and a Buddhist denominational counselor, as those numbers have warranted. To some degree it's a budget consideration, in trying to match the needs to what we can provide and our resources. It's probably fair to say that even where we have denominational counselors, they can't do everything that students need. In some cases, such as the Baptists, there are so many different kinds of Baptist that if you had a denominational counselor for every one of them, we'd have to have a new building. Even denominations that are more hierarchical than that still have geographical differences, diocesan differences.

Say we have a Jewish denominational counselor, we'll use this as an example: how do you decide how to choose this specific person, because Judaism is so wide in its variety and its approaches? The same goes, as you said, for various Christian denominations, but there's only one counselor for each. So, how do we decide on this here at HDS? Who chooses how the person gets appointed, because some of them have a very specific profile?

That's a very excellent question and I will come at it two different ways. One is that I've instituted that when we hire—for example, we just hired a person because we had a retirement from the Unitarian Universalist denominational counselor—we called for applicants and it's publicly advertised. Then we made it a short list selection and all of those short list folks were invited to the interview by my staff and also the students, the Unitarian Universalist students, who wrote a very fine report on their experience on the interview. We try to get as many of the stakeholders in the room to have a perspective and a voice. So that's one way we can come at it. I think the other way is more philosophical. In the Intro to Ministry Studies class, Stephanie and I start our students off with spiritual and intellectual autobiographies. They're very short, but people get a chance to tell us where they've come from. The trick of those is that we've instructed them from the very beginning to learn to tell your story in a way that leaves room for other people to tell theirs. I think of that in the same way as denominational counselors. For example, in the Jewish case, I don't expect Sally Finestone to be Orthodox. She's a rabbi, she wouldn't be Orthodox, but I do expect her to leave room in conversation for the Orthodox, Orthodoxy, and Orthodox students to tell their story and not be sort of normatively shunned to the side. It's a balance, but to me it's also very relevant to how we must live as religious people. The kind of notion that you can't say anything about yourself or have any perspective makes no sense, right; it's a bit common denominator reductionism. What Krister Stendahl used to say was, "How do I learn to sing my song to Jesus without calling other people dirty names?" In a place like this, that becomes a very important thing. In a world like this, that becomes a very important thing.

You have also had a crucial role these last few years in Admissions. Can you just describe your role and what you've seen happening these last few years in Admissions and how that has changed?

My role is modest. I consult in a particular way with Loida Feliz [Director of Admissions] when we're coming to the meetings where we're going to make decisions about grouping some people and so on, to help the applicants in terms of ones that are very obviously admitted and ones that we need to talk about more. But she runs the meeting and she does a fabulous job at it. I guess in some sense we share some duties of authority but it's a very collegial and consensus driven process. Sometimes we'll vote as a Committee on applicants, but largely we talk together and come to conclusions. So it's not something any one person has any special authority over. That said, I think I see my role as being very supportive of the Admissions department because they work very hard for us. I am among those who give some guidance as to the kinds of things that I think the faculty are particularly interested in and want to make sure are covered in recruiting. In that they're concerned with the way in which we think about applicants and even, I suppose, how the applications questions are drawn. Admissions handles all that, but in some sense the faculty have these students for two and three years, so who is it that the faculty hopes to have here? That profile is part of what I do as the faculty. Again, not nearly alone, but I think it's an important role.

What I've seen over the last few years is really excellent recruiting. I remember when I was on the road doing more recruiting—I just don't have the time to do that anymore—but I can remember going to some very nice schools that would say, "What's Harvard doing here? Harvard doesn't need to recruit." Some just said, "Why would you be here? Everybody knows Harvard! You don't have to recruit." That's simply not true. There are lots of other good schools out there to begin with. A lot of people may know the Harvard name, but they don't know much about this program and so in many respects I think that recruiting is an educational project. Also, for example, the diversity and explorations program that Maritza Hernandez had been running; it at least put them in conversation with people who never would even have thought of divinity school or thought of this divinity school. So, the flipside of "Everybody knows Harvard" is that a lot of people think, "Well that's not for me," right? So that's important, to disabuse that perspective.

The other thing I think of, because this program is complex, because it's about the diversity of ways in which we think about that, it's important to have an interpretation in the recruiting and interpretation of what the school is. I think that those are the kinds of things that Admissions can't do in a vacuum, right? They do a very great job, but how do we—as a faculty, as a school, as an administration—how do we want to interpret ourselves out there? What I would say is that over the last several years that interpretive process has been working, I think, very well. We're seeing very strong applicants. We're seeing very strong applicants for both programs and so it means an enormous amount to us as a school and faculty, to have the quality students that we do.

The faculty members that I talk to have taught in other places in many cases, and one of the things they always remark about is the quality of the students and how rewarding it is to teach them. Every once in a while one of them will quit—they are somewhat mortified to be the dullest person in the room—which is clearly not true but it does give some view of the estimation that we have of our students and then they go and do wonderful things. It's not just about an institution replicating itself. It's about some very important things about the way religion is voiced, is lived, is understood in the world. In some ways, I suppose you could say the number of graduates we have in the world is not huge, but they have an enormous impact actually and that's something that I think we're proud of and have some fiduciary responsibility about.

Professor Rose, can you something about your teaching role here? You've been teaching the Introduction to Ministry class, is that correct? Do you teach other classes as well?

Sure. The Intro to Ministry Studies class is one of the required classes. It's a co-taught class with me and Stephanie Paulsell, and we try to expose students to accounts of ministry from the beginning, as early as Gregory the Great. In other traditions, it may be novels, it may be essays, it may be biographies. It's quite a variety of literature, always sort of saying, "Here's an account." First of all, what it says to folks is that ministry studies have a history in literature. Then it's a matter of asking, "How do we engage these things that we are not?" Then to try to avoid the notion of, "Well, because it's not me, it's not relevant to me. I'm an X; I'm a Lutheran and that just doesn't fit for me, or I'm a Buddhist and that doesn't fit." Some of the most interesting students we've had … I shouldn't say most interesting students, but some of the most interesting kinds of responses have come from folks who are Buddhist saying, "Wow, Gregory the Great is really interesting to me." Clearly Gregory the Great is not going to be the same as they are in their religious expression, but that's what we want people to do; to engage, to be excited by, to learn from people unlike themselves, but who think about ministry. To ask the students to think about ministry perhaps a little differently from how they have all along.

Has that always been the same kind of course over the last few years or decades, or have you altered it? Do you have a different approach than the course that used to be here, a traditional kind of way of teaching?

It is a different course than the one that was introduced around the same time the new curriculum was introduced, in 2005 or 2006. It's funny, I never thought I would forget the date when we were going through it. But it is different. I think that the other course, which was called "Introduction to Theological Education for Ministry" was more of a topical course. You took a particular topic like sexuality and racism, things of that nature. There is something about narrative that works, because all of those topics are things that we run into in this class. But I would have to say that lots of times, particularly in the first term that some folks are here, they're brand new; they come in with a bunch of presuppositions and predispositions. They haven't learned a common language to talk together theologically and throwing out a lot of hot-button topics and asking them to wrestle with them would often end up in wrestling matches that weren't especially productive. It hasn't always been the case, but it happened enough. I think the narrative gives people a doorway in. I think it's been really a beneficial change.

What about the other classes you teach here?

For a number of years I taught a course in Administration and Leadership, partly because we had so many people going into nonprofit organizations and I got annoyed enough of people saying, "Well, I'm the person who came from divinity school. I have ideas, but I don't do the day-to-day administration." So you'd have these organizations with wonderful admissions that treated their people terribly because they just didn't have good administration. So that course is now taught, or a version of it is taught by Emily Click. So, I have taught that over a few years. I have taught a course in Ministry in the Digital Age and that is, in some sense, a two part course. Part of it is a course of learning about the variety of Biblical study software and how to use that if you're preparing for a preaching ministry, just because there are now libraries at your fingertips that you didn't have a few years ago and it can be a very huge help in doing a good job in preparing, or at least doing your research or sermon.

We talk about how to do websites and social media and all of those things, how to use technology in worship, just so people could get some hands-on work with those things. The other part is a more critical view of things like the use of technology. We ask questions like, "Is multitasking really good for your head? Are you really able to do it?" You know, some of the research would suggest that people aren't nearly as good at it as they think they are. We try to take a look at some of those things too. In some sense, as ministers, we're going to be consumers of those things or producers of some of them. We have to be and it's good to be. On the other hand, we're going to be working in congregations where some of those things are going to have troubling side effects.

Then the other course that I teach is a seminar on Dietrich Bonhoeffer. That grew out of a segment that I do in Intro to Ministry Studies. It's a heavy reading course because we read a lot of what he did right and we try to look at it from a ministerial perspective, but clearly as a theologian minister there are many, many interesting ways in which those two domains interact.

You're teaching ministry and you're a minister yourself, heavily involved in the religious life in the Divinity School. Do you participate in the wider religious life here are Harvard, and can you say something about that religious life? Are you involved in a Memorial Church at all?

I'm not, and that's partly because there's only so much one can do. I have a congregation, though a small one, that really becomes the focus for me beyond the Divinity School.

When I went from part-time to full-time here, Dean Thiemann and I agreed that I would be able to continue doing that ministry because I felt that I couldn't teach ministry based on memory, and without accountability, for very long. You know, others probably can, but for me it was that day to day, week to week accountability to the work of ministry that was important. I also find it's just a life giving work for me, a vocation in a true sense.

Where is your congregation?

Well, it used to be right up here in Porter Square, Mass Ave. right up where Lesley University is. We sold that building to Lesley. It was a great big arch of a building and we moved over to a place on the three corners of Somerville, Medford, and Arlington. So, it's quite near Tufts, near the Alewife Brook Parkway.

What denomination is that, if I may ask?

United Church of Christ.

Do you have people from this school coming over and doing internships there?

Yes. We've always had them over the years, when we were here in Cambridge, or over there; a number of Divinity School students have served. My current Associate Minister is a Divinity School graduate and our Christian education minister just graduated last year from here and we have a student intern this year.

We have a lot of connections and they're great because they bring great ideas and we hope they learn some things. A church life, when you get to face any organization close up, shows its imperfections. How one navigates those and deals with that is a huge part of developing into a professional life.

How do you see the future of all the different topics we've talked about: the admissions, the ministry, and the religious life here at HDS?

I think the Divinity School has, certainly for the foreseeable future, a very bright future. Our Admissions pool or applicants' pool is very strong. We've got a good faculty, we've got people who really love their work here and, from a variety of perspectives, are excellent colleagues. So it seems to me that the satisfaction that the students express with their education here is high. I have every reason to believe that as a school our future is very bright. What I do think is that the religious landscape is changing, and changing fairly rapidly. It's been coming on for a long time, but it's at one of those tipping points.

If you look at the demographics or the statistics of mainline Protestant denominations for example, the decline over the last forty to fifty years has been pretty consistent. You're seeing denominations continually shrink their central offices because of budget cuts. You see attendance down, you see fewer young people being brought up in the church. One set of statistics, for example, is really interesting. There were interviews where people were asked, "Did you go to church when you were twelve?" This was asked as a snapshot of people from twenty to ninety. What you saw was that people who were ninety had much higher percentages and went to church. The people who were twenty, much lower percentages.

How we see that unfold is a very common phenomenon in the church. You'd be brought up in the church, you'd go to conformation class, you'd fall away from the church as a late teenager in college, you get married, you might have children and you'd say, "Well we've got to bring the kids up back in the church!" And you'd go, kids would become part of Sunday school and you would begin to develop an adult spirituality. Other generations would have this hiatus but that depended on people who saw that as a piece of their own formation and experience. So, there this was motion of coming back. Well, if you're not brought up in it, you don't go back to it in the same way. So, I think we're seeing a significant difference that way. Another difference in the Sixties and Seventies was that a kind of anti-institutionalism hit the churches pretty hard. I think that's where some of the decline began. There was just this kind of notion that there are all these organizations that aren't of any relevance and that sort of thing. What I see with young people now is not that kind of antipathy. Where I'll see most young people will be weddings or funerals, weddings are obvious and funerals, I guess, obvious as extended families experience death. What I find is that they appreciate the church. They think we have this lovely building, it's not ostentatious at all, but it's a nice little arts and crafts building built in the Twenties. It's a sort of sweet place and they liked the service and they liked the kind of care they were held in, either in grief or joy. They'll remark about that and be pretty excited about it, but will have no intention whatsoever of going from there to being a church attender. It's just not part of their life.

Now, that's not everyone. Obviously we do have young people, but more and more I see that particular picture. So, what it means to me is that spirituality, spiritual life, and religion are things that many people find important in one way or another. It's not clear to me exactly how that's going to work itself out in the churches as they are composed right now. They are not going to disappear in a moment, but more and more churches close every year. So, it isn't an idle thing and certainly in Europe you're probably way ahead on that trajectory. It's going to be interesting to see the ways in which people engage spiritually, and especially engage beyond themselves as individuals spiritually. I have great hope that that's such a basic human need for thriving that we're not talking about a "God is dead" kind of future, but I think the changes in the next couple of generations are hard to predict right now.

Now that obviously raises some real questions for a school like this, right? We're in a very lucky place because many of our students are so bright and so capable and so imaginative and creative that they're perfectly prepared, both emotionally and intellectually, to go out and do different things. So, they might start in a church and they may do something else, but they may be part of changing the church to something entirely different. I don't think it's going to be an easy transition for everybody. My guess is that the next couple of generations are going to pretty interesting. Even the conservative denominations are seeing a decline and so I think it's just going to be very interesting to see what the next couple of generations are going to be like.

Yet here, your student population and student applications seem to be growing—that's the paradox.

It is the paradox and I think it speaks to the notion that people understand that there is something very deeply important about religious living in life. I mean, I would see that more clearly among our students now than I did twenty years ago. The kind of unapologetic sense of something at the core being important and it's not, for the most part, a navel-gazing kind of thing. People are interested in other people, other problems, and other people's problems. There's something very hopeful about the people we see. It is a paradox and where it leads, I'll be glad to know, but I probably would be able to watch it from the sideline by the time it has much impact.

Jack Jenkins

I am from Aiken, South Carolina. I'm a white male, a Protestant out of the South-east. I come from a family that is southern in the sense that I have roots in my family that go back before the Revolutionary War. We've been there for a long time. We're a typical family in the South but we're also progressive. That's been consistent in my family for a long time. I'm Presbyterian, Presbyterian Church U.S.A., not to be confused with Presbyterian Church America or Evangelical Presbyterian Church, or all these different versions. Also, I'm in the Harvard Divinity School and I play harmonica and ukulele.

Have you always been a Presbyterian, Jack?

I have, as long as I can remember. I was baptized a Methodist. I don't remember that though. I was born in Washington D.C. and then we moved to Spartanburg, South Carolina when I was very young. We were at a Baptist Church there, but I only kind of remember that. As soon as we got to Aiken, South Carolina, where I grew up and spent most of my life, we went to the Presbyterian church. We were only Presbyterian, honestly, because they had the best kids' program in the area.

So there was a kind of an egalitarian approach to that?

Precisely.

So, you grew up down south.

Yes, I went to a little college called Presbyterian College in South Carolina.

Is that an exclusively religious place?

It's a mixture of several things. I come from a military family. My Dad is military and then Mom's a crazy hippie. They love each other very much, but we don't know why! Our family is pretty close. My sister did more moving than I did. My sister was born in Panama and I had just had the two jumps from D.C. to Spartanburg, but we are a close family even in that regard. My sister went to Presbyterian College ahead of me and really recommended it. Part of the reason that it was so important for Lathem and I—that's my sister, Lathem—is that the Presbyterian church played such a big role in our upbringing. There were some youth conferences and retreats that we went to as high schoolers and middle schoolers. We were both on the youth council for our Presbytery, which is like a diocese in South Carolina, and so we were leading prayer retreats for others. Through all of those collective experiences, the people that really deeply influenced us when we were younger were these Presbyterian leaders.

I almost went to film school out of high school. I was going to go to FNC Film School down at Varsity University. Then I realized that, honestly, their program is designed so you get the one year as an undergrad and then three or four years full time as a film student, including summers. So, that's the price you pay for getting a full ride and for everything else. But I realized I didn't have anything to make films about. I was a relatively sheltered high school student, and so I wouldn't have been able to grapple with ideas that I didn't have yet. I wanted a little more education. I knew a lot of great folks in Presbyterian College, so there was that religious angle, but there was also this other reason.

During your liberal arts education, did you major in religion? If so, which aspect of religion did you focus on?

I had two majors. One was in History, but then my other major was in Religion/ Philosophy. At that point in time, they had a way that you could combine the two. I will say at Presbyterian College, I was an atypical religion student and religion major. Usually a religion major at my college means you've studied Christianity for quite some time. Even with a religion/philosophy degree, there's a lot of Christianity in that. There are a lot of philosophers that are also Christians, and so that would come up probably more often than it would have in other schools, precisely because it's Presbyterian College. Even though it's a small denomination, it still comes up in the place like PC. I really love and got into studying abroad and travel when I was at college, one of the cool things about our college is that it's actually cheaper to study abroad. So, it's been mandated since I've left. You either have to do an internship or study abroad, so I studied abroad three times during undergrad. I had only one full semester and I was just in New Zealand, and that was basically the archetypal studying abroad experiences with going places and drinking a lot. Honestly, that was an extension of another two summer programs that I've done in different places. One was in the United Kingdom and Ireland—we were studying Colonialism when we were there. Then I did a summer gig in Vietnam, where I was studying Communism and its connection to Buddhism. Thus New Zealand actually was an easy place for me study abroad for a first semester, but they also had some good Buddhism courses and instruction, so it was easier for me to do that. I was studying Buddhism. To answer your original question, the religion aspect of my religion degree was actually a lot more multi-faceted. My work was essentially a comparison of world religions, which was atypical for my college at the time. I don't think it's atypical anymore. At the same time, I was also very involved in religious life in and at my university. I was very involved with religious leadership and still doing things with the Presbyterian Church. So when I took the Christian courses and the theology courses that I did take, there was still the possibility of pursuing ordination and getting courses that would help me out for that as well.

So whilst you were still finishing your studies at an undergrad level—and traveling—you were seriously considering ordination?

I was seriously considering it, but by the time I graduated I'd convinced myself that I would never go to seminary. I would never be ordained, that was a far-fetched idea for me. There were folks who were going to go do that and they were great but, you know.

So what happened?

I graduated from college and I was originally going to go into the Peace Corps. I took a summer job at a conference center, just a summer job to kill time while I did all the medical rigmarole. I almost got a scholarship to go to Ireland to study Anthropology. Then realized I like Anthropology, but not enough to go to Ireland and get a degree in it, so it didn't work out. So I was going to do this Peace Corps gig and then they delayed my deployment by a couple of months. So I had time to kill after the summer. My sister got married and, long story short, she had a friend from her short time in politics who was at the wedding and her friend convinced me to drive to Iowa and start working for the Obama campaign. I started working for him and then I got to the Iowa Caucuses and it was amazing. The Peace Corps folks told me I could take a year for the campaign. They said call us back and we'll ship you back to Peru, which was probably where I was going to go. So I said all right. Then Barack kept winning and so I worked for Obama's campaign for about a year and a half in various capacities. I went all across the country in the United States and then I finished up during the General Election in Ohio. During that time period, I applied for Divinity School, which is a different story all together. After the closing of the Obama campaign, I did politics for a few more months.

You decided to apply for divinity school while working for Barack Obama?

Yes. I'll say that the president of my university had specifically asked me to think about going to HDS while I was in college—he's an HDS grad. I didn't know Harvard Divinity School existed when he took me out to lunch when I was at PC.

He just said, "think about this" and I said, "really? What? That's a thing?" So that was where the seed was planted. The story I tell, it's interesting, because that is not the reason I ended up sticking around here. The reason I was actually inspired to come to HDS was my work in politics. I spent a lot of time talking to people. As part of my job early on, I was a caucus educator in Iowa. About 50% of our supporters had never caucused before and caucusing is confusing no matter who you are, and so we just wanted to teach them how to caucus. I would to go to these people's homes, to talk about this thing that I didn't even know existed a few months before and then teach them how do it. Our supporters would come from all walks of life. A lot of them were poor and transient, so I walked into all of their homes and had a political conversation—but these are people so they're going to talk to you about what drives them, what inspires them and how they live their lives. I saw the direct effects that politics can have. I learned how these folks are oriented and that what guides their daily life is a faith—whether that's going to a church, or the sense of faith which is "spiritual and not religious."

I was leaving one primary and going through … I ended up in New Orleans, basically while I was going from one state to another. I had done relief work there after Hurricane Katrina and I wanted to go and see Ninth Ward, because that's where I had worked and because it was where it was hardest hit. So I had a buddy of mine there that was working for the Red Cross and I went and saw him, and we drove to the Ninth Ward. It still looked awful. A lot of the stuff had been cleaned up, but there wasn't really any new construction. There's still a lot of stuff and work to be done and it had been months or years at this point. I asked him, "You're the Red Cross guy, right? You don't fix these things?" He said, "Yeah, we don't necessarily go and fix all the houses. We do a lot feeding the workers." I said, "Who are you feeding, because it doesn't seem like it's working?" He told me, "OK, so you might have heard, the government bailed and the non-profits enforced for a while, but then they've got to sustain themselves and not all of them get to stick around for a long time. Even then, there's only a few of those. Most of the people we feed are church workers. They're here every weekend. It might be like a bunch of 80 year old grandmothers from Connecticut, but they have been here every single weekend since the hurricane and that's who we feed." It was just this moment for me where you saw the limits of all the different spheres, like government and non-profit. You know the people who were there in the midst of it, where the government and the non-profits couldn't even reach, were people of faith. I thought: that's really important and that's really cool. That's a world that I know. So, that's when I decided that if I got into divinity school, I would go. It was the only divinity school I applied to, mostly because I didn't have time to apply anywhere else. But they let me in that year. Then Barack kept winning so I deferred for another year.

Did you know early on that you wanted to do the three year MDiv program?

I didn't start the ordination process until after a year here at Harvard but I knew that it was a possibility. Also, even if I decided I didn't want to do that, which is a different conversation, the MDiv requires the field education placements. You can do them as an MTS student, but this way, there's this element of practical instruction that is a required part of the course work. The idea that you have to take three courses outside of your religious tradition, whilst also delving into your own tradition, felt valuable to me.

You've just mentioned ordination, yet during your last year as an undergrad you decided it wasn't right for you?

Yes.

But you started thinking about it again, after your experiences in politics and thinking about going back to a divinity school?

Yes.

What triggered that change?

It's funny, isn't it? There's a different part of the story even now. It's my tradition. It's a whole complement of things. One thing is that in my tradition, we have the really awesome situation where we like people to go to seminary, and that's great. The problem with that is going to seminary. But, we do—that's because we believe in the priesthood of all believers. We have that access open for folks to come and become ordained leaders in the churches. Admittedly, ordination isn't the only way to do that, but for me, working in an ordained capacity in a religious tradition allows you to access people around the world. You can have a practical influence, in terms of, for example, feeding the hungry, it also gives a spiritual credibility that allows you to do things you might not be able to do in a lay capacity. That's unfortunate, of course, and I'm the first person to critique that about my own tradition. In addition to that, there's the very real thing about spiritual discernment, you know? What does it mean to be called? What does it mean to be ordained? In my tradition, that's an open question right now, because historically ordination has only meant church ministry, being a professor, or being a missionary. There are people who do otherwise but you're going to have to fight for it. But now, we're talking about ordination as a broader concept, and now it's really interesting to be a part of that conversation as well. So those three or four different ideas were all percolating even when I got here and continue to percolate now.

It's odd to say this, given all of the critiques of "Godless Harvard," but my faith is far stronger than it's ever been. There's a spiritual development there that doesn't necessarily ... there's not a one-on-one correlation with stronger faith leading to wanting to pursue ordination. But for me, it kind of worked out that way. This was due to the tangible, spiritual experiences that I had here at HDS. Especially on the field education side that I chose, there's a call there. I'll be damned if I can figure out exactly what that call is to at the moment, but I did figure out this sense of call while I was a Harvard Divinity School. The cool thing about Harvard, though it can be frustrating for some, is that it's a great place to start that seeking process. There are some folks who just want to have things told to them. I don't operate that way, and so this is really a great place to kind of just discover.

Did you have to choose an area of focus?

If you aren't pursuing ordination, you do. It's a weird question for people who are on the ordination track because they're like, "What's your focus? You're being a minister but you don't really know what that means?" I've already answered that question, they're like, "What's your focus on?" I tell them, "I'm pursuing ordination at the PC (USA)" and that's usually enough. But what I wrote on my application was that I was looking at the confluence of media, religion, and service, those three things at once. That has technically remained true until today, but the easiest way to answer that for me now is by exploring ordination. Then Harvard makes you choose another religion that you'll study and for me that's Islam. We are required to take three courses outside of our tradition, and for me they have been about Islam.

Let's go back to your very first introduction to Harvard. Was this the first time you visited, or did you come to an open house or some other introductory activity?

I've been to two open houses. When I first got admitted, it was during the Obama campaign and I actually had a short window of time where I wasn't working on the campaign and was able to come and visit. I came with a friend of mine who was here at Harvard and so I crashed with her. The next year, I deferred for a year after that to stay on the campaign, so I didn't have to start in August. I saw the campaign all the way through to 2008. I came again in 2009. Those were the only two times not only that I'd been to Harvard, but to Boston. I hadn't been in this part of the country really, other than those two short trips. The second trip was only to figure out a place to live that summer. I came up for Admitted Student's Day, but I was also just trying to find a place for me to crash for the summer.

What were your first impressions?

The cool thing about it, and the part I was really excited about, was that you couldn't ignore the diversity. Everyone's question is, "Hey, who are you?" "Are you MTS or Mdiv?" Those were the questions you asked somebody immediately at orientation, and it just becomes all that after a while.

I was really impressed with that. You don't get that kind of diversity in some colleges—especially at my little college. Even traveling around the country, you find pockets of different homogenous cultures, but they aren't as diverse as you find here. That was really cool during orientation, seeing the spectrum of different kinds of people. I also realized how smart they all are, like really upfront. I think part of it is because at orientation everyone has the peacock feathers out, getting ready to strut their stuff. But truthfully, everyone's all worried about if they're going to make it here so they have to over-impress. But my first impression was of the academic integrity of a lot of these people and just the cool, raw diversity of Harvard.

Let's talk a little more about those first few days. Was this when you met your adviser? How did you find your initial classes?

So, funny thing about the adviser—I missed the part where you could choose one. I don't know how I missed it. So I just got a random person assigned to me. Professor Olupona was great, but he has nothing to do with anything I'm studying. But, for me, and for how I operate, it was fine, because for a while there, I just needed someone to sign my study card and Professor Olupona was great with that. It wasn't until last year that I switched over to another adviser. I met my original adviser, he seemed great. He does African religion, and he told me the whole story about this monkey in a castle and I was just randomly sitting listening to him for an hour. I remember the first courses. Everybody's so intense in that first semester. As I mentioned earlier—I don't know if it's just like that at any university or any institution—but everyone's on their game and trying to make sure all of their guns are blazing with anything they say in class. I had very different experiences though, because I had HTP which we had to take at the time—Histories, Theologies and Practices in Christianity. It is no longer offered as a course because it was controversial. HTP was controversial because it was trying to shove the entire Christian tradition—literally history, theologies and practices—into a one semester course. I don't actually know why the course was offered, I don't know if it was trying to like keep accreditation for certain things or impress certain people. But it was actually kind of good; it was a good bonding experience for our class, because everyone hated it, not that it was the professor's fault. The professors did, I think, an exemplary job, and one of them was my adviser then. They did the best that they could with what was handed to them, but I think they were going to face criticism no matter what they did.

Why is that?

Well, I think it was different things. Because some folks who aren't Christian felt it was weird that they were being forced to take "this course." Now they knew that upfront, this wasn't news to them. But they were like, "Really? I'm Buddhist, I want to do Buddhist studies." They really didn't even know about atonement theory, they don't need to know. At the same time, people were also frustrated just by the whole class, because when you try to cover the entire Christian tradition in one semester, you're going to be all over the map. Most of these folks come out of contexts where they're usually, at least, around a large number of Christian people. Everyone kind of has a familiarity with it, everyone has built-in knowledge. They were like, "You're grossly over-generalizing this one section of Christianity that I know really well." So, folks were just going to be upset. There were some minor protests at the end of the course regarding its validity. But apparently, it had been a contested course for quite some time. When they decided to get rid of it I don't think anyone shed a tear. Afterwards they just started something similar to it, but as an elective, as opposed to a required course. But what was cool about that class is that it forced people to engage with some material they'd never read before. Those were the most contentious course sections that I had my entire time at Harvard. With my first and second semesters, there were these required courses because a lot of folks were surprisingly challenged by the readings that were given to them, on a personal level, because the instructors were trying to look at these different things and bring in different readers and theologies and perspectives that challenged folks and so that was kind of cool. Then the objection came out against the other course, Introduction to Ministry Studies, where we would all sit around and talk about our personal, spiritual autobiographies. There was a lot of hugging and it was just this very different environment. What was interesting about that is that you really do get a balance between this really intense, almost aggressive academic world juxtaposed with what seemed like a very practice based, you know, "Let's talk about your spiritual autobiography, let's all hug and love each other" type situation. So that was a really cool balance during my first semester.

Any other specific experiences or courses worth mentioning during that first year?

Yes! Preaching for Social Change with Charles Adams was fantastic, because he was great. Even when he lectures, he's basically preaching. But the people who were in that class was what made it cool because, basically, I was the only white, straight, Christian male in the course, whereas everybody else had this, like, different flavor of tradition. We had Muslims in there, we had Baptists and Unitarians and everything you could think of, who had really amazing things to say and had things at stake in their sermons. For a year and a half after that class ended we still stayed in touch over the email list from the course, because we all preached together and grew close to each other. I really learned a lot from my fellow students. I think that was transformative for me because I think that courses like Preaching for Social Change constantly reminded me of how my peers are also amazing sources of information and knowledge and experience. I can just go talk to the person sitting next to me in the library and be like, "Can you translate this ancient Latin text?" And they can. That was a cool course in that regard, to kind of see the talent and the intellect, and just the awesomeness of my fellow students.

I intentionally took Harvey Cox's course. It's the course he still teaches, the only one he still teaches, which is basically a survey of American religion.

Yes, I took that course.

It was weird because I was the AV guy in the back. [Laughter]

I was also taking the course, but I did the final project on the emergent church. Harvey Cox lets you make videos, and so I made a video on that. Through the research of producing that documentary, I ended up finding a church I really loved. So that was The Crossing which is based out of Boston. The head priest, who's now leaving after six years, is the leader of this church community which is a kind of experimental, alternative church community. She's an HDS grad and actually used to work at HDS. When she was here, she was Buddhist; now she's an Episcopalian priest. [Laughter] So you know, a great HDS story. I didn't know that until after we finished the documentary. It's an Episcopal church but I'm Presbyterian, though that was not a hindrance there at all. They encouraged that I work there and the only person, honestly, on the leadership team for that church that was Episcopalian was the priest. Everyone else attends extensively Episcopal service, but the whole point is that it kind of problematizes conceptions of denominational tradition anyway. Anyway, I ended up working there and she has been one of my mentors, spiritually, since then. She has played a big part in my spiritual development over the past couple of years since then.

So, field education was essential?

It was, absolutely essential. It grounds everything else for me.

If we think about the methodology of regular courses, sections, and interactive classes—were you happy with the way religion is taught here at HDS? Did the content go deep enough on an intellectual level?

The short answer is yes. I know that I got a kind of religious instruction here that I would not get otherwise and I'm very glad for that. Let me begin with the affirmation that the great thing about HDS is that it offers perspective on religion that challenges you. I felt it was really helpful because of how much it challenged me. It doesn't allow you to get stuck in certain forms. In my tradition, there exist certain forms of dogmatism, or even just certain academic tropes that you're told are always correct, and you never second guess them. I've seen that just since interacting with all of my friends in other seminaries, especially the difference in how they are instructed and what that does to their understanding of religion. I feel that my instruction has been more far reaching because I've had to search, as opposed to just having to check these religious boxes which is definitely the case at Presbyterian seminaries. Not all of them, but a lot of them. At the same time, the one course I took on Calvinism, and I'm a Calvinist, was one of the best courses I've taken at HDS and it got really, really deep. But I remember, in that course, the ability of the instructor to invite my classmates to engage with both the academically rigorous and grounded, and the experience of faith for day-to-day people which was more experiential, was highly unusual for here. That's what also made the Preaching for Social Change class; everyone really loved that course. I was kind of scared because everyone who was in there was like, "This is so different from everything else." I was like, "Oh, it sucks because I really had to take this class," and I do think that's a valid critique. The truth is I had several courses at HDS and you don't want just experimental, you don't want just dry academics—the reality is they need each other. The cool thing about seminaries is that they are the one place where you mandate the academic part, because you're not going to ... you're not necessarily going to mandate that for a lot of churches on Sunday or just a limited experience for people. So I don't want to belittle that, as important as it is; I mean, it's awesome. But for me, it was important to have those two in conversation with one another and sometimes HDS errs on the side of, you know, if you're sitting on personal experience it's invalidated. Well, it's not invalidated but it's discouraged by the culture because it's not a pure academic argument, which I do not necessarily disagree with. But I think the courses that I've really enjoyed at HDS have made space to say, "You can do both and that's what religion can be for a lot of people." So ultimately, I got courses like that at HDS. But at the end of the day, the academic level was very high and I really valued that. It's Harvard and so you're going to run it whether you're here or in the Yard, meaning you're having some long nights.

Generally speaking, I think it's a higher intellectual level. I'm always encouraged by several of my fellow students and they're of a higher intellectual level. But Harvard, like any other institution, offers some courses where you're like, "Okay. Well, I'm not going to do any work for this class!"

Did you take any classes outside of the Divinity School, in any of the other schools here at Harvard?

I love doing that. I'm taking a couple of classes at the Yard right now. The Yard's really fun because if you get one of those courses where it's mostly undergrads, it's like this really fun, cultural thing to experience. You know they're these incredibly intelligent kids, but they are still kids and so that's really fun! [Laughter] It's great to have these folks you can struggle with over great intellectual ideas, but still be kids about it. There is a different culture there as well, in terms of how students interact with religion. When I've taken courses with undergrads, they're perfectly fine with just saying, "Well, this is stupid because this can't work in society," but at the same time, the professors are great and the Teaching Fellows are great. It's a very different culture again from the Kennedy School where I have had an interesting experience. I feel like they find out you're at the Divinity School and they let down their guard as if to say, "OK, I don't have to compete with you." Because they're like, "I'm not fighting with you for a job somewhere down the line." They are academic over there, but it's more of a professional, practical, cut-throat attitude that I experienced with the Kennedy School. However, they're really fun too. I've taken two to three-point-five courses at the Kennedy School and our course work is really related to theirs. We can take courses in any class at any school at Harvard, but a lot of those are just straight up cross-listed that are both Divinity courses as well as Kennedy School courses. I really enjoyed that because I come from a political background and so if someone misquotes what is politically true, I can also shoot that down or try my best to shoot it down in their context as well. It's also good to learn again from that whole school of knowledge. So, I really enjoyed it. It's a different environment, in the sense of this professional combativism, but I enjoyed the break from here as well.

If you're talking about both academic and "old school" professional competitiveness—aren't both ever present at this school?

They are, definitely.

Are people fighting to become a parish minister somewhere?

I think that happens a lot less. I mean, there's definitely academic competitiveness in here. But again, in a lot of ways, religious study is the ivory tower of all ivory towers. It's the first kind of academic study. It's so old and feels so old. You definitely get that academic antagonism here as well. I would argue that it's more nuanced than you're going to run into just through culture. If you're going to buy into the pluralism ideology and things like that, it affects a lot of how you interact with people. You can still basically shoot down their argument but we talked about HDSEs, the kinds of terminology that we would use. We would say, "I want to problematize" and "push back" and then, "I want to lift up everything you've said," these different kinds of code words that we use aren't used in other places. They have different code words or just don't have them because the point is to attack and break down, which is respected in some regards. I don't want to be absolutist about that, but it is in a lot of ways respected. I'm very aware of people in line for positions and jobs here. I think precisely because it's not a monoculture to begin with, it helps dispel some of that. I think we definitely run into academic competitiveness, and it's tough for a lot of people because you're competing with your friends a lot.

Earlier you were talking about the highly individualized nature of the Episcopalian program here. If everybody has been "sitting on their own island", how do you create a sense of community? How do you align students to be together and share experiences while everybody is working on their own projects?

This is, I think, the challenge of HDS as an institution—how do you go about building community? I think it kind of happened on its own in some respects. I had groups of friends who in our first year would just visit each other's houses of worship every week. You know, we'd go to one church, one synagogue, and one temple every other week for a while. What that does is create a very intentional shared experience. We got less intentional over time but it paid off in that we could go see friends preach or deliver a homily or run a workshop at a church or something like that and that's normal for us. We get used to that, but you have to be intentional about it. Other than that, I'll be the first to say that when I go look at my friends who are at seminaries, their communities have a very strong sense of identity. But, then again, they also have a very homogeneous group of people there. For me, it's like mostly white, middle to middle-upper-class suburban kids who are at seminaries, and we definitely have our fair of share that here. But we have more diversity of thought and perspective and intention. There are only about a third of us are who are in this, a little more than a third, and only a percentage of that wants to do ordination in their respective traditions. The majority of folks here are doing something else. A lot of them are doing the academics. A lot of them didn't really do academics, so you have diversity not only of people but also of interest. So finding those different things often becomes interesting—you form these smaller groups so this is not an academic group, this is an academic group. This is—you know, all six Presbyterians, all seven Methodists. But what I saw really early on, when I first got here, I realized that wasn't the case and that's actually why. That was one of the main reasons I started the Frisbee team. I'm not very good at Ultimate Frisbee, but it was an excuse to get people out. Not only of the library, but really just out of their specific groups where you can just find your little sphere of people who think just like you and never leave. By having a Frisbee team we're getting folks from all over HDS to come and play together. We have Muslims on the team, we have Lutherans on the team, and we have atheists on the team. We have academics. We have practitioners of all kinds. The community itself can be supportive of that. So when we're were playing Yale this next week, the folks are going to come and attend that and I feel like that's actually a bigger deal because we don't do things like that much here. In some ways Ultimate Frisbee is a silly and mostly harmless way for folks to kind of galvanize around each other and that was my answer to the question. But I think people have had different answers to that over time and I don't have a good solution to that. I think when it's a group of people who are all in their own worlds, you have to be very, very intentional about pulling them out of that.

Apart from your famous Frisbee activities, did you participate in other kinds of student activities outside of the academic and religious?

I'm part of a Presbyterian group. Community Tea happens once a week and it is a gathering on Tuesdays where they have tea and free food. I'm really glad that exists. So we can come in and it's … you're going to Harvard, right? They don't have coffee hour, they have tea. You're surrounded by portraits of old people in the room. But it does pull everybody and usually folks are coming out of classes. Even if they're there for 30 seconds just to get the food and leave, they still have to talk to someone. Then after everyone has been milling about for about 45 minutes they'll stop, everyone will move to the side, and they'll give announcements for the different groups. Those are often really fun and very, very funny and it's a festive time. That's really good because you get to connect. Also, there are several organizations that I've ended up helping out with solely through that. For example, Fiesole is a Creative Writing group that meets in the Rabinowitz Room and so I've been a part of that. There have been other religious groups that can say, "Hey, we need some musicians for this service we're doing!" So I'd play an egalitarian service as a result, things like that. Then of course, probably one of the best community things that we do at Harvard is the Theological Review at the end of each year. Other institutions do similar things, but what's cool about it is that we have this big roast of ourselves. Where people show up, everyone lines up and they do skits about Harvard—about fellow students, people would just sing songs, and there are even these certain songs that have been passed down for ten years. We would just keep playing them over and over and over again because there is some sort of sense of tradition. It is hilarious and it's an excellent way to kind of see how clever all these different people in this community really are. We have the HDS Ball as well, like everyone else we have a giant party at the end of every year and everyone dresses up. I don't know who's going to be the band this year but we usually have a great band, often consisting of several HDS students. It's about just having a good time. So we still have those aspects of community that define us and we can mark time only by having these meetings. Ultimately, I think there is a rich community here. Honestly, it's my experience that that sense of community has actually been bolstered since I've been here, especially outside of the traditional groupings. There's definitely been an increase in organizations that transcend that. You know, just outside a few minutes ago people were reading lines because there's an improv group. There's a film group, all these different things that people are starting to play with—they didn't exist previously, which I think is kind of cool.

Looking now to your own field of expertise, which is communication—has your thinking evolved during your time here at Harvard? Did you gain new insights, specifically on the topic of religion?

I worked as a reporter for the Religion News Service this past summer and I still technically am a reporter for them. My experience in HDS has been transformative for understanding religion because it's really easy to have a black and white depiction of what religion is and can be. And you know, you can run across a mindset like a pastor in a congregation, and that's it. Every religion works that way. People do it all the time from, like, different religions. For example, you can be Buddhist, where you assume Jesus is just, like, our Buddha. Then you can say, "Well, your Buddha is just like our Jesus." There's this whole thing, like, you can go get religious degrees and not break that mold too much in America. Whereas here at Harvard they break that for you the second you get here. They want to make sure you don't have that perspective because that's the only way you're going to be able to survive the pluralism, or their definition of pluralism, depending on which era of HDS's history you fall into. You encounter this dramatic diversity and so for me as a journalist, there's a crap-load of knowledge and different religious traditions, which is very helpful. But being able to recognize the contextual nature of religion, and being able to hear that out, is useful in journalism. If you have a different perspective on how religion works and functions, and how power works in and go back to journalism, you can really see alternative theories and theologies. It really makes a difference in how you write stories.

So, for example, I wrote a story based on an interview with a man from my home state, South Carolina. Jim DeMint is the darling of the Tea Party. One of their big guys, he wrote a book this past year called The Great American Awakening. The title is supposed to hark back to the second Great Awakening. It's the narrative of his experience with The Tea Party, but Jesus is mentioned every three seconds. I interviewed him about this and he said a lot of stuff off the record that has to stay off the record. But I can say that he and I actually got into lengthy theological conversation and a kind of conversation that I would not have been able to have had I not been here at HDS and had the primer of different kinds of theory, and different kinds of theology. An hour later I had an interview with another Senator, he's Jewish: Joe Lieberman. He wrote a book about Sabbath, right? So he and I had a conversation about how we understand Sabbath. Then I could honestly ask him some unsettling questions about defining religious practice. He really gave some great answers back. So religion is really helpful in journalism, because you know at the outset that not everybody works with the same definitions of religion. So you can go to interview someone and they start going off on what sounds like a complete tangent, but I know that that is contextual to their experience. It has a lot to do with power and concepts of power in their respective traditions, and I can write a better article because I am aware of that. So I can be more interdisciplinary with how I write my article because of the diverse environment at HDS. It paid off dividends in a big way, to the point where Religion News Service now has tried very hard to start to have just a steady trickle of Harvard Divinity School students to work with them. That's who they want, because what they appreciate is that we understand religion in a more nuanced and complicated way. It's more accurate to the spectrum of religion. It doesn't mean that you can't get that from other places, but they've been impressed with our ability to navigate what's seems difficult for other people who were writing about religion.

Is there anything else you'd like to say about your ordination, or about the field education here at Harvard Divinity School?

The ordination. I can say that I'm at a point right now where I'm probably not going to pursue parish ministry in terms of my ordination. That's an open question because of the political situation of my denomination, that escapes me right now. I'm waiting it all out, basically. But our tradition is definitely not closed off to different understandings of subordination. So I'm actually not mixed ordination. I have it, but I probably mixed the traditional round of that which ended up being a traditional parish ministry, at least for now, for coming out of this school. With the field education, I have had two very different experiences, one working at a church with an experience of church community, which I loved. I realized through this, that it is the best church community I can possibly imagine ever working for, and I still don't want to do it. I don't want to do this for the rest of my life. Also, the experience of working for the Religion News Service was a very different experience from working in a parish, but no less informative both for my professional and spiritual growth. I recommend field study and field education—if you're in Divinity and you're in MDS, I highly recommended it because Harvard will pay you to go do awesome things. Also, those are really great opportunities that can be really fulfilling.

If you could go back, and tell yourself something on that very first day you arrived on campus—what would that be?

What I would have liked to have told him was that if he was really thinking about not doing parish ministry, he could have taken Greek and Hebrew while he was here! I mean honestly, I would have switched. I would have taken three semesters of Hebrew and two semesters Greek if I could go back and do it.

I think if I could go back and talk to Jack circa 2009, I really would stress to him that it's important to know that you're going to be challenged and to help him understand what that's going to mean for him. And to recognize that it's going to shift a lot of new perspectives. Here, we talk a lot about people's shifts over time. I think a lot of people freak out because some other plans have changed and now they don't know where to go. I would tell myself to be more intentional about getting discernment, processing it and then moving forward with it. Also, there are a few classes I wouldn't take!

What does your future hold, Jack Jenkins?

I have a few job prospects coming out of here, which is great. I'm interested in journalism and blogging. Sojourners is talking to me about writing for them and working on their website. Another prospect involves working for a service organization based out of a church, Broad Street Ministries, which is down in Philadelphia. The newest one just came up this weekend. It's to do with the guy who made Teach for America. It's part of that and he's also an ordained Presbyterian minister, so he's looking at retro-fitting our entire denomination and in a really cool way. Hyperbolic, but at the same time he's not. [Laughter] Basically, all of my career options are either media related, or service related and so those are the two things.